Democracy in Plural Societies

Democracy in Plural Societies

A COMPARATIVE EXPLORATION

Arend Lijphart

NEW HAVEN AND LONDON YALE UNIVERSITY PRESS
1977

Designed by Thos Whitridge and set in Baskerville type.

Printed in the United States of America by the Vail-Ballou Press, Binghamton, N. Y.

Published in Great Britain, Europe, Africa, and Asia (except Japan) by Yale University Press, Ltd., London. Distributed in Latin America by Kaiman & Polon, Inc., New York City; in Australia and New Zealand by Book & Film Services, Artarmon, N.S.W., Australia; and in Japan by Harper & Row, Publishers, Tokyo Office.

Library of Congress Cataloging in Publication Data
Lijphart, Arend.
Democracy in plural societies.
Includes index.
1. Democracy. 2. Pluralism (Social sciences)
3. Underdeveloped areas—Politics and government.
4. Comparative government. I. Title.
JC421.L54 321.8 77-76311
ISBN 0-300-02099-6

To Yamile and Carlos Andrés

Contents

Acknowledgments

Comparativists and area or country specialists may not belong to a mutual admiration society, but they need each other's work for constructive and cumulative research in the social sciences. During the process of writing this broadly comparative study—ranging over political systems in six continents—I have acquired a renewed appreciation for and made extensive use of these specialists' contributions. The credit that is their due is given in the footnotes, but I wish to emphasize my indebtedness and gratitude to them here, too. I am deeply grateful also to the comparative scholars of what Hans Daalder has called the "incipient school" of consociational analysis; in addition to Daalder himself, this school includes Luc Huyse, Gerhard Lehmbruch, Val R. Lorwin, Kenneth D. McRae, Eric A. Nordlinger, G. Bingham Powell, Jr., and Jürg Steiner. Their research, paralleling mine but frequently diverging from my interpretations and conclusions, has been a constant source of inspiration and encouragement. I also want to express a special word of thanks to the scholars who assisted me by reading and criticizing sections of the penultimate draft of this book: Myron J. Aronoff, Herman Bakvis, Colin Campbell, F. C. Engelmann, Milton J. Esman, Herman R. van Gunsteren, Emanuel Gutmann, Theodor Hanf, Ulf Himmelstrand, Monte A. Horsford, René Lemarchand, Hin Seak Leng, R. William Liddle, R. A. J. van Lier, Val R. Lorwin, Kenneth D. McRae, Kenneth McRoberts, John Meisel, R. S. Milne, Richard Rose, Giovanni Sartori, J. H. Speckmann, John E. Trent, R. K. Vasil, Douglas Verney, Peter Verton, J. H. Whyte, and Steven B. Wolinetz.

My appreciation further extends to the Institute of International Studies in Berkeley for its generous financial support during the early stages of my research. Parts of the manuscript were drafted while I was a Visiting Research Fellow in the Department of Political Science, Research School of Social Sciences, of the Australian National University in Canberra in 1972 and a Fellow at the Netherlands Institute for Advanced Study in the Humanities and the Social Sciences in Wassenaar in 1974–75. I am very grateful for the opportunities for undisturbed reading, thinking, and writing that these fellowships provided. A grant from the Law Faculty of the University of Leiden enabled me to make a short research trip to Surinam and the Netherlands Antilles in 1975.

Earlier versions of several chapters and sections of this book were presented as papers at a number of professional meetings: the Symposium on Comparative Analysis of Highly Industrialized Societies in Bellagio, Italy, in August 1971, the Joint Work-in-Progress Seminars of the Departments of Political Science of the Institute of Advanced Studies and the School of General Studies of the Australian National University in Canberra in June 1972, the Ninth World Congress of the International Political Science Association in Montreal in August 1973, and the Workshop on the Politics of Multi-Cultural Societies of the European Consortium for Political Research in Louvain, Belgium, in April 1976. The many comments and suggestions that I received at these sessions have been extremely helpful. Finally, I acknowledge with gratitude the permission to reprint a few passages from my articles "Typologies of Democratic Systems," *Comparative Political Studies* 1, no. 1 (April 1968): 3–44; "Consociational Democracy," *World Politics* 21, no. 2 (January 1969): 207–25; and "The Northern Ireland Problem: Cases, Theories, and Solutions," *British Journal of Political Science* 5, no. 1 (January 1975): 83–106.

1 Plural Societies and Democratic Regimes

That it is difficult to achieve and maintain stable democratic government in a plural society is a well-established proposition in political science—with a history reaching back to Aristotle's adage that "a state aims at being, as far as it can be, a society composed of equals and peers."[1] Social homogeneity and political consensus are regarded as prerequisites for, or factors strongly conducive to, stable democracy. Conversely, the deep social divisions and political differences within plural societies are held responsible for instability and breakdown in democracies.

This study will examine a particular form of democracy—consociational democracy—which modifies the above proposition: it may be *difficult*, but it is not at all *impossible* to achieve and maintain stable democratic government in a plural society.[2] In a consociational democracy, the centrifugal tendencies inherent in a plural society are counteracted by the cooperative attitudes and behavior of the leaders of the different segments of the population. Elite cooperation is the primary distinguishing feature of consociational democracy; a number of closely related complementary characteristics will be analyzed in the next chapter.

Consociational democracy is both an empirical and a normative model. In the first place, it serves as an explanation of the political stability of a number of smaller European democracies on which the first part of this book (chapters 2 and 3) will focus: Austria, Belgium, the Netherlands, and Switzerland. These countries are now retreating from their high point of consocia-

1. Aristotle, *Politics*, trans. Ernest Barker (New York: Oxford University Press, 1958), p. 181.

2. The term "consociational" is derived from Johannes Althusius's concept of *consociatio* in his *Politica Methodice Digesta* (1603).

tional development. They reached their apogee of sharp plural divisions and close elite cooperation in the late 1950s and have been declining since then—not, it is worth emphasizing, as a result of the failure of consociational democracy, but because consociationalism by its very success has begun to make itself superfluous. We shall be concerned here with the four countries in their consociational phase of development. This means that "Austria" will usually mean Austria during the time of Catholic-Socialist elite cooperation embodied in the grand coalition, "the Netherlands" will refer to the Dutch case of consociationalism rather than present-day Holland, and so forth. For the same reason, the statistical and survey data used in the analysis will be from around 1960 as much as possible, instead of the most recent data.

A CHALLENGE TO DEMOCRATIC PESSIMISTS

Although consociationalism is a passing phase in the development of these four European countries, this phenomenon is by no means of merely historical interest. By their success in forging stable democratic regimes in severely divided societies, they constitute deviant cases not only in European politics but also on a world scale. In a study of 114 polities, Robert A. Dahl found that while 58 percent of those with a low degree of subcultural pluralism are polyarchies or "near-polyarchies," only 36 percent of those with moderate pluralism and 15 percent of those with marked or extreme pluralism can be so classified.[3] In particular, many non-Western countries are plagued by the twin problems of sharp cleavages of various kinds and political instability. The consociational experiences of Austria, Belgium, the Netherlands, and Switzerland provide concrete examples of how democracy can be a stable and effective system of government in plural societies. The second part of this study (chapters 5, 6, and 7) will deal with consociational democracy as a normative model

3. Robert A. Dahl, *Polyarchy: Participation and Opposition* (New Haven: Yale University Press, 1971), pp. 110–11.

that is of special importance to the plural societies of the Third World.

The argument that consociational democracy can serve as a normative model challenges the pervasively pessimistic mood of our times and is deliberately unconventional. It is based on the conviction that, after a period of excessive optimism about the prospects of democracy in the 1950s and early 1960s, the conventional wisdom of the 1970s is overly pessimistic. Of course, there have been too many democratic failures and too much violence in plural societies in recent years to warrant a sanguine view of the chances for democracy. But it is equally unrealistic to give in to complete despair. Pessimists can in good conscience reject or ignore the arguments and recommendations of this book only if they are fully convinced that consociational democracy is not merely improbable but completely impossible in the plural societies of the Third World—a view that is untenable when all the evidence is examined.

Democratic pessimists must also be warned that their pessimism entails the danger of becoming a self-fulfilling prediction: if politicians and political scientists are convinced that democracy cannot work in the plural societies of the Third World, they will not even try to introduce it or to make it work. Such a negative attitude therefore actually enhances the likelihood that nondemocratic forms of government will prevail.

DEFINITIONS

Most of the terms used so far are quite well known, widely used, and to a large extent self-explanatory. It may nevertheless be useful to provide definitions of the principal concepts in order to minimize the possibility of misunderstanding. First of all, a *plural society* is a society divided by what Harry Eckstein calls "segmental cleavages." He writes: "This exists where political divisions follow very closely, and especially concern lines of objective social differentiation, especially those particularly salient in a society."[4] Segmental cleavages may be of a religious, ideological,

4. Harry Eckstein, *Division and Cohesion in Democracy: A Study of Norway*

linguistic, regional, cultural, racial, or ethnic nature. A further characteristic, already implied by Eckstein's definition, is that political parties, interest groups, media of communication, schools, and voluntary associations tend to be organized along the lines of segmental cleavages. The groups of the population bounded by such cleavages will be referred to as the *segments* of a plural society.

Democracy is a concept that virtually defies definition. Suffice it to say that it will be used here as a synonym of what Dahl calls "polyarchy."[5] It is not a system of government that fully embodies all democratic ideals, but one that approximates them to a reasonable degree.

Political *stability* is an almost equally difficult and ambiguous term. It will be used in this study as a multidimensional concept, combining ideas that are frequently encountered in the comparative politics literature: system maintenance, civil order, legitimacy, and effectiveness.[6] The foremost characteristics of a stable democratic regime are that it has a high probability of remaining democratic and that it has a low level of actual and potential civil violence. These two dimensions are closely related; the latter can also be viewed as a prerequisite for, and as an indicator of, the former. Similarly, the degree of legitimacy that the regime enjoys and its decisional effectiveness are related both to each other and to the first two factors. Jointly and interdependently, these four dimensions characterize democratic stability.

The key concept of *consociational democracy* has already been provisionally defined and will be elaborated in the next chapter.

(Princeton: Princeton University Press, 1966), p. 34. See also Alan Zuckerman, "Political Cleavage: A Conceptual and Theoretical Analysis," *British Journal of Political Science* 5, no. 2 (April 1975):231–48; and R. A. Schermerhorn, *Comparative Ethnic Relations: A Framework for Theory and Research* (New York: Random House, 1970), pp. 123–27.

5. Dahl, *Polyarchy*, pp. 1–9, 231–49.

6. See Harry Eckstein, *The Evaluation of Political Performance: Problems and Dimensions*, Sage Professional Papers in Comparative Politics, no. 01-017 (Beverly Hills: Sage, 1971); and Leon Hurwitz, "Contemporary Approaches to Political Stability," *Comparative Politics* 5, no. 3 (April 1973):449–63.

Here it is important to emphasize that it is defined in terms of both the segmental cleavages typical of a plural society and the political cooperation of the segmental elites, and to distinguish it from two similar concepts that have been used in comparative analyses of consociationalism: Val R. Lorwin's "segmented pluralism" and Gerhard Lehmbruch's "concordant democracy." Lorwin focuses on the first characteristic and leaves open the question of elite responses and the consequences of deep cleavages; moreover, he restricts the term to cleavages of a religious and ideological nature. Lehmbruch defines concordant democracy as a strategy of conflict management by cooperation and agreement among the different elites rather than by competition and majority decision; this is the second feature of consociational government.[7] In other words, consociational democracy means segmented pluralism, if it is broadened to include all possible segmental cleavages in a plural society, and combined with concordant democracy. The examples that Lorwin and Lehmbruch mention, and also those that Eric A. Nordlinger examines in his comparative analysis of democratic conflict regulation in deeply divided societies, are the same as the four countries to be analyzed in the first part of this book.[8] The other cases considered by one or more of the three authors are Luxembourg, Lebanon, and Malaysia. The Luxembourg case is fully comparable to the four larger European consociational democracies but had to be omitted here on the pragmatic ground that it suffers from a dearth of adequate data for analysis. Lebanon and Malaysia will be examined in chapter 5 as relatively successful examples of consociational democracy in the Third World.

7. Val R. Lorwin, "Segmented Pluralism: Ideological Cleavages and Political Cohesion in the Smaller European Democracies," *Comparative Politics* 3, no. 2 (January 1971): 141–44; Gerhard Lehmbruch, "Segmented Pluralism and Political Strategies in Continental Europe: Internal and External Conditions of 'Concordant Democracy,'" paper presented at the Round Table of the International Political Science Association, Turin, September 1969, pp. 1–2. See also Gerhard Lehmbruch, *Proporzdemokratie: Politisches System and politische Kultur in der Schweiz und in Österreich* (Tübingen: Mohr, 1967).

8. Eric A. Nordlinger, *Conflict Regulation in Divided Societies*, Occasional Papers in International Affairs, no. 29 (Cambridge, Mass.: Center for International Affairs, Harvard University, 1972).

PLURAL SOCIETIES AND DEMOCRACY IN THE FIRST WORLD

The consociational type of democracy derives its significance as an empirical model from the contribution it makes to the understanding of Western democracies. It is inspired by the body of theorizing about democratic stability and in particular by Gabriel A. Almond's classic typology of political systems, first propounded in 1956, which is the major modern attempt to identify different types of democracies.[9] Because the consociational model represents a constructive effort to refine and build onto Almond's influential typology, it is necessary to take a close look at Almond's ideas. An additional important reason for doing so is that Almond not only identifies a number of significant variables and relationships that directly define his types but also integrates several related theories and concepts into the typology: overlapping and crosscutting memberships, party systems, separation of powers, and political development. These are of vital importance in the analysis of consociational democracy too.

In Almond's earliest formulation, political systems are classified into four basic categories: Anglo-American, Continental European, preindustrial or partly industrial, and totalitarian. The first two are types of democratic regimes, and these are distinguished according to the criteria of political culture and role structure. The Anglo-American systems are characterized by a "homogeneous, secular political culture" and a "highly differentiated" role structure, while the Continental European systems are characterized by a "fragmentation of political culture"—that is, they have mutually separated "political subcultures"—and a role structure in which "the roles are embedded in the subcultures and tend to constitute separate subsystems of roles."[10] In other words, the Continental European systems are plural societies. Britain and the United States

9. Gabriel A. Almond, "Comparative Political Systems," *Journal of Politics* 18, no. 3 (August 1956): 391–409; this article was reprinted without change in Gabriel A. Almond, *Political Development: Essays in Heuristic Theory* (Boston: Little, Brown, 1970), ch. 1.

10. Ibid., pp. 398–99, 407 (italics omitted).

exemplify the first, nonplural, type, and Weimar Germany, France, and postwar Italy the second. The distinction between these two types of democracy is maintained in the later (1966) and much more elaborate typology of political systems proposed by Almond in collaboration with G. Bingham Powell, Jr.[11]

Before discussing Almond's typology further, two cautionary remarks are in order. First, despite his geographically derived terminology, Almond does not use geographical location either as the fundamental or as an additional criterion for distinguishing between the Anglo-American and Continental European types of democracy. In fact, in the same article in which he proposes this typology, he specifically rejects any regional classification because it "is based not on the properties of the political systems, but on their contiguity in space," which is an irrelevant criterion.[12] Second, the cases that he classifies in his 1956 article and in subsequent writings are political systems as they operated in or until the 1950s and early 1960s and do not necessarily reflect the situation of the 1970s. This warning applies with special force to the British and American cases. Moreover, "France" means primarily the French Third and Fourth Republics.

In both of Almond's formulations, the patterns of the political cultures and the role structures are linked with the political stability of the countries under consideration. The Anglo-American type, with its homogeneous political culture and its autonomous parties, interest groups, and communications media, is associated with stability, and the Continental European type, with its fragmented culture and mutual dependence of parties and groups, with instability. The same relationship is stated implicitly in the "functional approach to comparative politics" proposed by Almond.[13] William T. Bluhm argues that it contains "a theory of the most efficient [i.e., stable] system" and

11. Gabriel A. Almond and G. Bingham Powell, Jr., *Comparative Politics: A Developmental Approach* (Boston: Little, Brown, 1966), pp. 217, 259–66.

12. Almond, "Comparative Political Systems," p. 392.

13. Gabriel A. Almond, "Introduction: A Functional Approach to Comparative Politics," in *The Politics of the Developing Areas*, ed. Gabriel A. Almond and James S. Coleman (Princeton: Princeton University Press, 1960), pp. 3–64.

comments that "the features of the most efficient order . . . look amazingly like those of the modern parliamentary democracy, and especially its British embodiment," or, in other words, the Anglo-American type.[14] To use Almond's own terms, the Continental European type is associated with "immobilism" and "the ever-present threat of what is often called the 'Caesaristic' breakthrough." This unstable type of government cannot easily sustain democracy and may lead to dictatorial rule; it even has, Almond says, a "totalitarian potentiality" in it. In his more recent work, the immobilism characteristic of the Continental European type of democracy is said to have "significant [and presumably unfavorable] consequences for its stability and survival." In contrast, the British system is described as "versatile," meaning that it "can respond more flexibly to internal and external demands than many, perhaps most, other systems."[15]

SEPARATION OF POWERS AND OVERLAPPING MEMBERSHIPS

Almond's scheme has close parallels with the separation-of-powers doctrine, which is also concerned with democratic stability—particularly with the probability that an initially democratic regime will maintain its true democratic nature. In his presidential address to the American Political Science Association in 1966, Almond contrasted the separation-of-powers theory with systems theory, and described the former as the "dominant paradigm" of political science in the eighteenth and nineteenth centuries, which is now replaced by the systems paradigm. On the other hand, he also emphasized the close connection between the two by calling the authors of the

14. William T. Bluhm, *Theories of the Political System: Classics of Political Thought and Modern Political Analysis* (Englewood Cliffs, N. J.: Prentice-Hall, 1965), p. 150. See also Stanley Rothman, "Functionalism and Its Critics: An Analysis of the Writings of Gabriel Almond," *Political Science Reviewer* 1 (fall 1971): 242–43, 246–47.

15. Almond, "Comparative Political Systems," p. 408; Almond and Powell, *Comparative Politics*, pp. 106, 262.

Federalist Papers "systems theorists."[16] This connection between separation of powers and Almond's functional approach is particularly important in this context because one of the criteria distinguishing Almond's Anglo-American and Continental European types is role structure: the degree to which the roles are autonomous—or *separate.*

The main difference between the separation-of-powers doctrine and Almond's scheme is that Almond extends the idea of separation of powers from the three formal branches of government (the legislative, executive, and judicial) to the informal political substructures (parties, interest groups, and the media of communication), and that he places much more emphasis on the latter (the input structures) than on the former (the output structures). The other differences are mainly terminological. Almond translates powers into functions, and separation becomes "boundary maintenance." Both separation of powers, according to the *Federalist Papers,* and proper boundary maintenance between political functions contribute to the stability of democratic systems. In Britain, an example of the Anglo-American type, there is "effective boundary maintenance . . . among the subsystems of the polity," but in France, representative of the Continental European type, one finds "poor boundary maintenance . . . among the various parts of the political system." French parties and interest groups "do not constitute *differentiated, autonomous* political subsystems. They *interpenetrate* one another," especially within the Catholic, socialist, and communist subcultures. Similarly, the Anglo-American and Continental European types are distinguished by the degree of autonomy of their media of communication. The United States, Britain, and the Old Commonwealth nations have "to the greatest extent autonomous and differentiated media of communication," whereas France and Italy "have a 'press' which tends to be dominated by interest groups and political parties."[17]

Just as the separation-of-powers doctrine is supplemented by

16. Gabriel A. Almond, "Political Theory and Political Science," *American Political Science Review* 60, no. 4 (December 1966): 875–76; Almond and Powell, *Comparative Politics,* p. 11.

17. Almond, "Functional Approach," pp. 37–38, 46 (italics added).

the idea of checks and balances, the boundary maintenance doctrine is supplemented by the twin concepts of "multifunctionality" and "regulatory role." Perfect boundary maintenance never occurs, according to Almond. The formal branches of government, parties, interest groups, and so on invariably perform more than just a single function: "All political structure, no matter how specialized, . . . is multifunctional." What is important, therefore, is not so much that, for instance, political parties are the only interest aggregators and perform no function other than interest aggregation, but that this function becomes their special responsibility. In modern specialized systems, of which the Anglo-American democracies are the prototype, there are certain structures "which have a functional distinctiveness, and which tend to perform what we may call a regulatory role in relation to that function within the political system as a whole."[18]

In addition to the convergence of the first criterion of Almond's typology—role structure—with the separation-of-powers doctrine, there is also a close connection between the second criterion—political culture—and the "overlapping memberships" proposition formulated by the group theorists Arthur F. Bentley and David B. Truman as well as the very similar crosscutting cleavages proposition of Seymour Martin Lipset. These propositions state that, when individuals belong to a number of different organized or unorganized groups with diverse interests and outlooks, their attitudes will tend to be moderate as a result of these psychological cross-pressures. Moreover, leaders of organizations with heterogeneous memberships will be subject to the political cross-pressures of this situation and will also tend to assume moderate, middle-of-the-road positions. Such moderation is essential to political stability. Conversely, when a society is riven with sharp cleavages and when memberships and loyalties do not overlap but are concentrated exclusively within each separate segment of society, the cross-pressures that are vital to political moderation and stability will be absent. As Truman states, if a complex society manages to avoid "revolution, degeneration, and decay [and] maintains its

18. Ibid., pp. 11, 18.

stability . . . it may do so in large measure because of the fact of multiple memberships."[19] Lipset argues that "the chances for stable democracy are enhanced to the extent that groups and individuals have a number of crosscutting, politically relevant affiliations."[20] And Bentley calls compromise "the very process itself of the criss-cross groups in action."[21]

In political culture terminology, overlapping memberships are characteristic of a homogeneous political culture, whereas a fragmented culture has little or no overlapping between its distinct subcultures. In Almond's typology, the stable Anglo-American systems have a homogeneous culture and the unstable Continental European systems have deep subcultural cleavages. Their immobilism and instability, Almond states, are a "*consequence* of the condition of the political culture." For instance, Almond and Powell describe the French system under the Fourth Republic as divided into "three main ideological families or subcultures," with the main parties, interest groups, and the media of communication "coordinated in ideological families." The result was that demands "piled up and were not converted into policy alternatives or enacted into law," and that there were long "periods of immobilism with brief periods of crisis-liquidation." Sometimes Almond and Powell themselves adopt the language of the overlapping memberships theory: in a nation like France, "the individual may be exposed to few of the kinds of 'cross-pressures' that moderate his rigid political attitudes."[22] And in *The Civic Culture* Almond and Sidney Verba state that "membership patterns differ from one country to the next. In the European Catholic countries, for example, the pattern tends to be ideologically cumulative. Family, church, interest group, and party membership tend to coincide in their ideological and policy characteristics and to reinforce one

19. David B. Truman, *The Governmental Process: Political Interests and Public Opinion* (New York: Knopf, 1951), p. 168.

20. Seymour Martin Lipset, *Political Man: The Social Bases of Politics* (Garden City, N. Y.: Doubleday, 1960), pp. 88–89.

21. Arthur F. Bentley, *The Process of Government: A Study of Social Pressures*, 4th ed. (Evanston: Principia Press of Illinois, 1955), p. 208.

22. Almond, "Comparative Political Systems," p. 408 (italics added); Almond and Powell, *Comparative Politics*, pp. 122, 263–65.

another in their effects on opinion. In the United States and Britain, however, the overlapping pattern appears to be more common."[23]

PLURAL SOCIETIES AND PARTY SYSTEMS

Almond's typology not only has intimate links with the separation of powers and overlapping memberships theories but also converges with the traditional dichotomous classification of democratic polities according to the number of parties operating in the system: two-party versus multiparty systems. It should be emphasized that this typology is commonly used to distinguish not only between party systems but between entire political systems. For instance, Sigmund Neumann argues that "these different party systems have far-reaching consequences for the voting process and even more so for governmental decision-making . . . A classification along this line [according to the number of parties], therefore, proves to be quite suggestive and essential."[24] And Maurice Duverger concludes that "the distinction between single-party, two-party, and multiparty systems tends to become the fundamental mode of classifying contemporary regimes."[25]

Both Duverger and Neumann stress that there is a close relationship between the number of parties and democratic stability. A two-party system, Duverger believes, not only "seems to correspond to the nature of things" because it can accurately reflect the natural duality of public opinion, but also tends to be more stable than a multiparty system because it is more moderate. In the former, one finds a "decrease in the extent of political divisions" which serves to restrict the demagogy of parties,

23. Gabriel A. Almond and Sidney Verba, *The Civic Culture: Political Attitudes and Democracy in Five Nations* (Princeton: Princeton University Press, 1963), pp. 133–34.

24. Sigmund Neumann, "Toward a Comparative Study of Political Parties," in *Modern Political Parties: Approaches to Comparative Politics,* ed. Sigmund Neumann (Chicago: University of Chicago Press, 1956), pp. 402–03.

25. Maurice Duverger, *Political Parties: Their Organization and Activity in the Modern State,* trans. Barbara and Robert North (London: Methuen, 1959), p. 393.

whereas in the latter there is an "aggravation of political divisions and an intensification of differences" coinciding with "a general 'extremization' of opinion."[26] Similarly, Neumann argues that a multiparty system, unlike the two-party system, does not have a "unifying and centralizing order" and, consequently, "does not hold great promise of effective policy formation."[27]

Almond argues that in modern developed political systems with proper boundary maintenance (that is, the Anglo-American type), interest aggregation is the foremost and distinctive function of the political parties, and that this function is in the "middle range of processing" and is supposed to transform the articulated interests "into a relatively small number of alternatives." The two-party system would appear to be ideally suited for this, and multiparty systems would appear to be less efficient aggregators. Nevertheless, at first Almond rejects the idea that his Anglo-American type is congruent with the two-party system and his Continental European type with the multiparty system: "The commonly used distinctions between one-party, two-party, and multi-party systems simply get nowhere in distinguishing the essential properties of the totalitarian, the Anglo-American, and the Continental European political systems."[28]

In his later writings, however, Almond implicitly accepts the congruence between his own typology (at least that part of the typology which deals with democratic systems) and the typology based on the number of parties: "Some party systems aggregate interests much more effectively than others. The *number of parties* is a factor of importance. Two-party systems which are responsible to a broad electorate are usually forced toward aggregative policies." On the other hand, "the presence of a large number of fairly small parties makes it increasingly likely that each party will merely transmit the interests of a special subculture or clientele with a minimum of aggregation." Two-party systems not only are the best aggregators but also contribute to effective boundary maintenance. It is desirable, according to

26. Ibid., pp. 215, 387–88.
27. Neumann, "Comparative Study of Political Parties," p. 402.
28. Almond, "Functional Approach," pp. 39, 40; Almond, "Comparative Political Systems," p. 397.

Almond, for aggregation structures to be differentiated from both the decision-making and the interest articulation structures, and "the competitive two-party system perhaps most easily secures and maintains this differentiation."[29] Both effective aggregation and proper boundary maintenance are directly related to democratic stability, and both are characteristic of the Anglo-American type of democracy.

DEVIANT CASES

The only major weakness in Almond's otherwise theoretically rich, well-integrated, and economically formulated typology is that he does not deal satisfactorily with the smaller European democracies. In the article in which he originally sets forth the Anglo-American and Continental European types with their distinctive qualities, the Scandinavian nations and the Low Countries are specifically excluded from the category of Continental European political systems, and Austria and Switzerland are not mentioned at all. For Scandinavia and the Low Countries, a separate category is set up which is not elaborated in detail. Almond merely says that these political systems "combine some of the features of the Continental European and the Anglo-American," and that they "stand somewhere in between the Continental pattern and the Anglo-American." In his later writings, he specifies more fully in what respects this third type of political system differs from the other two. Adopting the language of the number-of-parties typology, he distinguishes between the *crisis* or *immobilist* multiparty systems of France and Italy and the *working* multiparty systems of Scandinavia and the Low Countries. In the latter, at least some of the parties are broadly aggregative, such as the Scandinavian Socialist parties and the Belgian Socialist and Catholic parties.[30] This criterion is not very satisfactory, because it does not apply clearly to

29. Almond and Powell, *Comparative Politics*, pp. 102–03, 107 (italics added).

30. Almond, "Comparative Political Systems." pp. 392–93, 405; Almond, "Functional Approach," p. 42.

the Dutch parties, whereas the Italian Christian Democratic party does seem to fit it.

The second criterion for distinguishing the working multiparty system from the immobilist system is much more satisfactory, at least with regard to the Scandinavian countries: their "political culture is more homogeneous and fusional of secular and traditional elements." In fact, the Scandinavian countries do not differ significantly from the Anglo-American type in this respect. In *The Civic Culture,* Almond and Verba mention the Scandinavian countries together with England, the Old Commonwealth countries, and the United States as having "homogeneous political cultures."[31]

But a homogeneous political culture is not at all characteristic either of the working multiparty systems in Switzerland and the Low Countries or of the two-party Austrian system. Especially the Catholic, Socialist, and Liberal *familles spirituelles* (spiritual families) of Belgium and Luxembourg, the Catholic, Calvinist, Socialist, and Liberal *zuilen* (pillars or vertical groupings) of the Netherlands, and the Catholic, Socialist, and Liberal-National *Lager* (camps) of Austria are subcultures quite similar to the subcultures characteristic of Almond's Continental European type. In fact, these countries have even more thoroughly fragmented political cultures than France, Italy, or Weimar Germany, with a solid network of interpenetrating groups and communications media within each subculture and with even less flexibility and overlapping of membership between different subcultures. Lorwin's ranking of Western democracies according to their degree of segmented pluralism confirms this description: Austria, Belgium, Luxembourg, and the Netherlands are in the highest category of segmentation; the Continental European countries (in Almond's sense, that is, France, Italy, and Germany) together with Switzerland and the United States are in the medium category; and Britain, the Irish Republic, the Scandinavian states, Finland, and Iceland are ranked low on segmented pluralism.[32]

31. Almond and Verba, *Civic Culture,* pp. 28–29.
32. Lorwin, "Segmented Pluralism," p. 148.

The political stability of the consociational democracies must be explained in terms of an additional factor—cooperation by the leaders of the different groups which transcends the segmental or subcultural cleavages at the mass level—rather than by assigning them to an in-between position on the explanatory variable of political culture. It is for this reason that the experience of the European consociational democracies is of such great normative significance to plural societies in the Third World: they are stable democracies not because their societies are only mildly plural, but in spite of the deep segmental cleavages in their societies.

PLURAL SOCIETIES AND DEMOCRACY IN THE THIRD WORLD

A great many of the developing countries—particularly those in Asia and Africa, but also some South American countries, such as Guyana, Surinam, and Trinidad—are beset by political problems arising from the deep divisions between segments of their populations and the absence of a unifying consensus. The theoretical literature on political development, nation-building, and democratization in the new states treats this fact in a curiously ambivalent fashion. On the one hand, many writers implicitly refuse to acknowledge its importance. Walker Connor even charges that most of the leading theoreticians of nation-building "have tended to slight, if not totally ignore, problems associated with ethnic diversity."[33] On the other hand, the authors who do treat the question seriously tend to attach overriding importance to it. For instance, it constitutes the very first of Lucian W. Pye's famous syndrome of seventeen features that jointly characterize the non-Western political process. Pye states that the political sphere is not clearly differentiated from the sphere of social and personal relations in non-Western societies: "The fundamental framework of non-Western politics is a

33. Walker Connor, "Nation-Building or Nation-Destroying?" *World Politics* 24, no. 3 (April 1972): 319.

communal one, and all political behavior is strongly colored by considerations of communal identification."[34]

Such communal attachments are what Clifford Geertz calls "primordial" loyalties, which may be based on language, religion, custom, region, race, or assumed blood ties.[35] The subcultures of the European consociational democracies, which are religious and ideological in nature and on which, in two of the countries, linguistic divisions are superimposed, may also be regarded as primordial groups—if one is willing to view ideology as a kind of religion. All of these societies, Western and non-Western, will be referred to here as *plural* societies. And the definition of this term, supplied earlier in this chapter, closely approximates the meaning in which J. S. Furnivall used it. It is worth noting that Almond's and Furnivall's conceptual frameworks are fully compatible, because Furnivall explicitly included cultural differences as one of the characteristics of plural societies: "Each group holds by its own religion, its own culture and language, its own ideas and ways." He defines a plural society as one in which such "different sections of the community [live] side by side, but separately, within the same political unit." This concept is somewhat narrower than Geertz's because it does not include regional differentiation. Furnivall's plural society is one of geographical mixture but mutual social avoidance: "It is in the strictest sense a medley [of peoples], for they mix but do not combine."[36] The broader definition will be followed here because it fits the purposes of this study's broad comparative exploration best, despite the frequent criticism that the concept of plural society is too broad and encompasses too much.[37] At the same time, it is imperative to be alert to qualita-

34. Lucian W. Pye, "The Non-Western Political Process," *Journal of Politics* 20, no. 3 (August 1958): 469.

35. Clifford Geertz, "The Integrative Revolution: Primordial Sentiments and Civil Politics in the New States," in *Old Societies and New States: The Quest for Modernity in Asia and Africa,* ed. Clifford Geertz (New York: Free Press, 1963), pp. 109–13.

36. J. S. Furnivall, *Colonial Policy and Practice: A Comparative Study of Burma and Netherlands India* (Cambridge: Cambridge University Press, 1948), p. 304.

37. See, e.g., O. D. van den Muijzenberg, *De "plural society": Een onderzoek naar gebruik en bruikbaarheid als sociologisch begrip* (Amsterdam: Sociologisch-Historisch

tive and quantitative differences within the broad category of plural societies: differences between different *kinds* of segmental cleavages and differences in the *degree* to which a society is plural.

The second prominent characteristic of non-Western politics is the breakdown of democracy. After the initial optimism concerning the democratic prospects of the newly independent countries, based largely on the democratic aspirations voiced by their political leaders, a mood of disillusionment has set in. And, according to many observers, there is a direct connection between the two fundamental features of non-Western politics: a plural society is incapable of sustaining a democratic government. This relationship was already implicit in Furnivall's work. He applied the concept of plural society to colonial dependencies and argued that their unity was maintained by the nondemocratic means of colonial domination. It is also in accord with John Stuart Mill's gloomy assessment of the chances of representative democracy in plural societies: "Free institutions are next to impossible in a country made up of different nationalities. Among a people without fellow-feeling, especially if they read and speak different languages, the united public opinion, necessary to the working of representative government, cannot exist."[38]

This proposition is stated in its most unequivocal form by M. G. Smith. Domination by one of the segments is part of his definition of a plural society. But it is not merely a matter of definition. According to Smith, pluralism necessarily entails the maintenance of political order by domination and force: "Cultural diversity or pluralism automatically imposes the structural necessity for domination by one of the cultural sections. It . . . necessitates nondemocratic regulation of group relationships." This notion implies a dichotomous typology that closely resem-

Seminarium voor Zuidoost Azië, 1965), pp. 114–16; and Ira Katznelson, "Comparative Studies of Race and Ethnicity: Plural Analysis and Beyond," *Comparative Politics* 5, no. 1 (October 1972): 135–54. For a different view, see Michael F. Lofchie, "Political Theory and African Politics," *Journal of Modern African Studies* 6, no. 1 (May 1968): 10–15.

38. John Stuart Mill, *Considerations on Representative Government* (New York: Liberal Arts Press, 1958), p. 230.

bles Almond's classification of European political systems. One type consists of "integrated societies characterized by consensus and cultural homogeneity" and the other consists of "regulated societies characterized by dissensus and cultural pluralism." This implies that homogeneity is a prerequisite for democratic government, and it contains the concrete prediction that "many of the newly independent states may either dissolve into separate cultural sections, or maintain their identity, but only under conditions of domination and subordination in the relationships between groups."[39]

These ideas also have a prominent place in the political development literature. The concept of political development is a rather amorphous one and has been given a wide variety of definitions, but it has usually included (at least until the current mood of democratic pessimism set in) the two dimensions of democratization and national integration or nation-building in addition to the development of differentiated functions and specialized, efficient structures. Three further significant aspects of the notion of political development should be noted. In the first place, democratization and other dimensions of development are usually thought to be dependent on national integration. For instance, Pye argues that political development in general cannot advance far without a sense of deep identification with the total system. The importance of national integration in the development process sometimes leads to the complete equation of the two concepts: political development *is* nation-building.[40] Second, the prescription for policy-making which follows from this proposition is that nation-building must be accorded priority and must be the first task of the leaders of the developing states. Third, the usual view is that nation-building

39. This is Leo Kuper's summary of Smith's theory in "Plural Societies: Perspectives and Problems," in *Pluralism in Africa*, ed. Leo Kuper and M. G. Smith (Berkeley: University of California Press, 1969), p. 14.

40. Lucian W. Pye, "Identity and the Political Culture," in Leonard Binder et al., *Crises and Sequences in Political Development* (Princeton: Princeton University Press, 1971), p. 117; Lucian W. Pye, *Aspects of Political Development* (Boston: Little, Brown, 1966), p. 38. For a general review of the literature on nation-building, see Stein Rokkan, *Citizens, Elections, Parties: Approaches to the Comparative Study of the Processes of Development* (Oslo: Universitetsforlaget, 1970), pp. 46–71.

entails the eradication of primordial subnational attachments and their replacement with national loyalty. Leonard Binder argues that "national integration requires the creation of a cultural-ideological consensus of a degree of comprehensiveness that has not yet been seen in these [developing] countries."[41] This is also implied by Samuel P. Huntington's assertion that political modernization means national integration and that it involves "the replacement of a large number of traditional, religious, familial, and ethnic political authorities by a single secular, national political authority."[42]

An alternative approach to the study of political development is the center-periphery framework, but this approach does not provide an alternative interpretation of the nation-building process. Its innovative contribution is its emphasis on the crucial role of elites. In the authoritative formulation of the center-periphery approach by Edward Shils, the center is that part of society "in which authority is possessed," and the periphery is "the hinterland . . . over which authority is exercised." The center is also a "phenomenon of the realm of values and beliefs." This central value system is central, according to a circular definition, because "it is espoused by the ruling authorities of the society." The value system at the center is a consensual one, but attachment to it becomes attenuated in the periphery—which may presumably be quite heterogeneous and divided in its values. The implication of this model for plural societies is that there must be political domination by a center composed of one of the segments, or, alternatively, if domination is to be avoided, the creation of a national consensus in the sense of the "incorporation of the mass of the population into the central institutional and value systems."[43] These conclusions are identical with those of other theories of political development.

If, on the other hand, these conclusions are not implied, a

41. Leonard Binder, "National Integration and Political Development," *American Political Science Review* 58, no. 3 (September 1964): 630.

42. Samuel P. Huntington, *Political Order in Changing Societies* (New Haven: Yale University Press, 1968), p. 34.

43. Edward Shils, "Centre and Periphery," in Paul Ignotus et al., *Personal Knowledge: Essays Presented to Michael Polanyi on His Seventieth Birthday, 11th March 1961* (London: Routledge and Kegan Paul, 1961), pp. 117, 118, 124, 128.

series of troublesome questions arise with regard to the applicability of the center-periphery framework to plural societies. At the 1970 Unesco conference on nation-building, the participants generally agreed that the approach was useful as a descriptive and heuristic device but criticized its lack of clarity in dealing with regionally and culturally divided societies. The rapporteur summarized these points as follows:

What are the territorial implications of the model? If the 'centre' is a territorial concept, is there a single centre or could there be more than one? . . . What is the degree of social and cultural homogeneity requisite for a 'centre' to be accepted as a legitimate locus of authority and loyalty? To the extent that such homogeneity does not exist or there is resistance to the dominant centre from regional centres which may conceive of themselves as competing or even 'counter-centres,' is the former still to be conceived as a 'centre'?[44]

If these questions are indeed left unanswered by the center-periphery approach, it must be judged irrelevant for the study of plural societies. What Shils makes unmistakably clear, however, is that his concept of a center precludes any kind of pragmatic elite coalition. The central value system does not have to be completely and purely consensual and the ruling class may even be "relatively segmental," but there is always a sense of affinity based on a "common relationship to the central value system" that unites the different sectors, not just the "perception of a coalescent interest."[45] Hence the above questions cannot be resolved by means of a consociational explanation.

OVERDRAWN CONTRASTS BETWEEN THE FIRST AND THIRD WORLDS

The fundamental error committed by much of the theoretical literature on political development is to exaggerate the degree of homogeneity of the Western democratic states. Development is

44. Rajni Kothari, "Introduction: Variations and Uniformities in Nation-Building," *International Social Science Journal* 23, no. 3 (1971): 342.
45. Shils, "Centre and Periphery," p. 126.

generally viewed as the movement from the present condition of non-Western states or their condition at the time of independence to a desired or likely objective. This objective is the ideal type of a highly homogeneous Western society. Furnivall's analysis of plural societies already adhered to such a dichotomous view of Western and non-Western societies. In his earlier study of the Netherlands Indies, he stated that the plural society was not confined to the tropics and gave the examples of the racial cleavage in the United States, culturally divided Canada, and religiously divided Ireland.[46] But in his later work he drew a sharp "contrast between the plural society of tropical dependencies and the *unitary society that western people take for granted.*"[47] Furnivall's model of "normal homogeneous western states," however, does not apply to Western societies in general. It approximates Almond's Anglo-American type or, more specifically, an idealized version of British society. James S. Coleman criticizes the usual perspective on political development which assumes that the end product of development will be a "modern" polity. This perspective, he argues, betrays an "ethnocentric, Western-parochial normative bias."[48] A more fundamental weakness is that it is not really a Western-parochial but a British-parochial assumption.

Almond's conception of political development, together with his dichotomous typology of Western democracies, enables him to avoid this error. He states that the level of political develop-

46. J. S. Furnivall, *Netherlands India: A Study of Plural Economy* (Cambridge: Cambridge University Press, 1939), p. 446.

47. Furnivall, *Colonial Policy and Practice,* p. 307 (italics added). Here he described countries like the United States and Canada as societies with "plural features" but not plural societies (p. 305). Oliver C. Cox claims that the statements in *Colonial Policy and Practice,* published in 1948, must have been written at an earlier time than those in *Netherlands India,* published in 1939; see Cox, "The Question of Pluralism," *Race* 12, no. 4 (April 1971): 392, 400. Furnivall's distinction between plural societies and societies with plural features parallels M. G. Smith's distinction between plural and heterogeneous societies; see Smith, "Institutional and Political Conditions of Pluralism," in *Pluralism in Africa,* ed. Kuper and Smith, pp. 28–29.

48. James S. Coleman, "The Development Syndrome: Differentiation—Equality—Capacity," in Binder et al., *Crises and Sequences in Political Development,* p. 74. See also Ali A. Mazrui, "From Social Darwinism to Current Theories of Modernization," *World Politics* 21, no. 1 (October 1968): 70–75.

ment must be measured by the degree of role differentiation, subsystem autonomy, and secularization.[49] These are properties of the role structure and the political culture and are virtually the same concepts as are used to define the two classes of Western democracies. The Continental European type with its fragmented (that is, not homogeneous and secular) political culture and low subsystem autonomy should therefore be regarded as relatively underdeveloped compared with the Anglo-American type.

Furnivall and later writers are in agreement with Almond's argument concerning the political consequences of cultural homogeneity or pluralism but ignore the fact that many Western societies—Almond's Continental European systems—belong to the plural type. This error has been pointed out forcefully by at least one observer. Alfred Diamant protests against Pye's division of polities into Western and non-Western types: several of Pye's seventeen characteristics of non-Western politics, Diamant states, "could be used without change for a description of Austrian politics between the two World Wars." More generally, he argues, the Western ideal type based primarily on British consensual politics should be abandoned: "One could more successfully derive this ideal type from what Gabriel Almond has called the continental political system with its several sub-cultures. Non-Western political systems would become more comprehensible and less remote if we would use this continental type which is based on a multi-racial (multi-national) society, lacking in strong consensus."[50] But Diamant's warning has gone largely unheeded.

The second serious error in which political development theorists since Furnivall have persisted has been to ignore the fact that several plural societies in Europe have achieved stable democracy by consociational methods. Furnivall maintains that the Western experience does not provide a normative model for plural societies, whose problem "demands on appropriate

49. Almond and Powell, *Comparative Politics,* pp. 105, 306.

50. Alfred Diamant, "Is There a Non-Western Political Process? Comments on Lucian W. Pye's 'The Non-Western Political Process,' " *Journal of Politics* 21, no. 1 (February 1959): 125, 126.

technique outside the range of political science in the West. In the West the basic problem of applied political science is how best to ascertain and give effect to the common social will." He does not believe that the introduction of new governmental forms will enable the plural societies to achieve and maintain democracy, and he specifically rejects such a consociational device as communal representation because "it tends to impair and not to strengthen social will, and makes for sectional division and not for social unity." This pessimistic view inevitably leads him to the conclusion, still prevalent in the political development literature, that the creation of a national consensus is not only a prerequisite for democracy but also the first task to be performed by non-Western political leaders: "It is insufficient . . . merely to construct new machinery; *first* it is necessary to transform society. The functions of the Government are to create a common social will as the basis for a Government that shall represent the people as a whole. . . . The transformation of society is a prerequisite of changes in the form of Government."[51]

This prescription constitutes the third serious error in the prevalent approach to the question of political development, and it is the error with the gravest practical consequences. Although the replacement of segmental loyalties by a common national allegiance appears to be a logical answer to the problems posed by a plural society, it is extremely dangerous to attempt it. Because of the tenacity of primordial loyalties, any effort to eradicate them not only is quite unlikely to succeed, especially in the short run, but may well be counterproductive and may stimulate segmental cohesion and intersegmental violence rather than national cohesion.[52] The consociational alternative avoids this danger and offers a more promising method for achieving both democracy and a considerable degree of political unity.

51. Furnivall, *Colonial Policy and Practice,* pp. 489–90, 503, 546 (italics added).
52. Nordlinger, *Conflict Regulation,* pp. 36–39.

2 Consociational Democracy

Consociational democracy can be defined in terms of four characteristics. The first and most important element is government by a grand coalition of the political leaders of all significant segments of the plural society. This can take several different forms, such as a grand coalition cabinet in a parliamentary system, a "grand" council or committee with important advisory functions, or a grand coalition of a president and other top officeholders in a presidential system. The other three basic elements of consociational democracy are (1) the mutual veto or "concurrent majority" rule, which serves as an additional protection of vital minority interests, (2) proportionality as the principal standard of political representation, civil service appointments, and allocation of public funds, and (3) a high degree of autonomy for each segment to run its own internal affairs.

GRAND COALITION

The primary characteristic of consociational democracy is that the political leaders of all significant segments of the plural society cooperate in a grand coalition to govern the country. It may be contrasted with the type of democracy in which the leaders are divided into a government with bare majority support and a large opposition. British democracy is the clearest example of the latter type; the government-versus-opposition model will therefore also be referred to as the British model. The style of leadership in the consociational model is coalescent; in the British model it is competitive or, as Martin O. Heisler suggests, "adversarial."[1]

Grand coalitions violate the rule that in parliamentary sys-

1. Martin O. Heisler, ed., *Politics in Europe: Structures and Processes in Some Postindustrial Democracies* (New York: McKay, 1974), p. 52.

tems cabinets should have, and normally do have, majority support, but not the support of an overwhelming majority. A small coalition not only allows the existence of an effective democratic opposition, but it is also formed more easily because there are fewer different viewpoints and interests to reconcile. This common-sense notion is also in accord with William H. Riker's "size principle" based on game-theory assumptions. This principle states: "In *n*-person, zero-sum games, where side-payments [private agreements about the division of the payoff] are permitted, where players are rational, and where they have perfect information, only minimum winning coalitions occur." When applied to social situations similar to such games, this means that the "participants create coalitions just as large as they believe will ensure winning and no larger."[2]

The size principle is most useful in illuminating the nature of the grand coalition, because it stipulates the conditions under which a minimum winning coalition will occur and therefore also, by implication, the conditions for other kinds of coalitions such as the grand coalition. Riker states, for instance, that the size principle must be modified by the "information effect": minimum winning coalitions can be expected only when the players have perfect information, and larger coalitions become necessary to the extent that information is imperfect. Even more important is the zero-sum condition: "Only the direct conflicts among participants are included, and common advantages are ignored." When common advantages do play a role, the zero-sum condition does not apply and neither does the size principle. Not only is this logically true, but experimental evidence from small-group research also supports it. Riker found that the size principle was operative in games played by close friends who regarded the game as purely a game and had no difficulty in accepting its zero-sum condition, but that groups of less well acquainted persons did not tend to perceive the game as zero-sum—"considerations of maintaining the solidarity of the group and the loyalty of members to it" took precedence over it—and

2. William H. Riker, *The Theory of Political Coalitions* (New Haven: Yale University Press, 1962), pp. 32–33.

therefore tended to form larger than minimum winning coalitions. The zero-sum condition "implies a limit, namely that no outcome can disrupt the body. That is, no decision can be taken in such a way that losers would prefer to resign rather than acquiesce."[3]

In real political life, the zero-sum condition limits the application of the size principle to coalition-building in two kinds of societies: (1) homogenous societies with a high degree of consensus where common advantages are taken for granted, and (2) their polar opposites, societies marked by extreme internal antagonisms and hostilities. In other words, the size principle applies when the participants in the political process perceive politics either as a *game* or as all-out *war*. In intermediate situations, there is at least some pressure for enlarging the coalition and perhaps even creating a grand coalition.[4]

The metaphor of the game is aptly used by Gabriel A. Almond to characterize the Anglo-American democracies: "Because the political culture tends to be homogeneous and pragmatic, [the political process] takes on some of the atmosphere of a game. A game is a good game when the outcome is in doubt and when the stakes are not too high." This means that the adversarial style fits a homogeneous society very well. But, Almond continues, "when the stakes are too high, the tone changes from excitement to anxiety."[5] Because the political stakes are often high in plural societies, it is advisable not to conduct politics as if it were a game: a grand coalition is therefore more appropriate than the government-versus-opposition pattern.

The function of a grand coalition can also be clarified by

3. Ibid., pp. 29, 51, 88–89, 103. On the inapplicability of the majority rule in plural societies, see also Ronald Rogowski, *Rational Legitimacy: A Theory of Political Support* (Princeton: Princeton University Press, 1974), pp. 77–142.

4. Even in nonconsociational parliamentary systems, cabinet coalitions often deviate from the minimum winning norm. See Hans Daalder, "Cabinets and Party Systems in Ten Smaller European Democracies," *Acta Politica* 6, no. 3 (July 1971): 282–303; and Michael Taylor and Michael Laver, "Government Coalitions in Western Europe," *European Journal of Political Research* 1, no. 3 (September 1973): 205–48.

5. Gabriel A. Almond, "Comparative Political Systems," *Journal of Politics* 18, no. 3 (August 1956): 398–99.

placing it in the context of the competing principles of consensus and majority rule in normative democratic theory. On the one hand, broad agreement among all citizens seems more democratic than simple majority rule, but, on the other hand, the only real alternative to majority rule is minority rule—or at least a minority veto. Most democratic constitutions try to resolve the dilemma by prescribing majority rule for the normal transaction of business when the stakes are presumably not too high, and extraordinary majorities or several majorities over a period of time for the most vital decisions, such as for adopting or amending constitutions. They thus follow Jean Jacques Rousseau's advice that "the more grave and important the questions discussed, the nearer should the opinion that is to prevail approach unanimity."[6] In practice, majority rule works well when opinions are distributed unimodally and with relatively little spread—in other words, when there is considerable consensus and the majority and minority are in fact not very far apart. When the people are "fundamentally at one," Lord Balfour once said, they "can safely afford to bicker."[7] But, in a political system with clearly separate and potentially hostile population segments, virtually all decisions are perceived as entailing high stakes, and strict majority rule places a strain on the unity and peace of the system.

Even in countries that are neither plural nor consociational, a grand coalition may be installed as a temporary expedient to cope with a grave domestic or foreign crisis. For instance, Great Britain and Sweden, both belonging to the class of homogeneous and consensual democracies, resorted to grand coalition cabinets during the Second World War. It is also the solution that Robert A. Dahl had in mind when, at the height of the Watergate crisis in the United States, he proposed a bipartisan administration for the period between President Nixon's resignation and the inauguration of a new popularly elected chief executive. The interim

6. Jean Jacques Rousseau, *The Social Contract,* trans. G. D. H. Cole (New York: Dutton, 1950), p. 107.

7. Quoted in Carl J. Friedrich, *Constitutional Government and Democracy: Theory and Practice in Europe and America,* rev. ed. (Waltham, Mass.: Blaisdell, 1950), p. 422.

president should be someone "free of narrowly partisan attachments," and the cabinet posts should be "more or less evenly divided among Democrats and Republicans. . . . Ranking members of the White House staff would likewise be drawn more or less equally from the two parties." It is particularly interesting to note his justification of this proposal: "Although new and unfamiliar to Americans, everything in the proposal is perfectly consistent with both the letter and the spirit of the Constitution. In a number of other countries, Grand Coalitions have achieved unity and stability during critical transitional periods by stilling partisan passions and strengthening consensus."[8] Julius Nyerere also argues that political opposition may be harmful in times of crisis and correctly summarizes Western democratic practice in the following words: "In Western democracies, it is an accepted practice in times of emergency for opposition parties to sink their differences and join together in forming a national government."[9] In plural societies, of course, it is the nature of the society that constitutes the "crisis"; it is more than a temporary emergency and calls for a longer-term grand coalition.

This argument can be taken one step further. The government-versus-opposition norm prescribed by normative democratic theory appears to be a principle of exclusion: a large minority should be kept out of the government. But it is actually far less exclusive than it appears, because it is based on the assumption that minorities will become majorities, and that governments and oppositions will alternate. In the long run, therefore, every significant segment will have an opportunity to participate in the government. There are two ways to effect the transformation of minorities into majorities: (1) a sizable body of floating voters may transfer their support from the party or parties in the government to those in the opposition and thus give the opposition the majority needed to form a new government; (2) there may be a system of shifting government coalitions in which over a period of several years each party moves

8. Robert A. Dahl, "A Bipartisan Administration," *New York Times*, November 14, 1973.

9. Julius Nyerere, "One-Party Rule," in *The Ideologies of the Developing Nations*, ed. Paul E. Sigmund, Jr. (New York: Praeger, 1963), p. 199.

into and out of the government. The first mechanism cannot operate satisfactorily in plural societies: because the segmental cleavages are likely to be politically salient and to coincide with party system cleavages, the floating vote will be of negligible importance. The second method can work only when there are three or more minority parties that have no outspoken preferences for particular coalition partners. In such a situation of what Val R. Lorwin has termed *Allgemeinkoalitionsfähigkeit,*[10] shifting coalitions can be an alternative to a grand coalition; they may also be regarded as a diachronic grand coalition. But when there are two major segmental parties, two stable alliances of parties, or a majority party confronting two or more smaller parties, a grand coalition offers the only possibility of avoiding the permanent exclusion of the minority from the government.

A final argument in favor of instituting a grand coalition both in dichotomous party systems and in more complex party systems characterized by *Allgemeinkoalitionsfähigkeit* can be stated as a reply to Brian Barry's objection to the idea that the grand coalition is a vital instrument for the attainment of political stability in plural societies. Barry argues that the grand coalition is a mere epiphenomenon and that the crucial factor is the willingness to compromise, which does not necessarily have to be expressed in the form of institutionalized collaboration in a grand coalition:

> The willingness of the leaders of the Austrian People's Party in 1945 to offer a "grand coalition" and the willingness of the leaders of the Socialist party to accept the offer was deeply significant because it showed that they were prepared to act in an accommodating way. But the same attitudes might well have served to create a stable polity if the People's Party had formed a moderate government and the Socialist party a moderate opposition.[11]

It is true—in fact, almost tautological—that a moderate attitude

10. Val R. Lorwin, "Belgium: Religion, Class, and Language in National Politics," in *Political Oppositions in Western Democracies,* ed. Robert A. Dahl (New Haven: Yale University Press, 1966), p. 178.

11. Brian Barry, "The Consociational Model and Its Dangers," *European Journal of Political Research* 3, no. 4 (December 1975): 405.

and a willingness to compromise are prerequisites for the formation of a grand coalition. On the other hand, the prospect of participating in the government is a powerful stimulus to moderation and compromise, because it minimizes the risk of being deceived by the other parties or by one's own undue optimism concerning *their* willingness to be accommodating. By being in the government together, parties that do not quite trust each other have an important guarantee of political security. For this it is necessary, of course, to be in the coalition at the same time rather than in a diachronic grand coalition.

VARIETIES OF GRAND COALITIONS

The idea of grand coalition has so far been discussed in general terms without specifying its exact institutional form. The grand coalition cabinet is the prototypal consociational device, but a variety of other forms can serve the same function. The essential characteristic of the grand coalition is not so much any particular institutional arrangement as the participation by the leaders of all significant segments in governing a plural society.

Switzerland and Austria offer the best examples of the grand coalition in its prototypal form. In recent years, the Swiss seven-member federal executive body, the Federal Council, has been composed of members of the four main parties in proportion to their electoral strengths: two Radicals, two Socialists, two Catholics, and one member of the Peasants' party. The seven councillors also represent the different languages and regions. However, this "magic formula" was not achieved until 1959, when the underrepresentation of the Socialists was corrected by the addition of a second representative of this party to the Federal Council. The council was composed exclusively of Radicals until 1891. In that year, the first Catholic was elected to it, followed by a second representative from this party in 1919. A member of the Peasants' party entered the council in 1929, and the first Socialist was elected in 1943.[12]

12. Christopher Hughes, *The Parliament of Switzerland* (London: Cassell,

In the Austrian case, the ideal type of coalescent elites is approximated very closely. The grand coalition cabinet that ruled the country from 1945 to 1966 included carefully balanced delegations from the two overwhelmingly strong parties representing the Catholic and Socialist segments. Only the small Liberal-National segment was not represented.[13] In Belgium and the Netherlands, the grand coalition idea has not been institutionalized in the national executive. Although virtually all cabinets have been coalitions, several major parties have been in the opposition at various times. From 1918 to 1963, Belgian grand coalition cabinets including members of all three major parties governed the country for about one-fourth of the time. All other cabinets were shifting coalitions in which the Catholics played a pivotal role; they spent only 14 percent of the 1918–63 period in the opposition. The Liberals and Socialists were less frequent coalition partners, but they were nevertheless in the government for about three-fourths and more than one-half of the time respectively.[14] The political parties representing the four Dutch *zuilen* never joined in a grand coalition during Holland's consociational era from 1917 to 1967, but all cabinets were shifting coalitions with the pivotal Catholic party almost permanently represented in them. Moreover, most of these cabinets, although not grand coalitions, had a broad political base, that is, they were larger than minimal winning size. The only major deviation from this pattern is that the Socialists were kept out of the cabinet until 1939.

In Belgium and the Netherlands, the shifting cabinet coalitions were complemented by grand coalitions in other organs: permanent or ad hoc "grand" councils and committees with formally not much more than an advisory function, but with actually often decisive influence. The outstanding examples are the Dutch Social and Economic Council—one of the few exam-

---

1962), pp. 69–83. See also Max Petitpierre, "De quelques problèmes concernant le Conseil fédéral," in *Annuaire suisse de science politique,* vol. 7 (Lausanne: Association Suisse de Science Politique, 1967), pp. 7–16.

13. A Communist was included in the coalition from 1945 to 1947; see Karl-Heinz Nassmacher, *Das österreichische Regierungssystem: Grosse Koalition oder alternierende Regierung?* (Cologne: Westdeutscher Verlag, 1968), pp. 98–99.

14. Lorwin, "Belgium," app., pp. 414–15.

ples of an effective and powerful economic parliament—and the temporary grand coalitions of party leaders that concluded the "school pacts" settling the deeply divisive issue of state aid to religious schools in the Netherlands in 1917 and in Belgium in 1958. Even where the cabinet itself is a grand coalition, it may not be the only or the most important consociational organ. In Austria, the crucial decisions were made not by the grand coalition cabinet but by the small extraconstitutional Koalitionsausschuss (Coalition Committee) on which the top Catholic and Socialist leaders were equally represented. A similar extraconstitutional steering committee, superior to both cabinet and parliament, was the Petka in interwar Czechoslovakia. It started as a coalition of the leaders of the five principal Czech parties and later became an inner cabinet.[15]

These examples show that grand coalitions do not have to take the form of cabinets in parliamentary systems. On the other hand, this does not mean that all formal institutional arrangements permit the formation of grand coalitions with equal facility. Two of the traditional typologies of democratic regimes should be examined in this connection: parliamentary versus presidential systems, and republics versus monarchies. Because a presidential regime entails the predominance of a single leader it is less suitable to consociational government than a parliamentary regime with a collegial cabinet in which the various segments can be represented. But presidentialism and consociationalism are not completely incompatible. One solution is the familiar one of a diachronic grand coalition. Although Colombia cannot be considered a plural society, the agreement between its Liberal and Conservative parties to alternate in the presidency for a period of sixteen years (1958–74) provides an illustrative example. This *alternación* was complemented by equal representation *(paridad)* on all lower levels of government. Another possibility is to make an arrangement in which the presidency is linked with a number of other top executive posts

15. Rudolf Schlesinger, *Central European Democracy and Its Background: Economic and Political Group Organization* (London: Routledge and Kegan Paul, 1953), pp. 268–69. The Petka was not truly a grand coalition because it excluded the ethnic minorities.

such as those of the prime minister, deputy prime minister, and speaker of the assembly. Together these can then become a grand coalition, as in Lebanon. Dahl's proposal of a nonpartisan president and a bipartisan cabinet to cope with the Watergate crisis and its aftermath provides an additional (hypothetical) example.

Although the concentration of power in the hands of one person presents an obstacle to the introduction of a grand coalition, a different feature of presidential government may have a favorable influence: separation of powers. Three of the European consociational democracies—Austria, Belgium, and the Netherlands—have regular parliamentary arrangements in which the cabinet is dependent on the confidence of parliament and can be dismissed by parliament. Switzerland, however, combines separation of powers with a collegial "presidency": the seven-member Federal Council is elected by parliament for a period of four years, and, once elected, the councillors cannot be forced to resign.[16] This separation of powers has probably had a favorable, albeit limited, influence on the development and persistence of consociational government in Switzerland. Dahl argues that, in general, constitutional separation of powers tends to encourage cooperative and coalescent strategies: separation of powers and federalism "decrease the distinctiveness of the opposition and the chances for a strictly competitive contest between government and opposition."[17]

The plausibility of this argument is enhanced by the fact that the Dutch have adopted a series of largely informal practices which have softened strict parliamentarism into a kind of semiseparation of powers that has favorably influenced elite cooperation in the Netherlands. Although all cabinets since 1868 have been parliamentary cabinets, their semi-independent position is emphasized by the prevalent concept that they are the king's or queen's cabinets. Moreover, although cabinet members may speak in parliament, they may not be members of parliament and may not vote. Ministers are also primarily recruited

16. See Christian Dominicé, "Le système gouvernemental suisse comparé à d'autres types de gouvernements," in *Annuaire suisse,* 7:39–67.

17. Dahl, *Political Oppositions,* p. 351.

from outside parliament. Of all of the ministers who served between 1848 and 1858, only about a third had been members of parliament before they entered the cabinet.[18]

As a result of their autonomous or independent status, the Dutch and Swiss executive organs of government can perform a dual function in consociational democracy. Because of their broad composition—although, as stated earlier, Dutch cabinets have never been perfectly grand coalitions—they provide sites within which elite cooperation takes place. But, as a result of their special position above parliament and the parties, they can also act as impartial mediators among the rival groups.[19]

Whether a country has a republican or a monarchical type of government also affects the possibilities of forming grand coalitions. The most important aspect of a monarchy in a plural society is the degree to which it is a symbol of national unity and thus serves to counterbalance the centrifugal effects of segmental cleavages. A second important function is that it can provide a neutral head of state and obviate the necessity of finding a widely acceptable candidate for this position—a problem similar to that of finding a nonpartisan president in a presidential regime. Hans Daalder concludes that, on balance, the Dutch monarchy "has tended to play a substantial integrating function."[20] The same can be said concerning the Belgian kings, who are "the center of what national liturgy there is." The king is also "the one Belgian, who is not a Fleming or a Walloon or a Bruxellois."[21] On the other hand, although the monarchy has sometimes been a strongly unifying force in both countries—especially under King Albert in Belgium and during the latter part of Queen Wilhelmina's reign in the Netherlands—this has not always been the case. The royal question led to the Belgian

18. Mattei Dogan and Maria Scheffer-Van der Veen, "Le personnel ministériel hollandais (1848–1958)," in *L'année sociologique,* 3d ser. (Paris: Presses Universitaires de France, 1958), p. 100.

19. See Arend Lijphart, *The Politics of Accommodation: Pluralism and Democracy in the Netherlands* (Berkeley: University of California Press, 1968), pp. 134–37.

20. Hans Daalder, "The Netherlands: Opposition in a Segmented Society," in Dahl, *Political Oppositions,* p. 218.

21. Val R. Lorwin and Marc Vermang, "Conflict and Compromise in Belgian Politics," *De Christelijke Werkgever,* no. 12 (December 1964): 13.

general strike of 1950 and almost to a civil war. And the Dutch royal house has been a symbol of national unity but it has also traditionally maintained close ties with the Calvinist segment.

Although Austria and Switzerland have lacked the positive unifying force of a national monarchy, they have found ingenious equivalents for its second function. During the entire era of the Austrian grand coalition, the presidency was held by a Socialist while the chancellorship was in Catholic hands. This was not a deliberate consociational design by the elites, however, because, except in 1945, the president was popularly elected and both of the major parties actively contested the elections.[22] The Swiss presidency is rotated annually among the members of the Federal Council—another example of the diachronic form of grand coalition.

MUTUAL VETO

The most important method of consociational government—the grand coalition in one form or another—is complemented by three secondary instruments: mutual veto, proportionality, and segmental autonomy. All four are closely related to each other, and they all entail deviations from pure majority rule. The mutual veto, to be discussed first, represents negative minority rule.

Participation in a grand coalition offers important political protection for minority segments, but no absolute and foolproof protection. Decisions have to be made in grand coalitions, and when these are reached by majority vote, though the minority's presence in the coalition does give it a chance to present its case as forcefully as possible to its coalition partners, it may nevertheless be outvoted by the majority. When such decisions affect the vital interests of a minority segment, such a defeat will be regarded as unacceptable and will endanger intersegmental elite cooperation. A minority veto must therefore be added to the grand coalition principle; only such a veto can give each segment

22. Alexander Vodopivec, *Wer regiert in Österreich?* (Vienna: Verlag für Geschichte und Politik, 1962), pp. 25–32.

a complete guarantee of political protection. The minority veto is synonymous with John C. Calhoun's concurrent majority, which also had the protection of minority interests as its principal goal: it invests each segment with "the power of protecting itself, and places the rights and safety of each where only they can be securely placed, under its own guardianship. Without this there can be no systematic, peaceful, or effective resistance to the natural tendency of each to come into conflict with the others."[23]

The great danger of the minority veto is that it will lead to minority tyranny, which may strain the cooperation in a grand coalition as much as the outvoting of minorities. There are three reasons why this danger is not as serious as it appears. First, the veto is a *mutual* veto that all minority segments possess and can use; Calhoun uses the term "mutual negative" as an equivalent of concurrent majority. The too frequent use of the veto by a minority is not very likely because it can be turned against its own interests, too. Second, the very fact that the veto is available as a potential weapon gives a feeling of security which makes the actual use of it improbable: "By giving to each interest, or portion, the power of self-protection, all strife and struggle between them for ascendancy is prevented, and thereby . . . every feeling calculated to weaken the attachment to the whole is suppressed." Accordingly, Calhoun argues, each segment "sees and feels that it can best promote its own prosperity by conciliating the good will and promoting the prosperity of the others." Finally, each segment will recognize the danger of deadlock and immobilism that is likely to result from an unrestrained use of the veto: "Impelled by the imperious necessity of preventing the suspension of the action of government . . . , each portion would regard the sacrifice it might have to make by yielding its peculiar interest to secure the common interest and safety of all, including its own, as nothing compared to the evils that would be inflicted on all, including its own, by pertinaciously adhering to a different line of action.[24]

23. John C. Calhoun, *A Disquisition on Government,* ed. C. Gordon Post (New York: Liberal Arts Press, 1953), p. 28.

24. Ibid., pp. 37–38, 52. See also George Kateb, "The Majority Principle:

The mutual veto can be an informal and unwritten understanding or a rule that is formally agreed on and possibly anchored in the constitution. The Netherlands and Switzerland are examples of the informal application of the veto. In Austria, it was formally affirmed by the leaders of the Socialist and Catholic parties before each coalition government was formed: in the Coalition Committee, all decisions had to be made unanimously. In Belgium, the mutual veto has never been more than an informal principle in the relations among the Catholic, Socialist, and Liberal *familles spirituelles,* but it has received constitutional recognition with regard to questions involving the linguistic groups. Lode Claes wrote in the early 1960s: "Increasingly, in parliament and other gatherings, a majority decision is not regarded as sufficiently representative when a tabulation of votes for and against shows them not to be equally divided between the two parts of the country."[25] In 1970, this view was translated into a constitutional amendment: laws affecting the cultural and educational interests of the language groups can be passed only if majorities of both the Dutch-speaking and French-speaking parliamentary representatives give their approval. This entails a formal veto power for both linguistic segments.

PROPORTIONALITY

The principle of proportionality also represents a significant deviation from majority rule and, like the mutual veto, is closely interconnected with the grand coalition principle. Proportionality serves two important functions. First, it is a method of allocating civil service appointments and scarce financial resources in the form of government subsidies among the different segments. It can be contrasted with the winner-take-all principle of

---

Calhoun and His Antecedents," *Political Science Quarterly* 84, no. 4 (December 1969): 583–605; and Giuseppe Di Palma, *The Study of Conflict in Western Society: A Critique of the End of Ideology* (Morristown, N. J.: General Learning Press, 1973), pp. 10–13.

25. Lode Claes, "The Process of Federalization in Belgium." *Delta* 6, no. 4 (winter 1963–64): 45.

unrestrained majority rule. Because one of the motivations behind the formation of a minimum winning coalition is that the "spoils" of government can be divided among as small a number of participants as possible, the proportional allocation rule makes a minimum winning coalition less profitable and therefore less probable.

Proportionality, as a neutral and impartial standard of allocation, removes a large number of potentially divisive problems from the decision-making process and thus lightens the burdens of consociational government. An even more important function of proportionality relates to the decision-making process itself. Jürg Steiner defines the proportional model as one in which "all groups influence a decision in proportion to their numerical strength." In this respect, too, the proportionality and grand coalition rules are linked: "A roughly proportional distribution of influence in policy problems can usually only be assured if the decision is bargained over with the participation of all groups."[26] But proportionality adds a refinement to the grand coalition concept: not only should all significant segments be represented in decision-making organs, but they should also be represented proportionally. For instance, the Swiss "magic formula" for the composition of the Federal Council is a proportional formula. And in Austria the grand coalition cabinets were constituted in such a way as to reflect the electoral strengths of the two coalition partners as faithfully as possible.

The proportional composition of cabinets and other decision-making bodies does not solve the problem of how to achieve proportional influence when the nature of the decision is basically dichotomous: for instance, should a certain action be taken, yes or no? Unless there is a spontaneous unanimity, there will be winners and losers in such a situation: ultimately, the use of either majority rule or minority veto cannot be avoided. There is no solution to this dilemma, but there are two methods that can alleviate it and can be regarded as partial solutions. One is to link several issues and to solve them simultaneously by

26. Jürg Steiner, "The Principles of Majority and Proportionality," *British Journal of Political Science* 1, no. 1 (January 1971): 63.

reciprocal concessions: the usual terms applied to this method are logrolling, package deal, and, in Austria, *Junktim.*[27]

The other method is to delegate the most difficult and fateful decisions to the top leaders of the segments. The proportionality principle is a vital instrument in this process. In the ideal-type British model, majority rule applies both to the decisions of the voters and to the composition of the cabinet. The voters in each constituency select one candidate together with, ideally speaking, a clear set of policies. The cabinet, supported by the majority of these winning candidates, then executes the winning program. In this model, the basic decision is made by majority rule at the electoral level. The proportional model, in sharp contrast, *postpones* the decision by majority rule (or minority veto) as long as possible. As an electoral system, it merely translates voting strength into parliamentary seats as faithfully as possible, without requiring a set of policy decisions. Decisions are postponed again by the formation of a proportionally constituted grand coalition cabinet, and possibly of a still higher organ such as the Koalitionsausschuss and the Petka. This method of postponing the decisions to the highest levels entails the concentration of decision-making in the hands of a small group of top leaders. The advantage of this arrangement is that in intimate and secret negotiations the likelihood of achieving a package deal is maximized and that of the imposition of a veto minimized.

Strictly speaking, the polar opposite of the proportional method of postponing and delegating decisions is not British-type majority rule but majority rule without the intervention of elected representatives, such as in a referendum, especially when it is coupled with the initiative. Switzerland therefore exhibits a curious mixture of proportional delegation of decisions to the level of the national executive with occasional lapses into the polar opposite, direct democracy and majority rule—only slightly tempered by the fact that on constitutional questions both popular and cantonal majorities are required for passage.

There are two variations of the principle of proportionality

27. Gerhard Lehmbruch, *Proporzdemokratie: Politisches System und politische Kultur in der Schweiz und in Österreich* (Tübingen: Mohr, 1967), pp. 26–29.

that entail even greater deviations from majority rule: the deliberate overrepresentation of small segments, and parity of representation. The latter can also be regarded as the maximum extension of the former: the minority or minorities are overrepresented to such an extent that they reach a level of equality with the majority or the largest group. The practical effect of majority rule in the British model is to exaggerate the representation and influence of the majority. Parity and minority overrepresentation have the opposite effect. Both are devices for providing added protection and security to small segments. Parity is an especially useful alternative to proportionality when a plural society is divided into two segments of unequal size. In such a case, proportionality does not eliminate a majority-minority confrontation in decision-making bodies because it merely reflects segmental strengths. An example of a paritarian body is the Belgian cabinet which, according to the new constitutional provisions of 1970, must consist of equal numbers of Dutch-speaking and French-speaking ministers (not counting the premier) and in which the francophone minority is thus overrepresented.

SEGMENTAL AUTONOMY AND FEDERALISM

The final deviation from majority rule is segmental autonomy, which entails minority rule: rule by the minority over itself in the area of the minority's exclusive concern. It is the logical corollary to the grand coalition principle. On all matters of common interest, decisions should be made by all of the segments together with roughly proportional degrees of influence. On all other matters, however, the decisions and their execution can be left to the separate segments.

The delegation of rule-making and rule-application powers to the segments, together with the proportional allocation of government funds to each segment, is a powerful stimulus to the various segmental organizations. One aspect of the definition of a plural society is that the representative organizations of the society follow segmental cleavages. This means that segmental autonomy increases the plural nature of an already plural society. Daalder has criticized the interpretation of Holland's 1917 school pact and the settlement of the suffrage question—by ad hoc grand coalitions of party leaders on the basis of proportional principles—as a response to the tensions on these issues between the subcultures: "The great Pacification of 1917 was . . . not a response to Dutch *verzuiling* [segmental cleavages], but in many ways its prelude. Only after 1917 did the various Dutch groups develop their strong networks of subcultural interest organizations."[28] Actually, there is no contradiction here at all. The zuilen were present as distinct subcultures with often divergent interests before 1917, but their organizational networks were immeasurably strengthened by the application of subcultural autonomy and proportional subsidies from 1917 on. It is in the nature of consociational democracy, at least initially, to make plural societies more thoroughly plural. Its approach is not to abolish or weaken segmental cleavages but to recognize them explicitly and to turn the segments into constructive elements of stable democracy.

A special form of segmental autonomy is federalism, although federalism can also be applied in nonplural societies, of course. As a theory, federalism has a few significant parallels with consociational theory: not only the granting of autonomy to constituent parts of the state, which is its most important feature, but also the overrepresentation of the smaller subdivisions in the "federal" chamber. Federal theory can therefore be regarded as a limited and special type of consociational theory. Similarly, federalism can be used as a consociational method when the plural society is a "federal society": a society in which each segment is territorially concentrated and separated from the other segments, or, to put it differently, a society in which the segmental cleavages coincide with regional cleavages.[29] Because government at the subnational level is in practice always or-

28. Hans Daalder, "The Consociational Democracy Theme," *World Politics* 26, no. 4 (July 1974): 616.

29. See Michael B. Stein, "Federal Political Systems and Federal Societies," *World Politics* 20, no. 4 (July 1968): 721–47.

ganized along territorial lines, federalism offers an especially attractive way of implementing the idea of segmental autonomy.

Conversely, segmental autonomy may also be regarded as a generalization of the federal idea. An attempt was actually made to develop such a system of nonterritorial federalism by Otto Bauer and Karl Renner as a solution to the nationalities problem of the Austro-Hungarian Empire. They referred to their proposal as federalism on the basis of the "personality principle" in contrast to the usual territorial principle. Each individual should be able to declare to which nationality he wished to belong, and these nationalities would become autonomous *Kulturgemeinschafte.* Bauer explicitly drew a parallel between these proposed cultural communities and the frequently coexisting religious communities of Catholics, Protestants, and Jews, who independently take care of their own religious affairs.[30]

In the European consociational democracies, both territorial and nonterritorial federalism have played a significant role. The former type has been particularly important in Switzerland (which will be considered in more detail in the next chapter) and, increasingly since 1970, in Belgium. Where the segments are geographically too interspersed, segmental autonomy has been established on the personality principle: in the Netherlands, Austria, and, as far as the religious-ideological subcultures rather than the linguistic communities are concerned, in Belgium. Austria is formally a federal republic, but its system of segmental autonomy is mainly of the nonterritorial form. It should be noted that, although it is easier to delegate governmental and administrative responsibilities to territorially concentrated than to nonterritorial segments, autonomy has proved to be compatible with both approaches. Especially in the

30. Otto Bauer, *Die Nationalitätenfrage und die Sozialdemokratie* (Vienna: Wiener Volksbuchhandlung, 1907), pp. 353–63. See also Karl Renner, *Das Selbstbestimmungsrecht der Nationen in besonderer Anwendung auf Österreich* (Leipzig: Deuticke, 1918); Carl J. Friedrich, "Corporate Federalism and Linguistic Politics," paper presented at the Ninth World Congress of the International Political Science Association, Montreal, 1973; and Karl Aun, "Cultural Autonomy of Ethnic Minorities in Estonia: A Model for Multicultural Society?" paper presented at the Third Conference of Baltic Studies in Scandinavia, Stockholm, 1975.

realm of cultural affairs—education and communication—segmental autonomy in the Netherlands, Austria, and Belgium has become very extensive.

SECESSION AND PARTITION

One of the reasons why Eric A. Nordlinger excludes federalism, as well as segmental autonomy in general, from his set of conflict-regulating practices in plural societies is that it may encourage the breakup of the state: "The combination of territorially distinctive segments and federalism's grant of partial autonomy sometimes provides additional impetus to demands for greater autonomy," and, when these demands are refused, "secession and civil war may follow."[31] One answer to this argument is that the same objection could be raised to other elements of consociational democracy. For instance, the mutual veto or the threat of it can be invoked too frequently and insistently by one segment in order to wrest extraordinary concessions from the others, and such an abuse of the veto may provoke violent conflict. Another danger is a segment's insistence on changing proportionality to overrepresentation in its own favor, even when the objective conditions do not warrant it. In short, all of the consociational methods must be applied with caution and restraint. Second, it is hard to imagine that the imposition of a unitary and centralized democratic system would be able to prevent secession if the basic ingredient of separatist sentiment were strong.

A more fundamental rejoinder to Nordlinger's objection is that secession should not be regarded as an undesirable result of the tensions in a plural society under all circumstances. There are three types of solutions to deal with the political problems of a plural society while maintaining its democratic nature. One is

31. Eric A. Nordlinger, *Conflict Regulation in Divided Societies,* Occasional Papers in International Affairs, no. 29 (Cambridge, Mass: Center for International Affairs, Harvard University, 1972), p. 32. See also Charles D. Tarlton, "Symmetry and Asymmetry as Elements of Federalism: A Theoretical Speculation," *Journal of Politics* 27, no. 4 (November 1965): 861–74.

to eliminate or substantially reduce the plural character of the society through assimilation—a method with a low probability of success, especially in the short run. The second is the consociational solution which accepts the plural divisions as the basic building blocks for a stable democratic regime. Especially if the second solution should be very unlikely to succeed or if it was tried and failed, the remaining logical alternative is to reduce the pluralism by dividing the state into two or more separate and more homogeneous states.

The consociational model is an intermediate model that stands between the unitary British model and the model of international diplomacy; it resembles the latter particularly as far as the mutual veto and the freedom of action of its units are concerned. Secession into sovereign statehood goes a significant step beyond segmental autonomy, of course, but it is not incompatible with the basic assumptions underlying the consociational model. The model supports J. S. Furnivall's comment that a geographically intermingled plural society does not have the advantage of a federation, to which "the *remedy* [of secession] is open . . . if the yoke of common union should become intolerable."[32] Instead of being viewed negatively as a source of problems, the geographical concentration of segments in a plural society can be viewed as having the positive advantage of allowing the application of either federalism as a consociational device or partition as an ultimate solution. The real problem occurs when the segments are geographically intermingled. Such a situation excludes the possibility of territorial federalism as a form of segmental autonomy and limits the choice to less far-reaching forms of autonomy. And partition results in homogeneously constituted separate states only if it is accompanied by the resettlement of minority populations.

There are authors who advocate partition even under these unfavorable circumstances. A striking instance is the recommendation made at the end of the Second World War by Louis Wirth: "It will be wise in the forthcoming peace settlements to

32. J. S. Furnivall, *Netherlands India: A Study of Plural Economy* (Cambridge: Cambridge University Press, 1939), p. 447 (italics added).

recognize the importance in the drawing of national boundaries of the distribution of ethnic groups and to be prepared for the transference of people to more congenial states in case ethnic boundaries must be violated." In order to strengthen his argument, he pointed to the "valuable precedent" of the "fairly satisfactory exchange of Turkish, Bulgar, and Greek populations after the Graeco-Turkish war of 1919–23," and he concluded as follows: "In the light of these events, the minority question can no longer be considered insoluble."[33] A more recent example is Norman Pounds's discussion of partition, in which he recognizes the thorny problem of population exchanges, as well as the undesirability of multiplying the number of small states in the world, but nevertheless maintains that "partition and its consequences may be a small price to pay for [avoiding] internal strife and even civil war."[34]

The question of the costs of partition and resettlement—in terms of not only the necessary physical resources but also and particularly the human suffering involved—is a relative one and should be measured against the benefits; but it is clear that these costs should not be underestimated. On the other hand, partition is worthy of consideration as a serious possibility and deserves at least a fair hearing—which it is unlikely to receive in the contemporary antipartition mood among statesmen and scholars. As Samuel P. Huntington remarks: "The twentieth century bias against political divorce, that is, secession, is just about as strong as the nineteenth century bias against marital divorce. Where secession is possible, contemporary statesmen might do well to view it with greater tolerance."[35] Among scholars, the bias

33. Louis Wirth, "The Problem of Minority Groups," in *The Science of Man in the World Crisis,* ed. Ralph Linton (New York: Columbia University Press, 1945), p. 372.

34. Norman J. G. Pounds, "History and Geography: A Perspective on Partition," *Journal of International Affairs* 18, no. 2 (1964): 172.

35. Samuel P. Huntington, "Foreword" to Nordlinger, *Conflict Regulation,* p. vii. Moreover, the disadvantages frequently attributed to small size should not be exaggerated. Robert A. Dahl and Edward R. Tufte conclude that "a country's chances of survival do not depend significantly on its size"; see their *Size and Democracy* (Stanford: Stanford University Press, 1973), p. 122. And a factor analysis of 236 variables for 82 nations found that size (in terms of population) and wealth (GNP per capita) were *virtually unrelated* factors; see Jack Sawyer, "Dimensions of Nations: Size, Wealth, and Politics," *American Journal of Sociology* 73, no. 2 (September 1967): 145–72.

against political divorce is supported by the traditional notion in international relations theory that the root cause of conflict among states is the absence of a common government. Hedley Bull is one of the few theorists who have explicitly stated their disagreement with this pervasive assumption: "Formidable though the classic dangers are of a plurality of sovereign states, these have to be reckoned against those inherent in the attempt to contain disparate communities within the framework of a single government."[36] In the field of peace research, there is a similar tendency to frown on peace which is achieved by separating the potential enemies—significantly labeled "negative" peace—and to strive for peace based on fraternal feeling within a single integrated and just society: "positive" peace.[37]

DISADVANTAGES OF CONSOCIATIONAL DEMOCRACY

Because the consociational model serves not only as an empirical explanation of the political stability of a set of small European democracies but also as a normative example to plural societies elsewhere in the world, it is necessary to evaluate its real and alleged weaknesses. These are of two kinds: consociational democracy may be criticized for not being democratic enough and also for being insufficiently capable of achieving a stable and efficient government.

If one regards the presence of a strong opposition as an essential ingredient of democracy, consociational democracy is by definition less democratic than the British government-versus-opposition pattern; grand coalition government necessarily entails either a relatively small and weak opposition or the absence of any formal opposition in the legislature. This objection is not an entirely fair one: the ideal of a vigorous political opposition, which can be realized to a large extent in homogene-

36. Hedley Bull, "Society and Anarchy in International Relations," in *Diplomatic Investigations: Essays in the Theory of International Politics*, ed. Herbert Butterfield and Martin Wight (London: Allen and Unwin, 1966), p. 50. See also Arend Lijphart, "The Structure of the Theoretical Revolution in International Relations," *International Studies Quarterly* 18, no. 1 (March 1974): 1974): 41–74.

37. See Johan Galtung, "Violence, Peace, and Peace Research," *Journal of Peace Research* 6, no. 3 (1969): 183–86.

ous societies, cannot be used as a standard for evaluating the political performance of plural societies. Under the unfavorable circumstances of segmental cleavages, consociational democracy, though far from the abstract ideal, is the best kind of democracy that can realistically be expected. The objection is also mistaken: it presupposes that parties alternate in government and opposition. As discussed earlier, segmental cleavages tend to be inflexible and do not allow much movement of votes between parties. It cannot be considered very democratic to exclude the minority segment or segments permanently from participation in the government. It should also be pointed out that a grand coalition does not rule out opposition completely. As long as there is a parliament or other body to which a grand coalition is responsible, criticism may be directed not only against the entire coalition but even more so against individual members of the coalition by supporters of the other parties. This is what the Austrians called *Bereichsopposition* ("opposition to what is happening under the agreed-upon jurisdiction of the other party") during the era of Catholic-Socialist grand coalitions.[38]

Another set of criticisms of the democratic quality of the consociational model is that it falls short of the democratic trinity of liberty, equality, and fraternity. The segment to which an individual belongs stands between him and the national society and government, and the segment may be oppressively homogeneous. The consociational model resembles the "communal society" of William Kornhauser's typology, in which the intermediate groups are "inclusive" in the sense that they tend to "encompass all aspects of their members' lives."[39] A highly homogeneous and conformist society may have the same dampening effect on individual liberty. This is not paradoxical: consociational democracy results in the division of a plural society into more homogeneous and self-contained elements.

The separation of the different segments and the autonomy they have to run their own affairs also affects the ideal of

38. Otto Kirchheimer, "The Waning of Opposition in Parliamentary Regimes," *Social Research* 24, no. 2 (summer 1957): 127–56.

39. William Kornhauser, *The Politics of Mass Society* (New York: Free Press of Glencoe, 1959), pp. 83–84.

equality in at least two ways. First, consociational democracy is more concerned with the equal or proportional treatment of groups than with individual equality. Second, segmental isolation and autonomy may be obstacles to the achievement of societywide equality. Regional inequalities tend to be greater in federally organized democracies than in unitary ones, and among sovereign states than within federal states.[40] In this respect, too, the consociational model stands in between the British model and the model of international politics. On the other hand, segmental separateness is not at all incompatible with segmental equality. As a matter of fact, the Catholic, Calvinist, and Socialist subcultures and their organizations in the Netherlands are often described as emancipation movements, and they have by and large achieved their goals of a full and equal role in Dutch national life within the framework of consociational democracy. Separation may tend toward, but does not inherently lead to, inequality.

Consociationalism is not an ideal regime in terms of the third element of the democratic trinity either. Fraternity means "positive" peace, and the mere "negative" peace of consociational democracy pales by comparison. But peaceful coexistence should not be belittled. The relevant question is not which of the two is in abstract terms the more desirable objective but which goal is realistically attainable. Positive and fraternal peace are obviously more worthy goals to strive for than mere peaceful coexistence, but in a plural society democratic peaceful coexistence is vastly preferable both to nondemocratic peace and to an unstable democracy rent by segmental strife.

A final objection to the democratic quality of consociational democracy is that it requires what Nordlinger calls "structured elite predominance" and, conversely, a passive and deferential role of all nonelite groups. Segmental leaders have the difficult task of, on the one hand, reaching political accommodations with and making concessions to the leaders of other segments and, on the other hand, maintaining the confidence of their own

40. See David R. Cameron and Richard I. Hofferbert, "The Impact of Federalism on Education Finance: A Comparative Analysis," *European Journal of Political Research* 2, no. 3 (September 1974): 225–58.

rank and file. It is therefore helpful if they possess considerable independent power and a secure position of leadership. But this does not entail a semidictatorial position. Nordlinger points out that structured elite predominance does not "necessarily or even usually involve the subjugation of nonelites. [It] is usually tempered with a good measure of responsiveness to nonelite wishes and demands. In open regimes nonelites generally set distinct outer limits to their leaders' demands and control."[41] Nor is consociational democracy incompatible with a considerable degree of participation in segmental organizations by nonelite members of the segment. In fact, Lorwin writes that the segmented pluralism of the five small European democracies he analyzes "has, on the whole, made for more, rather than for less, participation in voluntary associations." One of the obvious reasons is that, "all other things being equal, the more pluralism in an area of socioeconomic association, the larger number of posts to fill at all levels."[42] Moreover, the elitism of consociational democracy should not be compared with a theoretical—and naive—ideal of equal power and participation by all citizens but with the degree of elite predominance that is the norm in democratic regimes of all kinds. This may still reveal a difference but not a glaring contrast.

Perhaps the most serious and fundamental criticism of consociational democracy concerns not its undemocratic character but its potential failure to bring about and maintain political stability. Several of its characteristics may lead to indecisiveness and inefficiency: (1) Government by grand coalition means that decision-making will be slow. It is much easier to reach agreements in a small coalition with a narrower range of policy outlooks than in a large coalition spanning the entire range of a plural society; this is one of the reasons why, *ceteris paribus*, minimum winning coalitions are more likely to form than grand coalitions in the first place. (2) The mutual veto involves the further danger that decision-making may be completely im-

41. Nordlinger, *Conflict Regulation*, pp. 73–74.

42. Val R. Lorwin, "Segmented Pluralism: Ideological Cleavages and Political Cohesion in the Smaller European Democracies," *Comparative Politics* 3, no. 2 (January 1971): 157–58.

mobilized. It may therefore produce the very stagnation and instability that consociational democracy is designed to avoid. (3) Proportionality as a standard of recruitment to the civil service entails a higher priority to membership in a certain segment than to individual merit, and may thus be at the expense of administrative efficiency. (4) Segmental autonomy has a price in the literal sense of the word: to the extent that it requires the multiplication of the number of governmental and administrative units as well as the establishment of a large number of separate facilities for the different segments, it makes consociational democracy an expensive type of government.

The gravest problem is that of immobilism; by comparison the problems of administrative inefficiency and cost are relatively minor. It should be pointed out, however, that the characteristics of consociationalism responsible for these minor disadvantages may have positive functions with regard to the pace and effectiveness of decision-making. For instance, Steiner argues that in Switzerland "by virtue of the federal structure demands are split up among different political levels," which contributes to a "relatively small input of demands" at the national level and, consequently, to the alleviation of the burdens of decision-making at that level and a lower probability of immobilism.[43] Similarly, the principle of proportionality is a convenient and time-saving method for allocating resources and appointments.

Furthermore, a distinction must be drawn between short-term and long-term effectiveness. In the short run, an adversarial system may be a great deal more decisive and effective in a plural society than a consociational democracy. But the price that probably has to be paid for this favorable result is the increasing antagonism and suspicion of those segments that have been denied participation in the government and that, rightly or not, feel unjustly treated. Short-term efficiency is therefore likely to lead to a breakdown in the long run. Conversely, consociational democracy may appear slow and ponderous in the short run but has a greater chance to produce effective decisions over time, particularly if the leaders learn to apply

43. Steiner, "Principles of Majority and Proportionality," p. 69.

the mutual veto with moderation. The experience of the European consociational democracies shows that deadlock and immobilism are not at all inevitable.

A final criticism involves the question of both democratic quality and democratic stability. The government-versus-opposition pattern has the advantage that dissatisfied citizens can cast their vote against the government without voting against the regime. In the consociational model, government and regime coincide. Dissatisfaction with governmental performance therefore quickly turns into disaffection from the regime. Although this is indeed a serious weakness, it does not have to be fatal. If voter disaffection is mobilized by new political parties, these may be antisystem or antiregime parties but they are not necessarily antidemocratic. And because the typical electoral system of consociational democracy is proportional representation, it is easy for new parties to gain a voice in the political process. This is what happened when consociational democracy began to break down in the Netherlands in the late 1960s. The relative ease with which consociationalism can be discarded makes the persistence of a democratic regime more likely. This argument can also serve as a final reply to the various charges of the insufficiently democratic character of consociational democracy: when these weaknesses are felt to be increasingly onerous, and particularly when they are regarded as less and less necessary because a society has become less plural, it is not difficult to move from a consociational to a more competitive democratic regime.

3 Favorable Conditions for Consociational Democracy

Consociational democracy entails the cooperation by segmental leaders in spite of the deep cleavages separating the segments. This requires that the leaders feel at least some commitment to the maintenance of the unity of the country as well as a commitment to democratic practices. They must also have a basic willingness to engage in cooperative efforts with the leaders of other segments in a spirit of moderation and compromise. At the same time, they must retain the support and loyalty of their own followers. The elites must therefore continually perform a difficult balancing act. There are two vital matters: not just, in Hans Daalder's words, "the extent to which party leaders are more tolerant than their followers," but also the extent to which they "are yet able to carry them along."[1] The term "followers" here does not refer primarily to the mass public, which tends to be rather passive and apolitical almost everywhere and therefore does not present a great danger to the possibilities of elite accommodation, but refers more specifically to the middle-level group that can be described as subelite political activists.[2]

The role of leadership is clearly a crucial element in consociational democracy. Stanley Hoffmann's complaint that "efforts at theory have produced a glut of typologies and models of political systems, often at a level of abstraction that squeezes out the role and impact of political leaders,"[3] obviously does not apply to

1. Hans Daalder, "Parties, Elites, and Political Developments in Western Europe," in *Political Parties and Political Development,* ed. Joseph LaPalombara and Myron Weiner (Princeton: Princeton University Press, 1966), p. 69.

2. Rodney P. Stiefbold, "Segmented Pluralism and Consociational Democracy in Austria," in *Politics in Europe: Structures and Processes in Some Postindustrial Democracies,* ed. Martin O. Heisler (New York: McKay, 1974), pp. 147–55.

3. Stanley Hoffmann, "Heroic Leadership: The Case of Modern France," in *Political Leadership in Industrialized Societies: Studies in Comparative Analysis,* ed. Lewis J. Edinger (New York: Wiley, 1967), p. 108.

the consociational type of democracy. The emphasis on the role of the elite has the theoretical advantage of aiding in the explanation of political stability in systems where one would have expected instability. The *explanatory* power of this type is therefore quite considerable, but its *predictive* power is for the same reason rather limited. Elite behavior seems to be more elusive and less susceptible to empirical generalization than mass phenomena. If a consociational mode of democracy has been in operation for some time, an analysis of its institutional mechanisms and the elite's operational code would yield some grounds for predicting its successful continuation. But to predict whether an unstable democracy can or will become stable by adopting consociational practices is much more difficult, because this entails a deliberate change in elite behavior.

Both the explanatory and predictive power of the consociational model can be improved, however, by identifying the conditions that are conducive to overarching elite cooperation and stable nonelite support. On the basis of a comparative examination of the four European cases of consociational democracy and other Western democracies, the following factors appear to be particularly important in this respect: a multiple balance of power, small size of the country involved, overarching loyalties, segmental isolation, prior traditions of elite accomodation, and—although much more weakly and ambiguously—the presence of crosscutting cleavages. To the extent that these factors contribute to cooperation among segmental leaders and loyal support by the followers in the segments, they are conditions that are helpful not only in establishing consociational democracy in a plural society but also, once it is established, in maintaining and strengthening it.

It is also worth emphasizing that the favorable conditions that will be discussed in this chapter are factors that are helpful but neither indispensable nor sufficient in and of themselves to account for the success of consociational democracy. Even when all the conditions are unfavorable, consociationalism, though perhaps difficult, should not be considered impossible. Conversely, a completely favorable configuration of background conditions greatly facilitates but does not guarantee consociational choices or success. As Gabriel A. Almond concludes in one of his recent works, "choices in politics are constrained but indeterminate." This conclusion may be disappointing for "political *science*, but for political problem solving there may be cause for satisfaction." Consociational theory fits what Almond calls the "*political* science literature that stresses room for maneuver, ranges of freedom, the place for risk-taking."[4]

THE BALANCE OF POWER

A multiple balance of power among the segments of a plural society is more conducive to consociational democracy than a dual balance of power or a hegemony by one of the segments, because if one segment has a clear majority its leaders may attempt to dominate rather than cooperate with the rival minority. And in a society with two segments of approximately equal size, the leaders of both may hope to win a majority and to achieve their aims by domination instead of cooperation. Robert A. Dahl's conclusion regarding a dual balance is the following: "Even in a system with two unified parties . . . strict competition is not inevitable. Yet the temptation to shift from coalition to competition is bound to be very great, particularly for the party that believes it could win a majority of votes. Hence coalition in a two-party system imposes severe strains and probably tends to be an unstable solution."[5] Gerhard Lehmbruch confirms this conclusion on the basis of the Austrian grand coalition that had to operate in a dual balance of power: "The bipolar structure of the coalition reinforced their antagonisms."[6] And, conversely, Daalder attributes the success of consociationalism in the Nether-

4. Gabriel A. Almond and Robert J. Mundt, "Crisis, Choice and Change: Some Tentative Conclusions," in *Crisis, Choice and Change: Historical Studies of Political Development,* ed. Gabriel A. Almond, Scott C. Flanagan, and Robert J. Mundt (Boston: Little, Brown, 1973), p. 649.

5. Robert A. Dahl, *Political Oppositions in Western Democracies* (New Haven: Yale University Press, 1966), p. 337.

6. Gerhard Lehmbruch, "A Non-Competitive Pattern of Conflict Management in Liberal Democracies: The Case of Switzerland, Austria and Lebanon," in *Consociational Democracy: Political Accommodation in Segmented Societies,* ed. Kenneth D. McRae (Toronto: McClelland and Stewart, 1974), p. 95.

lands partly to the minority status of all subcultures: "The divisive effects of segmentation are softened by the circumstance that none of the subcultures has much chance of acquiring an independent majority."[7] The "power" that may or may not be in equilibrium here primarily means the numerical strength of the segments, which in a democracy can be expressed as electoral strength and translated into parliamentary seats—although the influence of unequal economic power or cultural predominance may also be an important factor.

The notion of a multiple balance of power contains two separate elements: (1) a balance, or an approximate equilibrium, among the segments, and (2) the presence of at least three different segments. Together these two elements mean that all segments are minorities. When they are considered separately, however, two objections may be raised against them. First, the requirement of a "multiple" power configuration of "at least" three segments implies that there should preferably be as many groups as possible. Actually, a society with relatively few segments, say three or four, constitutes a more favorable base for consociational democracy than one with relatively many segments, and a much more favorable base than a highly fractionalized society. The reason is that cooperation among groups becomes more difficult as the number participating in negotiations increases. According to the same argument, however, a dual segmentation of a society should be better than a triple one. But the problem of a duality is that as already noted, it entails either a hegemony or a precarious balance. An additional reason why a moderately multiple configuration is preferable to a dual one is that it does not lead as easily to an interpretation of politics as a zero-sum game. If there are only two segments or subcultures, Jürg Steiner writes, "a gain for one is easily perceived as a loss for the other. With many subcultures, it is not very clear who loses if one of the subcultures improves its position. This may lead to a logrolling situation in which each subculture cares

7. Hans Daalder, "The Netherlands: Opposition in a Segmented Society," in Dahl, *Political Oppositions,* p. 219.

primarily about its own gains and nobody considers the possible costs of a decision."[8]

But Steiner's argument should not be stretched too far: it also appears to imply that the more segments there are the better off a society is, as, in fact, a few authors have suggested. For instance, Donald L. Horowitz contrasts the situation of a few large groups in which "the demands of one group tend to be made at the expense of another" with the profusion of dispersed small groups in which "the center has some flexibility and can sometimes grant the demands of one group without necessarily injuring the interests of others." Moreover, he states, the proliferation of many groups may allow the center to intervene as a "neutral arbiter."[9] If this "center" is a grand coalition, it will indeed improve its effectiveness if it can act as an impartial mediator in addition to its negotiating and bargaining tasks. But the latter tasks are more fundamental and are likely to be impeded by the participation of too many segments. The optimal number of segments therefore remains about three or four.

The second objection to the idea of a multiple configuration of power is that it is merely an indirect way of stating that the presence of a majority or near-majority segment is an unfavorable factor. It is true, of course, that the more segments there are the smaller is the chance that one will have majority status, but there is no certainty that there will not be one such dominant group. Only when the element of balance is added, is there a guaranteed all-minority situation. Unfortunately, when the two conditions are linked, they become too stringent. For instance, a quadruple configuration of power in which the segments contain 40, 25, 25, and 10 percent of the total population, respectively, is an all-minority situation but not a multiple balance. The solution is to use the size of the largest segment (majority, minor-

8. Jürg Steiner, *Amicable Agreement versus Majority Rule: Conflict Resolution in Switzerland*, rev. ed. (Chapel Hill: University of North Carolina Press, 1974), p. 268.

9. Donald L. Horowitz, "Three Dimensions of Ethnic Politics," *World Politics* 23, no. 2 (January 1971): 238. See also Robert Melson and Howard Wolpe, "Modernization and the Politics of Communalism: A Theoretical Perspective," *American Political Science Review* 64, no. 4 (December 1970): 1121–22.

ity, or approximately 50 percent) as a separate criterion, and to give it the greatest weight. The other two elements—balance or imbalance and two, few, or many segments—remain as subsidiary criteria.

Table 1 presents the various combinations of the three ele-

TABLE 1. Relative Sizes and Numbers of Segments in Descending Order of Conduciveness to Consociational Democracy

	Size of Largest Segment	Number of Segments	Relative Sizes of Segments	Hypothetical Examples (in %)	Index of Fragmentation (*F*)
1.	Minority	Few	Balance	33–33–33	.67
2.	Minority	Few	Imbalance	45–30–25	.64
3.	Minority	Many	Balance	20–20–20–20–20	.80
4.	Minority	Many	Imbalance	45–15–15–15–10	.72
5.	50%	Two	Balance	50–50	.50
6.	50%	Few	Imbalance	50–30–20	.62
7.	50%	Many	Imbalance	50–15–15–10–10	.68
8.	Majority	Two	Imbalance	60–40	.48
9.	Majority	Few	Imbalance	60–20–20	.56
10.	Majority	Many	Imbalance	60–10–10–10–10	.60

ments in descending order of their potential contribution to consociational democracy. Because three categories of two of the variables and two of the third variable are considered in the table, there are theoretically eighteen different combinations. But several combinations turn out to be contradictory because the three variables are not unrelated. For instance, if there is a majority segment there can be no power equilibrium; if the largest segments is a minority, there have to be at least three segments; and so forth. The order is based on the assumption that the size of the largest segment is the most significant variable, that the number of segments is the next in importance, and that the distribution of power is the least important factor. The relative importance of the last two variables ought to be reversed in some cases, however, particularly if a case is extreme on one of the variables. For instance, combination 4 with a not overly severe imbalance may be preferable to combination 3 with an extremely large, although balanced, number of groups. Moreover, combination 5—the dual balance—may be preferable to a combination 4 that is characterized by an extremely large number of groups and an extreme imbalance.

No attempt was made to fashion a quantitative index to measure the combined impact of the three variables. The table does present a series of hypothetical examples and the corresponding values on Douglas W. Rae and Michael Taylor's index of fragmentation (*F*). This index defines fragmentation as the probability that a randomly selected pair of individuals in society will belong to different groups. The index can vary between 0 and 1. The value is zero for a completely homogeneous society, because the probability of belonging to different groups is obviously nil. The other extreme is the hypothetical case of a society where each individual belongs to a different group; this situation yields an index of one.[10] The index will be used frequently later in order to measure the degree of homogeneity or heterogeneity in different plural societies. It should be noted here that the index does not capture the combined effect of the three aspects of the balance of power: it goes up as the segments become more balanced in size, but it goes down as the number of segments decreases.

10. Douglas W. Rae and Michael Taylor, *The Analysis of Political Cleavages* (New Haven: Yale University Press, 1970), pp. 22–23. Fragmentation, *F*, is identical to Rae's index of party system fractionalization and Greenberg's measure of linguistic diversity (*A*), and is the complement of the Herfindahl-Hirschman index. See Douglas W. Rae, *The Political Consequences of Electoral Laws* (New Haven: Yale University Press, 1967), pp. 55–58; Joseph H. Greenberg, "The Measurement of Linguistic Diversity," *Language* 32, no. 1 (March 1956): 109–15; and Marshall Hall and Nicolaus Tideman, "Measures of Concentration," *Journal of the American Statistical Association* 62, no. 317 (March 1967): 162–68. For discussions of *F* and similar indices, see John K. Wildgen, "The Measurement of Hyperfractionalization," *Comparative Political Studies* 4, no. 2 (July 1971): 233–43; Raimo Väyrynen, "Analysis of Party Systems by Concentration, Fractionalization, and Entropy Measures," in *Scandinavian Political Studies*, vol. 7 (Oslo: Universitetsforlaget, 1972), pp. 137–55; Allen R. Wilcox, "Indices of Qualitative Variation and Political Measurement," *Western Political Quarterly* 26, no. 2 (June 1973): 325–43; and N. David Milder, "Definitions and Measures of the Degree of Macro-Level Party Competition in Multiparty Systems," *Comparative Political Studies* 6, no. 4 (January 1974): 431–56.

Austria and the Netherlands fit the categories of table 1 quite neatly. Of the three Austrian subcultures, the Liberal-National is of negligible size and the large Catholic and Socialist *Lager* are about equally strong: a bipolar balance (combination 5). The relative sizes of the four Dutch *zuilen* have been estimated to be 34 (Catholic), 32 (Socialist), 21 (Protestant), and 13 percent (Liberal).[11] Holland can therefore be placed in the second combination. Switzerland cannot be assigned without difficulty. As indicated earlier, it has a lower degree of segmented pluralism than the other consociational democracies. A clear sign of this is that its segments cannot be identified as sharply and easily as those of the other three countries. There are Catholic, Socialist, and Radical (that is, Liberal) political parties, but these do not unambiguously represent subcultures. When Steiner speaks of political subcultures in Switzerland, he applies the term to much smaller groupings. The crosscutting of language and religious groups creates separate subcultures, and these are further divided into "cantonal subcultures." He emphasizes that these groups are "genuine subcultures rather than mere statistical groups."[12] The claim that each canton has its own distinct subculture, and that there are consequently more than twenty-five Swiss subcultures, is probably exaggerated, but Switzerland should in any case be classified as a society with "many" rather than "few" segments and can therefore be classified in category 4.

Belgium is the country that is the most difficult to place. Because the Catholic, Socialist, and Liberal *familles spirituelles* are all minorities, in decreasing order of magnitude, category 2 appears to be the most appropriate one. But the Catholic subculture is close to majority status, and the Belgian case therefore also approximates combination 6. This has been an important factor in Belgian politics; as Lucien Huyse points out, it is striking that the most turbulent episodes in the development of the royal question and the school conflict were preceded by electoral

11. Arend Lijphart, "Verzuiling," in *Verkenningen in de politiek,* ed. Andries Hoogerwerf, 3d ed., 2 vols. (Alphen aan den Rijn: Samsom, 1976), 2: 31–32.

12. Steiner, *Amicable Agreement,* p. 255. See also Gordon Smith, *Politics in Western Europe: A Comparative Analysis* (London: Heinemann, 1972), p. 18.

victories of the Catholic party.[13] A further complication is the bipolar linguistic division. The two language communites are afraid of being dominated by the other: the French-speaking Belgians fear the numerical superiority of the Flemings, and the Flemings fear and resent the economic and cultural dominance of the French-speaking segment. In this respect, Belgium fits combination 5. But because the linguistic cleavage does not coincide with the subcultural divisions, it is probably best to consider Belgium as an instance of combination 4 with relatively many minority segments.

It is significant that all four of these consociational democracies can be assigned to the top five categories of table 1, and that none of them has a dominant majority segment. But the evidence is not unambiguous. The grand coalition in Austria was started in spite of the electoral victory of the Catholics in 1945, although it must be admitted that the success of the party was due less to inherent Catholic strength than to the temporary disenfranchisement of a large number of Austrians. And, in nine of the Swiss cantons where the Catholic party has an absolute majority, the cantonal executives are nevertheless grand coalitions just like all other cantons without majority parties.[14] Hence one cannot conclude that the presence of a majority segment is an absolute barrier to consociationalism.

MULTIPARTY SYSTEMS

In plural societies with free elections, the salient social cleavages tend to be translated into party system cleavages; the political parties are likely to be the organized political manifestations of the segments. The presence of such segmental parties is favorable to consociational democracy. They can act as the political representatives of their segments, and they provide a good

13. Lucien Huyse, *Passiviteit, pacificatie en verzuiling in de Belgische politiek: Een sociologische studie* (Antwerp: Standaard, 1970), pp. 231–32.

14. Roger Girod, "Geography of the Swiss Party System," in *Cleavages, Ideologies and Party Systems: Contributions to Comparative Political Sociology*, ed. Erik Allardt and Yrjö Littunen (Helsinki: Academic Bookstore, 1964), pp. 139–40.

method of selecting the segmental leaders who will participate in grand coalitions. Parties are not the only structures that can perform this function; in plural societies with regionally concentrated segments and a federal constitution, the function of representation may instead, or in addition, be performed by the state governments or the state representatives in the national legislature and executive.

Given both the probability and desirability of segmental parties, it follows from table 1 that multipartism with relatively few parties is optimal for a plural society. This proposition challenges the traditional wisdom that two-party systems are superior to multiparty systems.[15] For instance, when a division into two major segments is politically expressed as a two-party system, as in Austria, this dual pattern is less conducive to consociational democracy than a multiparty system. Gabriel A. Almond and G. Bingham Powell argue that the two-party system of Austria, unlike the Italian multiparty system, has managed to aggregate interests rather effectively, and that this "has served to reduce . . . the relative strain on the Austrian system."[16] When one explains the stability of Austrian democracy in terms of the consociational model, however, one arrives at the opposite conclusion: Austria's stability was largely due to the cooperation of the rival elites in a grand coalition, and the two-party system, especially in the earlier years, was a strain on this overarching cooperation rather than a support for it.

On the other hand, the proposition is in accord with Giovanni Sartori's elaboration of the number-of-parties typology. He divides the multiparty systems into moderate and extreme multiparty systems. Counting only the major parties—those with either "coalition potential" or "blackmail potential" (such as the French and Italian Communist parties)—and omitting the small, marginal ones, "three or four . . . is the normal number" of parties in moderate multiparty systems. For extreme multipartism, "a minimum of five parties is required," and Sartori adds in a footnote that "the very interactions of more than four parties

15. See the discussion of party systems in chapter 1.

16. Gabriel A. Almond and G. Bingham Powell, Jr., *Comparative Politics: A Developmental Approach* (Boston: Little, Brown, 1966), p. 111.

help to explain a centrifugal pattern of development." The line between four-party and five-party systems is, according to Sartori, the essential dividing line rather than the distinction between two-party and multiparty systems. Otherwise, he agrees with Maurice Duverger's and Sigmund Neumann's assertions, cited in chapter 1, of a relationship between the number of parties and the stability of democracy. Both two-party and moderate multiparty systems are centripetal, whereas extreme multiparty systems are centrifugal, according to Sartori: "When the drive of a political system is centripetal one finds moderate politics, while immoderate or extremist politics reflects the prevalence of centrifugal drives." Extreme multiparty systems, of which postwar Italy, France especially under the Fourth Republic, Weimar Germany, and the Spanish Republic from 1931 to 1936 are given as examples, are "conducive to governmental deadlock and paralysis."[17]

In his later writings, Sartori retreats from drawing the dividing line between moderate and extreme multiparty systems at exactly the point of transition from a four-party to a five-party system. For instance, he defines the moderate system as one in which "the relevant parties are three, four, or *at most five.*" And elsewhere he states that the threshold is "around five" and not necessarily or precisely "at five."[18] Duverger makes a similar distinction between types of multiparty systems: tripartism, quadripartism, and, when there are five or more parties,

17. Giovanni Sartori, "European Political Parties: The Case of Polarized Pluralism," in *Political Parties and Political Development,* pp. 139, 153–55, 161. See also Gunnar Sjöblom, *Party Strategies in a Multiparty System* (Lund: Studentlitteratur, 1968), pp. 28, 174–75. Michael Taylor and V. M. Herman found that government stability, crudely operationalized as the duration of a cabinet in office, is negatively correlated with both the number of parliamentary parties and party system fragmentation; see their "Party Systems and Government Stability," *American Political Science Review* 65, no. 1 (March 1971): 29–31.

18. Giovanni Sartori, "Opposition and Control: Problems and Prospects," *Government and Opposition* 1, no. 2 (January 1966): 152 (italics added); and Sartori, "The Typology of Party Systems: Proposals for Improvement," in *Mass Politics: Studies in Political Sociology,* ed. Erik Allardt and Stein Rokkan (New York: Free Press, 1970), p. 337. See also Sartori, *Parties and Party Systems: A Framework for Analysis* (Cambridge: Cambridge University Press, 1976), pp. 119–216.

polypartism—which appears to correspond to Sartori's extreme multipartism.[19]

In a plural society with segmental parties, therefore, moderate multipartism presents the most favorable condition for consociational democracy—in line with Sartori's ideas. But a few qualifications must be added to this apparent convergence. First, the argument in favor of moderate multiparty systems is limited to plural societies only. In homogeneous countries, a two-party system will be more stable and effective than a multiparty system, and it also has considerable advantages in terms of the quality of democracy. In particular, it permits a pure government-versus-opposition pattern and a clearly accountable government—provided that the government is a cabinet dependent on majority support from the legislature, that the two parties are cohesive entities, and that they form one-party rather than coalition cabinets.

Second, moderate multipartism is a favorable factor only on the condition that all parties are minority parties; furthermore, it is helpful if they are not too unequal in size. In this respect, there is another contrast with Almond's ideas about party systems. He likes two-party systems best and his next preference is for multiparty systems in which at least one party is large and broadly aggregative. One of his examples is the Belgian Catholic party—the near-majority status of which has actually had a disruptive effect, as pointed out earlier in this chapter.[20] Finally, in plural societies that are not moderately segmented—that is, those with either only two or more than five or six significant segments—a two-party or an extreme multiparty system is preferable to moderate multipartism. The most important criterion is that the political parties clearly and separately represent all of the segments. An additional merit of proportional representation is that it allows the formation of segmental parties, and that it does

19. Maurice Duverger, *Political Parties: Their Organization and Activity in the Modern State,* trans. Barbara and Robert North (London: Methuen, 1959), pp. 234–39.

20. See also Leon D. Epstein, *Political Parties in Western Democracies* (New York: Praeger, 1967), pp. 73–76.

not artificially force the establishment of larger but less representative parties.

SIZE AND CONSOCIATIONAL DEMOCRACY

A striking characteristic of the European consociational democracies is that they are all small countries. The largest, the Netherlands, had a population of less than twelve million in 1960. In fact, of the nine countries that Lorwin classifies as having a high or medium degree of segmented pluralism, five are small (the Low Countries, Austria, and Switzerland) and four are much larger (France, Italy, Germany, and the United States)—and all of the smaller states have become consociational democracies in contrast to all of the large ones.[21] What is the explanation of this strong empirical relationship? Small size has both *direct* and *indirect* effects on the probability that consociational democracy will be established and will be successful: it directly enhances a spirit of cooperativeness and accommodation, and it indirectly increases the chances of consociational democracy by reducing the burdens of decision-making and thus rendering the country easier to govern. The direct and indirect effects of smallness derive both from the *internal* characteristics of small countries and from their *external* position vis-à-vis other and especially larger and more powerful countries in the international arena.

The *direct internal* effect of smallness is that the elites are more likely to know each other personally and to meet often; this increases the probability that they will not regard politics as a zero-sum game and hence, as discussed in chapter 2, that they will choose coalescent instead of adversarial styles of decision-making. Steiner formulates this argument as follows: "In smaller states the political elite is, compared to bigger states, relatively small. Hence the probability is greater that the members of the political elite will interact relatively frequently." This is likely to

21. Val R. Lorwin, "Segmented Pluralism: Ideological Cleavages and Political Cohesion in the Smaller European Democracies," *Comparative Politics* 3, no. 2 (January 1971): 148.

lead to a relatively high level of mutual goodwill, which in turn makes the political leaders "prefer not to perceive politics as a zero-sum game, in which a strategy of 'all-or-nothing' is applied. For the winners in such a game would forfeit the loser's goodwill, and this would entail high costs relative to the rewards to be gained."[22] It should be noted that this argument differs from the earlier argument that partition, which will generally result in the creation of smaller states, can be a solution to the problems of plural societies under certain circumstances. The result of this kind of partition is countries that are more stable because they are internally more homogeneous. But the better chances of achieving political stability that small plural societies have are not the result of their greater social homogeneity but of their more closely linked elites—as well as of the other effects of small size to be discussed presently. Moreover, the direct internal effect of small size on the possibilities of consociational democracy is not linear. When a country is very small, its reservoir of political talent will also be quite small. Because consociational democracy requires an exceptionally able and prudent leadership, smallness is a favorable factor only to a certain limit.

The *direct external* effect of the size factor is that small countries are more likely to be and feel threatened by other powers than larger countries. Such feelings of vulnerability and insecurity provide strong incentives to maintain internal solidarity. The political leaders will tend to draw together and their followers are also more likely to approve of intersegmental cooperation in the face of grave external threats. It is striking that in all of the consociational democracies the crucial steps toward this type of regime were usually taken during times of international crisis or specific threats to the country's existence. In Austria and the Netherlands, the inception of consociational democracy can be traced plainly to a particular short span of time in their political histories, and it occurred without exception during, and also partly because of, an international emergency. Austria's government by grand coalition was primarily a response to the

22. Jürg Steiner, "The Principles of Majority and Proportionality," *British Journal of Political Science* 1, no. 1 (January 1971): 65.

civil strife of the First Republic, but it was inaugurated, significantly, while Austria was occupied by the Allied powers after the Second World War. The comprehensive peaceful settlement of internal differences that paved the way for consociational democracy in the Netherlands was concluded in 1917, when the First World War was raging near its borders. In Belgium and Switzerland, consociational practices were adopted more gradually, but also partly under the influence of foreign threats. Belgian "unionism" (Catholic-Liberal grand coalitions) began during the country's struggle for independence but became infrequent when the nation's existence appeared to be secure. It was resumed again during the First World War, soon followed by the important step of admitting the Socialists to the consociational government. This final step of admitting the Socialists to the grand coalition was not taken until much later in Switzerland, but it also happened during a world war: in 1943.[23]

There is one important qualification that must be added to the proposition that foreign threats tend to impress on quarreling elites the need for unity and solidarity: such a threat must be perceived as a common danger by all of the segments in order to have a unifying effect. In particular, as Lehmbruch points out, when the internal divisions between the segments correspond with the international lines of conflict, "this results in the internal replication of international conflicts, especially in the case of religious and ethnic conflicts."[24] The coincidence of domestic and foreign cleavages was a factor of some importance for Belgium in both world wars: the linguistic and cultural affinity of Flanders to Germany and of Wallonia to France exacerbated the country's linguistic-regional conflict. In Switzerland, the French-German linguistic cleavage was also affected, but less

23. In most cases, the changes brought about under the influence of external threats have proved quite durable. This contrasts with the finding of Karl W. Deutsch et al., that the effects of foreign military threats on integration were never very strong and not always positive, and that, even when positive, "their effects were transitory." See their *Political Community and the North Atlantic Area: International Organization in the Light of Historical Experience* (Princeton: Princeton University Press, 1957), pp. 44–46.

24. Gerhard Lehmbruch, "Consociational Democracy in the International System," *European Journal of Political Research* 3, no. 4 (December 1975): 382.

seriously and only in the First World War. The only truly disastrous consequence of a foreign threat against a small European plural society was that of the German pressures for *Anschluss* on Austria: the First Republic "was torn apart by external pressures following the fault lines of the new state's precarious political structure.[25] On the whole, however, external threats have enhanced the solidarity of consociational democracies.

The *indirect* effects of small size concern the problems of decision-making. The stability of any regime can be considered in terms of the balance between its capabilities and the demands placed on it. Any government is more likely to be stable if it does not have to carry too heavy burdens. This is of particular importance in consociational democracies because the management of the segmental divisions is a slow and cumbersome process that requires much of the leaders' energies and skills. Smallness reduces the load on the decision-making system. Here again, a distinction must be made between internal and external aspects: the burdens of making domestic policy and those of foreign policy-making.

As far as the *indirect internal* aspects are concerned, smaller countries are easier to govern than large ones because they tend to be less complex: the number and variety of groups and individuals whose interests and attitudes have to be taken into consideration are fewer. This is what Ernest S. Griffith has in mind when he argues that "democracy is more likely to survive, other things being equal, in small states," and when he characterizes small states as "more manageable."[26] It is hard to make precise comparisons among states with regard to their complexity and the consequent burdens of decision-making, but the available theory and data support Griffith's assertion. Robert A. Dahl and Edward R. Tufte reach the following conclusions after a thorough evaluation of the evidence: "Other things being equal—particularly the socioeconomic level of a country—the larger a country, the greater the number of organizations and subunits it will contain, and the greater the number of organized

25. Lorwin, "Segmented Pluralism," pp. 149–50.

26. Ernest S. Griffith, "Cultural Prerequisites to a Successfully Functioning Democracy," *American Political Science Review* 50, no. 1 (March 1956): 102.

interests or interest groups it will contain." This means that among democracies, all other things again being equal, "the larger the country, the more complex its policy-making processes will be."[27]

An even more important reduction of the decision-making load of a small state results from the *indirect external* effect of small size: a small state's limited power on the international scene, its tendency to abstain from an active foreign policy, and, as a result, its greater chance of avoiding difficult choices in this realm. This advantage is maximized when a small country follows a policy of neutrality, particularly if it does so not so much by its own choice—which entails a potentially difficult decision—as by international dictate. All four European consociational democracies have had neutrality imposed on them at one time or another by the explicit or implicit agreement of the major foreign powers.[28] If a small country is a plural society, its size and its plural nature, which entails the danger of internal conflict spilling over into the international realm, jointly increase the likelihood of imposed neutrality.

Lehmbruch goes so far as to argue that, because "the preservation of internal equilibrium presupposes a reduction of external demands on the political system," the consociational type of decision-making "seems to work in small states only."[29] Daalder criticizes this conclusion and states that one of the questions that must be studied before small size can be accepted as an absolute prerequisite for successful consociationalism is the question "whether an active stance in international politics by larger states (with all its consequences for internal politics) is a matter of inescapable fate or of political choice."[30] There is indeed no inevitability about the relationship between size and foreign policy activism, but the overall tendency is abundantly clear. For instance, a recent systematic study of the participation of large

27. Robert A. Dahl and Edward R. Tufte, *Size and Democracy* (Stanford: Stanford University Press, 1973), p. 40.

28. Hans Daalder, "The Consociational Democracy Theme," *World Politics* 26, no. 4 (July 1974): 610.

29. Lehmbruch, "Non-Competitive Pattern of Conflict Management," p. 96.

30. Daalder, "Consociational Democracy Theme," p. 611.

and small states in international affairs confirms that "large states do exhibit a higher level of international activity than small states." As expected, the level of socioeconomic development is also a factor of importance, but "size is more important than development in accounting for differences in the level of international activity."[31] Another indication of the same tendency is Dahl and Tufte's finding that, the larger a country is in terms of population, the more it spends per capita on defense. This relationship is especially strong among democratic countries. And again, although the level of development (here measured in terms of gross national product per capita) is also related to the level of defense expenditure, size remains the strongest predictor by far.[32]

A final criticism of the proposition that a low foreign affairs load is a favorable condition is Brian Barry's assertion that "there seems to be no reason why 'consociationalism' should make the conduct of foreign affairs especially difficult and it is significant [that] most non-consociational countries have all-party coalitions in wartime, presumably the better to deal with external threats."[33] The weakness in this argument is the failure to distinguish between the direct and the indirect external effects of small size and between the normal conduct of foreign affairs and the management of severe crises and wars. Of course, wars entail the making of the most fateful decisions, but their favorable effect is of a direct nature—unifying a country's political leaders as well as their followers—while their potential damaging indirect effect of overloading the decision-making process does not present a serious risk, because the management of the war is likely to be given top priority, and other problems are likely to be ignored or postponed.

31. Maurice A. East, "Size and Foreign Policy Behavior: A Test of Two Models," *World Politics* 25, no. 4 (July 1973): 564. For a critical review of the concept of small states in international politics, see Peter R. Baehr, "Small States: A Tool for Analysis?" *World Politics* 27, no. 3 (April 1975): 456–66.

32. Dahl and Tufte, *Size and Democracy*, pp. 122–28.

33. Brian Barry, "Political Accommodation and Consociational Democracy," *British Journal of Political Science* 5, no. 4 (October 1975): 484.

THE STRUCTURE OF CLEAVAGES

When one analyzes the effects of social cleavages upon governmental performance and political stability, the first and most important distinction that has to be made is that between homogeneous societies without major cleavages and significantly plural societies. But plural societies must be distinguished further on the basis of several aspects of their cleavage structures: the number of cleavages and the degree of fragmentation that they cause, the extent to which different cleavages crosscut or coincide, the types and intensities of cleavages, the countervailing effects of overarching loyalties, and finally the manner in which segmental cleavages and party system cleavages are related.

Let us first take a look at the number, types, and fragmentation of the basic cleavages in the four consociational democracies. The major ones are class, religious, and—in Belgium and Switzerland—linguistic cleavages. Because all four are highly industrialized societies, their class structures may be regarded as basically similar.[34] But there are important differences with regard to the other two variables. Table 2 indicates the extent to which religion and language divide the four societies. The measure used was Rae and Taylor's index of fragmentation (F).[35] It is not a simple task to collect the data on religious and linguistic fragmentation. The figure for linguistic fragmentation in Belgium given in table 2 is based on the 1947 census data, in which 60.1 percent of the population was found to be Dutch-speaking and most of the remainder French-speaking. But these data are generally regarded as unreliable. Because of the political sensitivity of the linguistic issue, the question concerning language was not repeated in the 1961 census. However, one can estimate

34. One indicator is nonagricultural employment as a percentage of the population of working age: Austria, 49.2 percent (1951); Belgium, 53.0 percent (1960), the Netherlands, 52.0 percent (1947); Switzerland, 62.8 percent (1960). See Bruce M. Russett et al., *World Handbook of Political and Social Indicators* (New Haven: Yale University Press, 1964), p. 182.

35. Rae and Taylor, *Analysis of Political Cleavages*, pp. 30–33.

TABLE 2. Religious and Linguistic Fragmentation in Four Consociational Democracies (c. 1960)

	Religious Fragmentation	Linguistic Fragmentation
Austria	.19	.03
Belgium	.06	.48
Netherlands	.64	.02
Switzerland	.50	.40

SOURCES: Adapted from Bruce M. Russett et al., *World Handbook of Political and Social Indicators* (New Haven: Yale University Press, 1964), pp. 134–35, 249–54; data supplied by the Federal Statistical Office in Berne, and estimates by the author.

the strengths of the respective linguistic groups on the basis of the population of the different regions. Flanders contained 51.3 percent of the Belgian population in 1961, Wallonia 33.1 percent, and bilingual Brussels 15.6 percent. Since approximately 80 percent of the Bruxellois speak French, the ratio of Flemings to French speakers in the whole country is about 54.4 to 45.6 percent (disregarding the very small German-speaking minority of about half a percent).[36] This estimate yields an index of fragmentation of 0.50, very close to the index presented in table 2.

The Swiss census data on language are complete and reliable, but here another problem presents itself: should the index of fragmentation be based on the total resident population or only on the Swiss citizens? In most countries, the difference would not be great, but the number of foreigners living in Switzerland is very large: 10.8 percent of the population, according to the 1960 census. The citizen population is linguistically more homogeneous than the total population, mainly as a result of the large number of Italians living in Switzerland: of all Italian

36. See Georges Goriely, "Rapport introductif sur 'Bruxelles et le fédéralisme,'" *Res Publica* 13, no. 3–4 (1971): 407–13.

speakers only 38.6 percent are Swiss citizens. The index of linguistic fragmentation for the whole population is 0.47; for citizens only it is 0.40. The latter figure is included in table 2 (and the rule of restricting the analysis to citizens will also be followed in the tables below) because it is the more relevant datum with regard to the political consequences of cleavages. It should be noted that both indices are lower than the index for Belgium, in spite of the fact that more languages are spoken in Switzerland. But in Belgium the two linguistic groups are more nearly equally balanced, whereas the German speakers constitute almost three-fourths of the Swiss population: 74.4 percent of the citizens, and 69.4 percent of the total population.[37]

Austria and the Netherlands are almost completely homogeneous as far as language is concerned. The 1951 census in Austria found 98.7 percent German speakers. A question on language has never been included in any Dutch census. There is a Frisian-speaking minority in one of the northern provinces, but Dutch is also spoken by nearly everyone, so that the Netherlands can be estimated to be at least 99 percent linguistically homogeneous.

The indices of religious fragmentation in table 2 are based on a threefold classification of Roman Catholics, other Christian, and people adhering to other faiths or without church affiliation. The Netherlands and Switzerland are highly fragmented in this respect, whereas Austria and Belgium are more nearly homogeneous. Religious fragmentation in Switzerland would be slightly higher if foreigners were included in the calculation: 0.52 instead of 0.50. The threefold classification of religions is not satisfactory in the Dutch case, because there are significant differences within the Protestant category between the generally more liberal Dutch Reformed Church and the Orthodox Reformed Church. A fivefold classification (Catholics, Dutch Reformed, Orthodox Reformed, other Protestants, no religion)

37. The corresponding percentages of the other language groups are as follows: French, 18.9 percent (total population) and 20.2 percent (citizens); Italian, 9.5 and 4.1 percent respectively; Romansh, 0.9 and 1.0 percent; and other languages, 1.4 and 0.3 percent.

produces a higher index of fragmentation: 0.71. However, this is still not a completely satisfactory classification, because religiosity should be taken into account in addition to church affiliation. A threefold classification that is partly based on estimates concerning regularity of church attendance has the greatest political relevance: practicing Catholics (34 percent), orthodox Calvinists (21 percent), secular people (45 percent).[38] This yields a fragmentation of 0.64, which, as it happens, is the same index as the one presented in the table.

The religious homogeneity of Austria and Belgium is more apparent than real. Austria is 89.4 percent and Belgium 96.8 percent Catholic, but both countries have in fact sharp religious cleavages between practicing and nonpracticing Catholics. At most about one-half of the population of each country attends church regularly. If religiosity as well as church affiliation is taken into account, the religious fragmentation of the two countries is somewhere between 0.45 and 0.50. The failure to include religiosity also gives Austria and Belgium misleadingly low ratings on Marie R. Haug's composite "index of pluralism," based on five variables from the Cross-Polity Survey: language, religion, race, sectionalism, and interest articulation by nonassociational groups. Austria is given the lowest possible overall rating and is included in the category of "negligible pluralism." The Netherlands is in the next category of "moderate pluralism"; Belgium follows next with "marked pluralism," and Switzerland is in the fourth and last category, "extreme pluralism."[39] Because of their linguistic diversity, Belgium and Switzerland should indeed be rated higher than Austria and the Netherlands on an overall index of pluralism, but the four countries do not differ sufficiently to string them out along the entire range of such an index.

38. Lijphart, "Verzuiling," pp. 31–32.

39. Marie R. Haug, "Social and Cultural Pluralism as a Concept in Social System Analysis," *American Journal of Sociology* 73, no. 3 (November 1967): 298–99. The basic data are in Arthur S. Banks and Robert B. Textor, *A Cross-Polity Survey* (Cambridge, Mass.: M.I.T. Press, 1963), app. A.

CROSSCUTTING CLEAVAGES

When there are two or more cleavages, one must examine how they relate to each other and, in particular, whether they tend to crosscut or to coincide. In practice, perfectly crosscutting and perfectly coinciding cleavages occur rarely, but differences in the degree to which they crosscut can be critically important for two reasons. In the first place, the way in which cleavages cut across each other affects the chances for consociational democracy because it affects the numbers and relative sizes of the segments and thus the balance of power among them. Second, crosscutting can have important consequences for the intensity of feelings generated by the cleavages. According to the theory of crosscutting or overlapping memberships which, as indicated earlier, is one of the theoretical bases of Almond's typology, crosscutting entails cross-pressures that make for moderate attitudes and actions.[40] For a somewhat different reason, the extent to which various cleavages cut across the socioeconomic cleavage is especially important. If, for example, the religious cleavage and the social class cleavage crosscut to a high degree, the different religious groups will tend to feel equal. If, on the other hand, the two cleavages tend to coincide, one of the groups is bound to feel resentment over its inferior status and unjustly meager share of material rewards.

The extent of crosscutting in the four consociational countries was measured on the basis of the Swiss census data collected in 1960 and data from surveys conducted in Belgium and the Netherlands in 1956, in Switzerland in 1963, and in Austria in 1967.[41] Two measures of the extent of crosscutting were used.

40. See chapter 1. G. Bingham Powell, Jr., found confirmation of this theory in his Austrian community study; see *Social Fragmentation and Political Hostility: An Austrian Case Study* (Stanford: Stanford University Press, 1970), esp. pp. 37–38. For critiques of the theory, see Peter W. Sperlich, *Conflict and Harmony in Human Affairs: A Study of Cross-Pressures and Political Behavior* (Chicago: Rand McNally, 1971); and Eric A. Nordlinger, *Conflict Regulation in Divided Societies,* Occasional Papers in International Affairs, no. 29 (Cambridge, Mass.: Center for International Affairs, Harvard University, 1972), pp. 93–104.

41. The Swiss census data are unpublished figures supplied by the Federal

The first is the angle of crosscutting, which can vary from 90° (perfect crosscutting at a right angle) to 0° (perfect coincidence of the cleavages). For instance, religious and class cleavages crosscut at a right angle when the ratio of middle-class Protestants to lower-class Protestants is the same as the ratio of middle-class to lower-class Catholics. The angle is 0° when all Protestants belong to the middle class and all Catholics to the lower class.[42]

A graphical presentation of the crosscutting of the major cleavages is attempted in figure 1. Occupations, classified into

---

Statistical Office in Berne. The Austrian survey data (N=1,990) were made available by the Institut für Empirische Sozialforschung in Vienna. The Swiss survey data (N=2,066) were collected by the Institut Suisse d'Opinion Publique in Lausanne. The Belgian (N=979) and Dutch surveys (N=991) were conducted as part of the four-nation Unesco study "Common Ideas about Foreign Peoples." For other secondary analyses of the Unesco data, see Erich Reigrotzki and Nels Anderson, "National Stereotypes and Foreign Contacts," *Public Opinion Quarterly* 23, no. 4 (winter 1959–60): 515–28; Nels Anderson, "Opinion on Europe," *European Yearbook*, vol. 5 (The Hague: Nijhoff, 1959), pp. 143–60; and Marten Brouwer, "International Contacts and Integration-Mindedness," *Polls* 1, no. 2 (summer 1965): 1–11. A weakness of the Belgian and Dutch surveys (and also of the Swiss survey) is that the representativeness of the samples is not entirely satisfactory. In particular, manual workers are seriously underrepresented. See Heidi Sauer, *Quantitative Data on Common Ideas about Foreign Peoples: Comparative Sample Survey of Factors Affecting National Stereotypes and Prejudices* (Cologne: Unesco Institute for Social Sciences, 1958). In the Swiss survey, the occupation variable does not include husband's occupation in the case of housewives and previous occupation in the case of retired people. Because occupation was used as the indicator of social class position, the usable proportion of the sample for this purpose became overwhelmingly male (75.7 percent). Finally, a disadvantage of the Austrian survey is that it was taken in 1967, when the era of grand coalitions had already ended. In order to check the reliability of the survey data, an effort was made to compare the indices of fragmentation and crosscutting based on census data against the same indices computed from the survey data, whenever both sets of data were available. The two sets of figures were very close in all instances, as shown below. The census-based indices are given first: Religious fragmentation in the Netherlands: 0.64 and 0.61. Religious fragmentation, Switzerland: 0.50 and 0.50. Linguistic fragmentation, Switzerland: 0.40 and 0.44. Index of religious and linguistic crosscutting, Switzerland: 0.48 and 0.49. Angle of crosscutting, Switzerland: 61° and 56°. Party system fragmentation, Austria: 0.59 (based on the 1962 election results) and 0.53.

42. When the four frequencies in a 2 × 2 table are labeled f_{11}, f_{12}, f_{21}, and f_{22}, and $f_{11}f_{22} \leqslant f_{12}f_{21}$, the formula is as follows:

$$\text{Angle} = \frac{f_{11}f_{22}}{f_{11}f_{22} + f_{12}f_{21}} \cdot 180°.$$

FIG. 1. Crosscutting Cleavages in Four Consociational Democracies

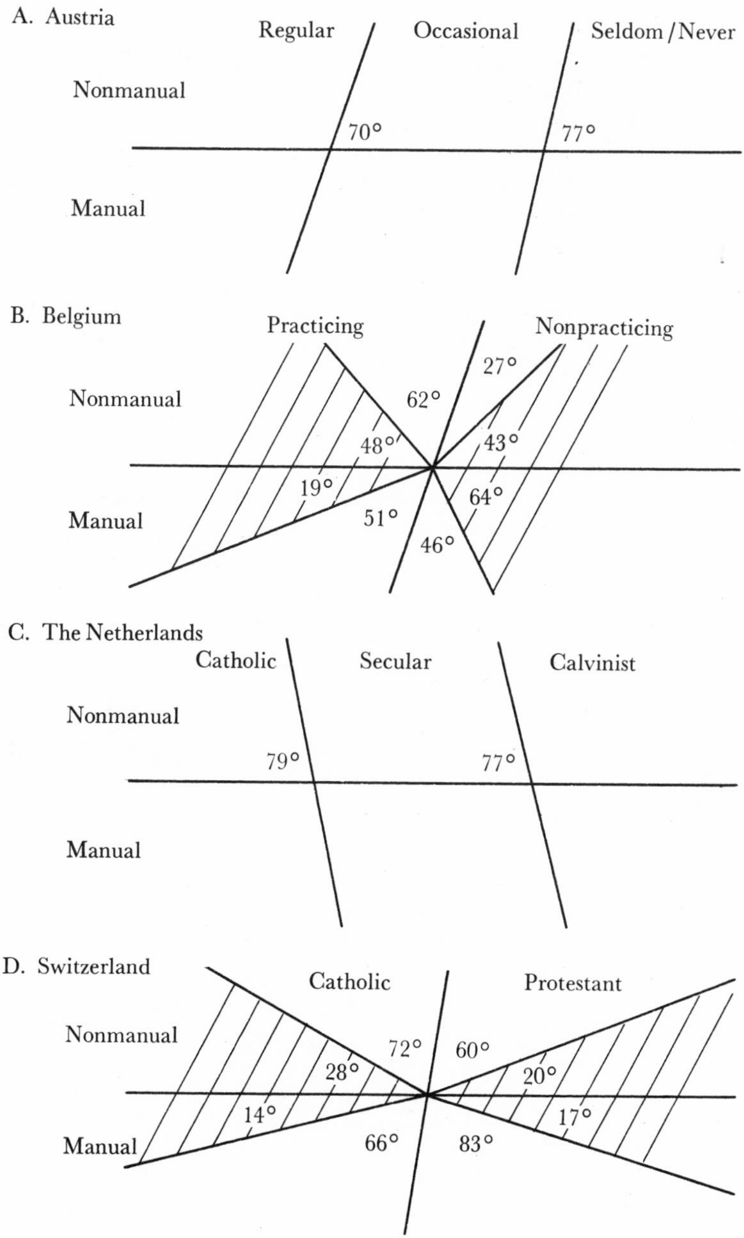

manual and nonmanual categories, were used as indicators of social class position.[43] The Austrian respondents were further classified according to whether they reported regular, occasional, or less frequent church attendance. Because the angle of crosscutting can be calculated only for dichotomous cleavages, the first line of religious cleavage is based on a comparison between regular churchgoers and all others, the second line on a comparison of regular and occasional churchgoers with those attending seldom or never. A similar procedure was followed in the Dutch case. In both countries religious and class cleavages come close to cutting across each other at right angles.[44] This conclusion is also applicable to the Belgian and Swiss cases, in which the angles are 70° and 80° respectively. In order to represent the relationship of the linguistic cleavage to the other two cleavages, a picture should be drawn of three planes crosscutting each other in three-dimensional space, but this would probably cause more confusion than enlightenment. Instead, the four angles resulting from the intersection of class and religion were divided on the basis of the strengths of the linguistic groups. The French speakers are in the shaded areas. Language clearly appears to cut across the other two cleavages to a high degree.

The exact angles of crosscutting between all pairs of dichotomized cleavages are presented in table 3. For Austria, religiosity was dichotomized into regular churchgoers and all others. For the Netherlands, the dichotomy is secular versus Catholics and Calvinists; this yields a perfect right angle (90°). The dichotomy for language in Switzerland is German versus the other three official languages. Table 3 confirms the impressions derived from figure 1 that language cuts across both religion and class in Belgium as well as in Switzerland, but three qualifications should be added. The 75° angle of linguistic and class crosscutting in Belgium does not sufficiently reflect the remnants of the socially inferior position of Flemish in the

43. The criteria for classification were taken from Robert R. Alford, *Party and Society: The Anglo-American Democracies* (Chicago: Rand McNally, 1963), pp. 69–71.

44. This is in accord with Powell's finding in the community of Hallein; see his *Social Fragmentation*, pp. 24–25.

TABLE 3. Crosscutting Cleavages in Four Consociational Democracies (c. 1960)

	Index of Crosscutting (*XC*)			Angle of Crosscutting		
	Relig. and Class	Relig. and Lang.	Lang. and Class	Relig. and Class	Relig. and Lang.	Lang. and Class
Austria	.50	—	—	70°	—	—
Belgium	.49	.48	.50	70°	55°	75°
Netherlands	.51	—	—	90°	—	—
Switzerland	.50	.48	.50	83°	61°	71°

SOURCES: Calculated from census data supplied by the Federal Statistical Office in Berne (1960), the Unesco survey data on Belgium and the Netherlands (1956), Austrian survey data supplied by the Institut für Empirische Sozialforschung (1967), and Swiss survey data supplied by the Institut Suisse d'Opinion Publique (1963).

nineteenth century, expressed well in the phrase cited by Lorwin: "French in the parlor; Flemish in the kitchen." Second, the 55° angle between the religious and linguistic cleavages in Belgium is the lowest value of table 3; it reflects the greater religiosity of the Flemings. But this finding should be considered in the light of the following comment by Lorwin: "In the Belgian self-image, Wallonia has become dechristianized while Flanders has remained Catholic. The reality is more nuanced, although the self-image is one form of reality. The contrast is chiefly between industrial-and-urban and rural-and-small-town populations. Walloon rural areas have retained their Catholicism but in the large Flemish cities the Church has lost most industrial workers."[45] Nevertheless, it is an exaggeration to state that in Belgium the "religious divisions reinforce, and tend to follow the

45. Val R. Lorwin, "Belgium: Religion, Class, and Language in National Politics," in Dahl, *Political Oppositions,* pp. 158–59. See also the estimates of religious practice in Flanders and Wallonia in Jean Meynaud et al., *La décision politique en Belgique* (Paris: Colin, 1965), pp. 24–25.

same lines as, the divisions of language" and to contrast Belgium with Switzerland where "the religious cleavage, instead of coinciding with the linguistic boundaries, cuts across them."[46] Finally, the position of the relatively small group of Italian-speaking Swiss citizens is not reflected either in figure 1, in which they could not be represented because of their small number, or in table 3, where they are combined with the French speakers and Romansh speakers. Because the vast majority of the Italian-speaking population is Catholic, the linguistic cleavage (Italian speakers versus all others) and the religious cleavage cut across each other at an angle of only 6°.

The other measure of crosscutting presented in table 3 is Rae and Taylor's index of crosscutting (*XC*). They define *XC* as "the proportion of all pairs of individuals whose two members are in the same group of one cleavage but in different groups of the other cleavage." An advantage of this measure is that the cleavages do not have to be dichotomized. It can vary from zero, when the two cleavages coincide completely, to a maximum that depends in a complex way on the extent of fragmentation of the two crosscutting cleavages but is generally not much higher than 0.50.[47] All of the indices of crosscutting in table 3 are quite high and very close to each other in value.

According to the theory of crosscutting cleavages, the moderating effect of such divisions depends first of all on the extent to which they cut across rather than coincide with each other, but also on the intensities of the cleavages or, more precisely, on their differential intensities. The crosscutting of cleavages of equal intensity may merely lead to the formation of a number of antagonistic groups among which cooperation is extremely difficult. In such a case, Dahl argues, crosscutting has a disintegrating effect: "Unifying effects cannot occur if all the cleavages are felt with equal intensity. Conciliation is encouraged by crosscutting cleavages *only* if some cleavages are less significant than others."[48] This is also E. E. Schattschneider's view: conflict

46. Leslie Lipson, *The Democratic Civilization* (New York: Oxford University Press, 1964), p. 152.
47. Rae and Taylor, *Analysis of Political Cleavages*, pp. 92–95, 99–103.
48. Dahl, *Political Oppositions*, p. 378n.

and cleavages of unequal intensity result in "a system of domination and subordination of conflicts," and in a process that "is not to divide and divide and divide to infinity but to divide and unify as a part of the same process."[49]

The theory of consociational democracy does not rely on the presence of crosscutting cleavages as a primary explanation of the political stability of plural societies. But crosscutting divisions of equal or unequal intensities are a factor of subsidiary importance, and they may or may not be favorable to consociationalism. When the cleavages are equal, they result in separate internally homogeneous segments that are not strongly subject to cross-pressures. The only effect that this type of division has on the chances of consociational democracy is that it creates a society with several segments. If this means an all-minority situation with not too many segments rather than a bipolar situation, it is a favorable effect; if it means a highly fractionalized society, this is not a favorable result. Unequal cleavages entail fewer segments that are less homogeneous internally. The cross-pressures within the segments will encourage moderate attitudes. But here, as we shall see, the problem arises of how the less intense cleavages are represented politically and how the issues affecting the less intense cleavages are resolved.

OVERARCHING LOYALTIES

The conflict potential of cleavages also depends on the degree to which their inherent intensities are moderated by overarching loyalties. As Harry Eckstein points out, "if division and cohesion were a zero-sum . . . the amount of cohesion could be inferred from the divisions."[50] But divisive and cohesive forces—cleavages and overarching loyalties—may operate simultaneously, and the conflict potential of cleavages depends on the combined effect of the two forces. Overarching loyalties may

49. E. E. Schattschneider, *The Semisovereign People: A Realist's View of Democracy in America* (New York: Holt, Rinehart and Winston, 1960), pp. 67–68.

50. Harry Eckstein, *Division and Cohesion in Democracy: A Study of Norway* (Princeton: Princeton University Press, 1966), p. 67.

produce cohesion for the entire society or for particular segments. An example of the latter is the unity in the Dutch Catholic and Calvinist subcultures. Even though, as we have seen, the religious and class cleavages of the Netherlands crosscut at virtually right angles, the class cleavage has not fragmented the Catholic and Calvinist segments. The explanation lies in the cohesive force of the religious bonds rather than the weakness of the class cleavage. In the secular segment, where no such unifying force exists, the class cleavage forms the boundary between separate Socialist and Liberal subcultures. Similarly, the integrative power of Catholicism in Belgium has been stronger than the class cleavage among practicing Catholics. But class differences do divide Socialists and Liberals. The interaction of cleavages and overarching loyalties thus determines the number and nature of the segments in a plural society.

Overarching loyalties are even more important if they provide cohesion for the society as a whole and thus moderate the intensities of all cleavages simultaneously. Nationalism is potentially such a cohesive force. Not only its strength is important, but also the question of whether it truly unites the society or instead acts as an additional cleavage by providing a loyalty to a "nation" that is not coterminous with the state. Nationalism is not strong in any of the four consociational countries. It is probably strongest in the Netherlands, a country with a long history as an independent nation in approximately its present geographical contours. In Switzerland, local attachments tend to outweigh national allegiance.

National sentiment in Belgium is weaker, according to Lorwin, than in any other European country.[51] But Austria is not very different from Belgium in this respect. An opinion poll conducted in 1956 revealed great confusion on the question of national identity: approximately half of the respondents believed that the Austrians constituted a nation, but the other half regarded themselves as part of the German nation.[52] To a significant extent these different opinions coincided with the major

51. Lorwin, "Belgium," p. 176.

52. Rodney P. Stiefbold et al., *Wahlen und Parteien in Österreich: Österreichisches Wahlhandbuch,* 3 vols. (Vienna: Verlag für Jugend und Volk, 1966), 2: 584–85.

segmental cleavage. William T. Bluhm states that in 1945 Catholics and Socialists had "different conceptions of the meaning and values of Austria as a community, different conceptions of Austrian identity." The major Catholic leaders were deeply attached to the values of the old empire and "thought of Austria in a total cultural sense, not only as a political community. Most of the Socialists, by contrast, had been cultural as well as political Pan-Germans."[53] Another example of the phenomenon of a nationalism that focuses on a nation which is not the national state is Flemish nationalism. In Flanders, the Flemish national symbols evoke more enthusiasm than the Belgian ones, which may even have a negative connotation for many Flemings.[54]

REPRESENTATIVE PARTY SYSTEMS

Political parties are the principal institutional means for translating segmental cleavages into the political realm. Hence the relationship of party system cleavages to the other major cleavages in society is of great importance. Table 4 presents the extent of crosscutting between the party system cleavages and the religious, class, and linguistic cleavages in the four consociational democracies. Only the major parties were taken into consideration: the Catholic, Socialist, and Liberal or Radical parties in all four countries, the two Protestant parties in the Netherlands and the Swiss Peasants' party.[55] Crosscutting is again shown in terms of both the index (*XC*) and the angle. For the purpose of calculating the angles, the parties were grouped into two alterna-

53. William T. Bluhm, *Building an Austrian Nation: The Political Integration of a Western State* (New Haven: Yale University Press, 1973), p. 63.

54. A royal house can be a particularly important symbol of nationalism and national unity; see the discussion in chapter 2.

55. For Switzerland, it is not easy to decide which parties are the "major" ones. The four parties included in table 4 are the major ones at the federal level and are represented in the Federal Council. But at the cantonal level several other parties have seats on the executive bodies. On the Swiss party system, see Erich Gruner, *Die Parteien in der Schweiz* (Berne: Francke, 1969); and Jürg Steiner, "Typologisierung des schweizerischen Parteiensystems," in *Annuaire suisse de science politique,* vol. 9 (Lausanne: Association Suisse de Science Politique, 1969), pp. 21–40.

TABLE 4. Crosscutting of Party System Cleavages and Religious, Class, and Linguistic Cleavages (c. 1960)

	Index of Cross-cutting (*XC*)	Angle of Crosscutting	
		Relig. vs. Secular Parties	Soc. vs. Nonsoc. Parties
Austria			
Parties and religion	.41	18°	18°
Parties and class	.45	39°	38°
Belgium			
Parties and religion	.26	4°	7°
Parties and class	.47	60°	41°
Parties and language	.49	72°	71°
Netherlands			
Parties and religion	.22	4°	8°
Parties and class	.52	89°	62°
Switzerland			
Parties and religion	.37	2°	44°
Parties and class	.56	84°	50°
Parties and language	.62	74°	89°

SOURCE: See table 3.

tive dichotomies—religious versus secular and socialist versus nonsocialist parties—and the values of the angle of crosscutting are given for both dichotomies.[56]

In all four countries, there is a very strong relationship between party preference and religion. Practicing Catholics in Belgium and the Netherlands give overwhelming support to the Catholic party, across class and linguistic cleavages. The same pattern holds, although not quite so strongly, for Austria and Switzerland. The Dutch Protestants give strong support to the

56. The religious dichotomy for the Netherlands is secular people versus Catholics and Calvinists. For the Catholic versus non-Catholic dichotomy, the angles of crosscutting are 3° and 4° respectively. The Italian speakers in Switzerland are not included in table 4.

Protestant Anti-Revolutionary party and the Christian Historical Union. Support for the Socialist and Liberal parties tends to follow the class cleavage. Among the Belgian nonchurchgoers, the Dutch secular group, and the Swiss Protestants, the manual workers generally support the Socialists and high proportions of the people in nonmanual occupations support the Liberals. The language differences of Belgium and Switzerland have little influence on party choice.[57]

Both the values of *XC* and the angles of crosscutting are lowest for the crosscutting of parties and religion in all four countries. Class and party crosscutting follows next, and linguistic and party crosscutting approaches a right angle most closely in Belgium and in Switzerland with only a single small exception. Generally, then, the party system cleavages tend to coincide with the religious cleavages, to coincide partly and crosscut partly with the class cleavage, and to crosscut almost perfectly with the linguistic cleavages. Which pattern is more favorable for consociational democracy? Seymour Martin Lipset argues that "a stable democracy requires a situation in which all the major parties include supporters from many segments of the population. A system in which the support of different parties corresponds too closely to basic social divisions cannot continue on a democratic basis, for it reflects a state of conflict so intense and clear-cut as to rule out compromise."[58] This statement is borne out, for example, by the crosscutting character of the Dutch religious parties. The fact that these parties are heterogeneous

57. For more recent data on electoral behavior, see Nicole Delruelle, René Evalenko, and William Fraeys, *Le comportement politique des électeurs belges* (Brussels: Éditions de l'Institut de Sociologie, Université Libre de Bruxelles, 1970); A.-P. Frognier, "Distances entre partis et clivages en Belgique," *Res Publica* 15, no. 2 (1973): 291–311; Keith Hill, "Belgium: Political Change in a Segmented Society," in *Electoral Behavior: A Comparative Handbook,* ed. Richard Rose (New York: Free Press, 1974), pp. 29–107; Henry H. Kerr, Jr., *Switzerland: Social Cleavages and Partisan Conflict,* Professional Papers in Contemporary Political Sociology, no. 06-002 (London:Sage, 1974); Arend Lijphart, "The Netherlands: Continuity and Change in Voting Behavior," in Rose, *Electoral Behavior,* pp. 227–68; and Werkgroep Nationaal Verkiezingsonderzoek 1972, *De Nederlandse kiezer '72* (Alphen aan den Rijn: Samsom, 1973).

58. Seymour Martin Lipset, *Political Man: The Social Bases of Politics* (Garden City, N. Y.: Doubleday, 1960), p. 31.

with regard to class has had a strongly moderating effect on the intensity of socioeconomic conflict or potential conflict of this nature. On the other hand, the fact that none of the Dutch parties is religiously heterogeneous has not prevented the resolution of religious issues by consociational means.

The Belgian case offers the best opportunity to compare the consequences of different forms of aggregation by political parties, because it has three clearly and unambiguously different patterns of relationships between parties and social cleavages: an institutionalized cleavage (religion), a semi-institutionalized cleavage (class), and a noninstitutionalized cleavage (language). Derek W. Urwin compares the resolution of the schools issue—a religious conflict—with the failure to find a solution for the linguistic issue, and concludes that the Belgian party leaders could reach a compromise on the schools issue because of the "institutionalization of the division through strong party organization"—that is, because of, not in spite of, the almost perfect coincidence of the party system cleavage and the religious cleavage. On the other hand, an institutionalized dialogue on the language issue has not developed because "the linguistic cleavage has not historically been translated into the party system."[59] Lorwin makes this point even more forcefully when he states that the first reason why the linguistic issue is so intractable is the following: "The sentimental and practical interests of the two linguistic communities are not effectively organized. . . . There are no recognized representatives qualified to formulate demands, to negotiate, and to fulfill commitments."[60] The Belgian sociologist A. van den Brande also supports this argument and suggests that the lack of institutionalization of the linguistic issue is one of the reasons why this conflict occasionally becomes violent—"searching for other channels where the political ones fail."[61]

59. Derek W. Urwin, "Social Cleavages and Political Parties in Belgium: Problems of Institutionalization," *Political Studies* 17, no. 3 (September 1970): 326, 336.

60. Lorwin, "Belgium," p. 174.

61. A. van den Brande, "Elements for a Sociological Analysis of the Impact of the Main Conflicts on Belgian Political Life," *Res Publica* 9, no. 3 (1967): 462.

There is an additional reason why the crosscutting of the party system cleavage and the linguistic cleavage has been an obstacle to the resolution of the conflict. Just as cross-pressures on the individual voter may lead him to cast a moderate vote or to abstain from voting altogether, so a cross-pressured party may be either moderate or inactive on the issue in question. Thus crosscutting can result in immobilism. Eckstein argues that, in general, this is a weakness of systems characterized by crosscutting cleavages: such systems, he states, "are always likely to be more durable than effective" because the result of crosscutting generally is "to keep decisions from being taken, due to lack of pressures for them or due to the fact that pressures mutually cancel one another."[62] Similarly, Schattsschneider argues that "a great number of potential conflicts . . . cannot be developed because they are *blotted out* by stronger systems of antagonism."[63]

On the whole, the evidence indicates that crosscutting may be conducive to consociational democracy, but its influence is not very strong and not even always positive. The only unambiguously favorable types of crosscutting are the crosscutting of class cleavages with various kinds of segmental cleavages—producing segments with approximate economic equality—and the "crosscutting," or rather overlap, of societywide overarching loyalties. The discussion of federalism in the next section will present another opportunity to evaluate the role of crosscutting, but this will not lead to a change in the conclusion concerning its marginal importance.

SEGMENTAL ISOLATION AND FEDERALISM

As shown in chapter 1, the four European cases of consociational democracy are characterized by an even more clearly fragmented political culture than the systems belonging to Al-

62. Eckstein, *Division and Cohesion*, pp. 193–94. Van den Brande suggests that, because of the many cross-pressures on the Belgian voter, "obligatory voting is not an accident in Belgium"; see his "Elements for a Sociological Analysis," p. 465.

63. Schattschneider, *Semisovereign People*, p. 68 (italics added).

mond's Continental European type. This appears to be paradoxical, because one would expect instability to increase as fragmentation increases. On the other hand, clear boundaries between the segments of a plural society have the advantage of limiting mutual contacts and consequently of limiting the chances of ever-present potential antagonisms to erupt into actual hostility. Quincy Wright argues that "ideologies accepted by different groups within a society may be inconsistent without creating tension." The danger of great tension arises only when these groups "are in close contact."[64] David Easton argues in a similar vein that efforts to homogenize a fragmented system may not be the best way of achieving a stable, integrated system: "Greater success may be attained through steps that conduce to the development of a deeper sense of mutual awareness and responsiveness among *encapsulated* cultural units."[65] And Lorwin makes the following remark about Belgium, which is equally applicable to the other consociational democracies: "If meaningful personal contacts with people of other subcultures are few, so are the occasions for personal hostility."[66]

This argument appears to contradict the widely held notion—one of the theoretical bases of overlapping memberships theory—that mutual contacts between different people and groups foster mutual understanding. This discrepancy can be resolved by making a distinction between essentially homogeneous societies, where increased contacts are likely to lead to an increase in mutual understanding and further homogenization, and plural societies, where close contacts are likely to lead to strain and hostility. Walker Connor makes this distinction when he argues that "increased contacts help to dissolve regional cultural distinctions within a country such as the United States. Yet, if one is dealing not with minor variations of the same culture, but with two quite distinct and self-differentiating cultures, are not increased contacts between the

64. Quincy Wright, "The Nature of Conflict," *Western Political Quarterly* 4, no. 2 (June 1951): 196.

65. David Easton, *A Systems Analysis of Political Life* (New York: Wiley, 1965), p. 250 (italics added).

66. Lorwin, "Belgium," p. 187.

two apt to increase antagonisms?"[67] This proposition can be refined further by stating both the degree of segmented pluralism and the extent of mutual contacts in terms of continua instead of dichotomies: the volume and intensity of contacts must not exceed the commensurate degree of homogeneity. In the words of Karl W. Deutsch, a transaction-integration *balance* is necessary because "the number of opportunities for possible violent conflict will increase with the volume and range of mutual transactions."[68]

A plural society tends to be organized along segmental cleavages, and these separate organizations entail a degree of segmental isolation that is conducive to consociational democracy. On the other hand, as we have seen, the consociational method of segmental autonomy substantially furthers the development of organizational networks within each segment. It may therefore be more proper to regard the segmental isolation resulting from separate political and social organizations as a method than as a precondition of consociational democracy. There is, however, one especially important type of segmental isolation that is definitely not "created" by consociational democracy: segmental isolation along geographical lines. Here, too, consociationalism can increase the degree of separateness by applying segmental autonomy of a territorial kind: federalism. The fact that two of the consociational democracies are federations offers an opportunity to investigate to what extent they have taken advantage of the federal method.

Switzerland is divided into 25 cantons—or, strictly speaking, 19 cantons and 6 half-cantons—and Austria is divided into 9 *Länder*. Especially in Switzerland it is important to analyze the cantonal level as well as the national level, because Switzerland is highly decentralized. A useful indicator of the relative importance of the national government compared with the governments at lower levels is the percentage of all government revenues (including social security and public enterprises) that is

67. Walker Connor, "Self-Determination: The New Phase," *World Politics* 20, no. 1 (October 1967): 49–50.

68. Karl W. Deutsch, *Political Community at the International Level* (Garden City, N. Y.: Doubleday, 1954), p. 39.

spent by the national government. The figures, based on 1959 data, are 61 percent for Switzerland and 84 percent for Austria. Other Western federal states have percentages between these two: Canada, 65 percent; West Germany, 74 percent; and the United States, 77 percent. Switzerland has the lowest percentage, but the percentage for Austria comes close to the percentages in a number of unitary states in Western Europe.[69] Decentralized government also means decentralized politics; as Roger Girod states, "on the whole Swiss political life is mainly on a cantonal basis."[70]

What is the effect of the division into cantons and Länder on the fragmentation and crosscutting of the major cleavages? How does the national cleavage structure compare with those of the cantons and the Länder? Let us first look at the Swiss case. Table 5 presents several measures of fragmentation and crosscutting for each of the 25 cantons (listed in descending order of population) and for the whole country, based on the 1960 census data. All noncitizens are excluded, as are all persons speaking a language other than the four official ones and persons who cannot be classified as either Protestant or Catholic.[71] The measures of fragmentation are Rae and Taylor's index F, and a very simple indicator of fragmentation, or rather of homogeneity: the size of the largest group. The Protestants are the largest religious group in Switzerland, with 58.1 percent of the population. Almost all cantons are more homogeneous in this respect; only in Geneva, Solothurn, and Graubünden does the largest group constitute a smaller percentage of the population than the national percentage. Measured in terms of the index of religious fragmentation, only Graubünden is more fragmented than the country as a whole.[72] As far as linguistic fragmentation is con-

69. Russett et al., *World Handbook,* pp. 64–65.

70. Girod, "Geography of the Swiss Party System," p. 133.

71. The exclusion of noncitizens reduces the population by 10.6 percent. The exclusion of the other two groups leads to another 1.6 percent reduction. Hence, table 5 is based on 87.6 percent of the total resident population in 1960.

72. The index of religious fragmentation in table 5 differs slightly from the same index for Switzerland given in table 2 because table 5 is not based on the total citizen population (see fn. 71, above).

cerned, there are three cantons (Valais, Fribourg, and Graubünden) that are more fragmented than the nation as a whole. All other cantons are more homogeneous in this respect. Religious and linguistic fragmentation are combined in the fifth and sixth columns of table 5. The first of these columns presents the largest of the eight religious-linguistic groups. The other column is the index of fragmentation calculated on the assumption that religion and language form a single variable with eight categories. Again only Graubünden turns out to be more fragmented than the country as a whole.

The angle of crosscutting in table 5 is based on the Protestant-Catholic dichotomy and a linguistic dichotomy of the largest linguistic group versus all others. For the nation and most of the cantons this means German versus the other three languages. The only exceptions are Vaud, Geneva, Valais, Fribourg, and Neuchâtel, where French is the dominant language, and Italian-speaking Ticino. Only three cantons have values of *XC* and eight cantons have angles of crosscutting that exceed the values for the whole country.

Table 6 summarizes the figures for the 25 cantons by providing the means and weighted means of the various measures of fragmentation and crosscutting. The weighted means—weighted by the population sizes of the cantons—are the most appropriate summary measures if we want to compare the cantons collectively with the whole nation. According to all of the measures, the federal division of the country has the effect of creating cantons considerably more homogeneous, and with considerably less crosscutting by the two cleavages, than the nation itself. This is not in accord with the norm of crosscutting cleavages theory, which prescribes that federal boundaries should crosscut rather than follow basic social cleavages; in Lipset's words: "Democracy needs cleavage *within* linguistic or religious groups, not *between* them."[73]

As far as the linguistic question is concerned, the Swiss formula for the management of relations between the different groups contains the following elements: (1) increasing the

73. Lipset, *Political Man,* p. 92 (italics added).

TABLE 5. Religious and Linguistic Fragmentation and Crosscutting in the Swiss Cantons (citizens only), 1960

	Religious Fragmentation		Linguistic Fragmentation		Relig. and Ling. Fragmentation		Relig. and Ling. Crosscutting	
	Largest group (in %)	Index (*F*)	Largest group (in %)	Index (*F*)	Largest group (in %)	Index (*F*)	Index (*XC*)	Angle
Berne	84.7	.26	84.3	.27	77.4	.38	.24	13°
Zurich	74.4	.38	95.9	.08	72.6	.42	.38	35°
Vaud	79.4	.33	87.7F	.22	70.6PF	.46	.38	69°
Aargau	58.4	.49	98.2	.04	57.6	.50	.49	66°
St. Gallen	60.1C	.48	98.5	.03	59.0CG	.50	.48	75°
Lucerne	86.2C	.24	98.3	.03	84.9CG	.26	.25	61°
Basel-City	66.1	.45	93.9	.12	63.5	.50	.44	47°
Geneva	56.8	.49	82.7F	.29	46.5PF	.64	.50	83°
Solothurn	56.4C	.49	97.0	.06	54.6CG	.52	.49	79°
Valais	96.2C	.07	64.3F	.46	62.2CF	.50	.47	69°
Ticino	92.8C	.13	88.6I	.21	87.5CI	.23	.12	2°
Fribourg	86.5C	.23	64.9F	.46	62.2CF	.54	.39	16°
Thurgau	67.2	.44	98.6	.03	66.7	.45	.44	41°
Graubünden	53.0	.50	60.0	.54	41.2	.74	.44	29°
Neuchâtel	77.8	.35	85.9F	.25	68.0PF	.50	.40	59°
Basel-Country	73.5	.39	96.5	.07	71.8	.42	.39	43°
Schwyz	93.8C	.12	98.7	.03	92.6CG	.14	.14	82°

TABLE 5. *(Continued)*

	Religious Fragmentation		Linguistic Fragmentation		Relig. and Ling. Fragmentation		Relig. and Ling. Crosscutting	
	Largest group (in %)	Index (*F*)	Largest group (in %)	Index (*F*)	Largest group (in %)	Index (*F*)	Index (*XC*)	Angle
Schaffhausen	79.1	.33	97.7	.05	78.2	.35	.32	26°
Zug	83.6C	.27	97.7	.05	81.4CG	.31	.30	86°
Appenzell A.R.	83.5	.28	99.0	.02	83.0	.29	.28	28°
Glarus	68.0	.44	98.0	.04	67.3	.45	.43	36°
Uri	92.6C	.14	98.2	.04	91.1CG	.16	.16	55°
Obwalden	96.6C	.07	99.1	.02	95.8CG	.08	.08	36°
Nidwalden	92.4C	.14	98.8	.02	91.4CG	.16	.15	59°
Appenzell I.R.	96.4C	.07	99.7	.01	96.1CG	.08	.07	58°
Switzerland	58.1	.49	74.7	.40	46.5	.68	.48	61°

SOURCE: Calculated from census data supplied by the Federal Statistical Office.

NOTE: Unless otherwise specified, the largest group is Protestant (column 1), German-speaking (column 3), and both Protestant and German-speaking (column 5). In other cases the following abbreviations are used to indicate the religious and/or linguistic character of the largest groups: P = Protestant, C = Roman Catholic, G = German, F = French, and I = Italian.

TABLE 6. Fragmentation and Crosscutting in Switzerland: Cantonal Averages and National Totals (1960)

	Cantons Mean	Cantons Weighted Mean	Switzerland
Religious fragmentation:			
Largest group (%)	78.2	75.4	58.1
Index of fragmentation (*F*)	.30	.34	.49
Linguistic fragmentation:			
Largest group (%)	91.3	89.9	74.7
Index of fragmentation (*F*)	.14	.17	.40
Religious and linguistic fragmentation:			
Largest group (%)	72.9	69.5	46.5
Index of fragmentation (*F*)	.38	.43	.68
Crosscutting:			
Index (*XC*)	.33	.36	.48
Angle	50°	46°	61°

SOURCE: See table 5.

homogeneity of the constituent units of the federation by means of maximum possible territorial segregation of the different groups, and (2) placing all functions in which language may become a sensitive issue, such as educational, intellectual, and artistic matters, under cantonal instead of federal jurisdiction. It is significant that the federation has four official languages but that only three cantons are officially bilingual (Berne, Fribourg, and Valais) and one trilingual (Graubünden).

There are, of course, several cantons that are not linguistically homogeneous. How can their civil peace be explained? An examination of the deviant case of the separatist movement in the Bernese Jura can throw significant light on the question. Why has only Berne experienced serious language conflict, and not the other three formally bilingual and trilingual cantons? Steiner's explanation is based on balance of power considerations. He argues that the main source of discontent in the Bernese Jura is that the French-speaking Catholic inhabitants are a minority in every respect. Both in the country as a whole and in Berne, German-speakers and Protestants form majorities.[74] An examination of table 5 and of some of the data not reproduced in the table bears out this argument. French-speaking, Italian-speaking, and Romansh-speaking Catholics are the groups that are minorities in both respects within the country. Within the present cantons, they are never in this double minority position. French-speaking Catholics are a clear majority in Valais and Fribourg (62.2 percent in both cantons), and they constitute a substantial minority only in Berne, Vaud, Geneva, and Neuchâtel (7.8, 17.1, 36.2, and 17.9 percent respectively). The last three cantons have French-speaking majorities so that their French-speaking Catholics are in a majority in one respect. Italian-speaking Catholics are an overwhelming majority in Ticino (87.5 percent), and a substantial minority (8.7 percent)—like the Romansh-speaking Catholics (19.3 percent)—in Graubünden. Here these two groups appear to be in a double minority position because the canton has a majority of German-speakers and Protestants. But Graubünden is a rather special case in that it has a high degree of decentralization within the canton; James A. Dunn states that it might almost be called "cantonal federalism."[75]

Steiner's balance-of-power argument receives further support from the results of the 1959 and 1974 referenda on the question of forming a separate canton in the Jura region. Only three Jurassian districts in the north voted in favor; these districts have Catholic and French-speaking majorities and are therefore in a double minority position. The other four districts all voted against a separate canton, and, significantly, none of them are in a double minority situation: the northern district of Laufen is German-speaking and Catholic and the three Southern districts have French-speaking and Protestant majorities.[76]

74. Steiner, *Amicable Agreement,* p. 256.

75. James A. Dunn, Jr., " 'Consociational Democracy' and Language Conflict: A Comparison of the Belgian and Swiss Experiences," *Comparative Political Studies* 5, no. 1 (April 1972): 20.

76. Various data on the religious and linguistic composition of the Jurassian

An additional explanation may be found in the fact that the religious and linguistic cleavages in the canton of Berne tend to coincide rather than crosscut. Both the index and the angle of crosscutting in Berne are much lower than for Switzerland as a whole and also considerably lower than the averages for the cantons (see tables 5 and 6). In the other cantons that are relatively heterogeneous in both respects. (i.e., whose indices of religious and linguistic fragmentation are both greater than 0.20), and where consequently the extent of crosscutting is an important factor, there is in fact considerable crosscutting These cantons are Vaud, Geneva, Fribourg, Graubünden, and Neuchâtal. In all five, both the index and the angle of crosscutting exceed those found in Berne. Moreover, these measures for Berne are well below the averages for the cantons, whereas the same measures for the other five cantons are almost all above the cantonal averages.

If a separate Jurassian canton should be set up—comprising either the entire Bernese Jura or more probably, in view of the 1974 referendum, only the three northern separatist districts—its French-speaking Catholic residents would exchange their double minority position in the canton of Berne for a double majority position. Dahl states that the solution of a separate canton "appears to be quite in the Swiss scheme of mutual guarantees."[77] Dividing a canton would indeed not be an unprecedented step. Three cantons have been divided in Swiss history: Unterwalden into Obwalden and Nidwalden in the fifteenth

---

districts are provided in François-L. Reymond, "La question jurassienne et l'évolution du mouvement séparatiste, 1959–1964," in *Annuaire suisse de science politique*, vol. 5 (Lausanne: Association Suisse de Science Politique, 1965), esp. pp. 35–36. See also Kurt B. Mayer, "The Jura Problem: Ethnic Conflict in Switzerland," *Social Research* 35, no. 4 (winter 1968): 707–41; Michel Bassand, "Changement social et antagonismes sociaux: Aspects sociologiques de la 'question jurassienne,'" *Les intérêts du Jura* 43, no. 8 (August 1972): 163–82; Kenneth D. McRae, *Switzerland: Example of Cultural Coexistence*, Contemporary Affairs, no. 33 (Toronto: Canadian Institute of International Affairs, 1964), pp. 57–61; and William R. Keech, "Linguistic Diversity and Political Conflict: Some Observations Based on Four Swiss Cantons," *Comparative Politics* 4, no. 3 (April 1974): 387–404.

77. Robert A. Dahl, *Polyarchy: Participation and Opposition* (New Haven: Yale University Press, 1971), p. 119n.

century because of the difficulties of communication between the two parts of the canton; Appenzell in 1597 because of the Catholic-Protestant division; and Basel in 1833 because of urban-rural tensions. Dunn calls the splitting of a canton in two one of the "oldest conflict resolution techniques" of the Swiss.[78]

It is interesting to note that Belgium has also moved in the direction of a semifederalism entailing both functional and territorial separation in order to find a solution for its linguistic problem. In recent years, the linguistic cleavage has become more and more institutionalized by the party system. The Flemish, Walloon, and pro-French Bruxellois linguistic parties are based on this line of cleavage. The older parties that used to cut across the linguistic boundary have now also become deeply divided by it. The two regional wings of the Catholic party are now virtually separate parties. And the same tendency among Socialists and Liberals is very strong. Urwin states that an observer of the 1968 election "could have been excused for mistaking regional wings of the parties for independent parties."[79]

The constitutional amendments adopted in late 1970 formally recognize the linguistic cleavage by dividing all members of parliament into two separate Cultural Councils that serve as parliaments within the area of cultural and educational autonomy granted to each linguistic community. Laws affecting cultural autonomy must be passed with a two-thirds majority including the concurrent majority of each language group. And the French-speaking minority can appeal any bill that threatens its interests to the cabinet, which is composed of equal numbers of Dutch speakers and French speakers. Bilingual Brussels is governed by a similar arrangement. It appears that, at last, the interests of the linguistic communities are being effectively organized and represented by means of this semifederal structure.[80]

78. Dunn, " 'Consociational Democracy' and Language Conflict," p. 32.

79. Urwin, "Social Cleavages and Political Parties in Belgium," p. 338.

80. See A. Coppé et al., *Herverdeling van de politieke macht* (Brussels: Reinaert, 1972); Luc Huyse, "Un regard sociologique sur la question linguistique en Belgique," *Septentrion* 3, no. 3 (1974): 23–25; Martin O. Heisler, "Institutionalizing Societal Cleavages in a Cooptive Polity: The Growing Importance of the Output Side in Belgium," in Heisler, *Politics in Europe*, pp. 178–220; and James

The First and Second Austrian Republics have both been federal states. Federalism was written into the constitution at the insistence of the Catholic party, although the Socialists preferred a unitary state. By 1929, however, the positions of the two parties were completely reversed. The Catholics, who had been in power since 1922, were eager to strengthen the central government, whereas the Socialists became defenders of the autonomy of the Länder, particularly Socialist Vienna. In 1945, both parties returned to their original points of view. As a result, Austria has become a federal but not a highly decentralized state.[81]

Table 7 presents the fragmentation and crosscutting of the different cleavages for the Länder as well as for Austria as a whole. Religious fragmentation was computed on the basis of a survey question concerning regularity of church attendance. The indices of religious fragmentation vary little among the Länder. The only *Land* with a strikingly low index is Vorarlberg, a stronghold of the Catholic party, where church attendance is high. Party system fragmentation was computed on the basis of the 1962 election results. The Catholic party received 45.4 percent of the vote and the Socialists 44.0 percent. The Catholics received the highest number of votes in all Länder except Vienna and Carinthia. In order to calculate the angles of crosscutting between party system cleavages, religious cleavages, and class cleavages, only the two major parties were considered.[82]

The striking overall result is that neither fragmentation nor crosscutting is much affected by the federal division. The weighted means, which here again are probably the most meaningful averages, hardly differ from the values for the whole country. Austrian federalism is clearly not an embodiment of the consociational method of segmental autonomy. Instead, the *Lager* and their ancillary structures perform this function, and

---

A. Dunn, Jr., "The Revision of the Constitution in Belgium: A Study in the Institutionalization of Ethnic Conflict," *Western Political Quarterly* 27, no. 1 (March 1974): 143–63.

81. Alfred Diamant, *Austrian Catholics and the First Republic: Democracy, Capitalism, and the Social Order, 1918–1934* (Princeton: Princeton University Press, 1960), pp. 83–85, 259–60; Kurt Steiner, *Politics in Austria* (Boston: Little, Brown, 1972), pp. 98–106.

82. This leads to some slight discrepancies with the figures reported in table 4.

TABLE 7. Fragmentation and Crosscutting in Austria: Länder Averages and National Totals (c. 1965)

	Länder Mean	Länder Weighted Mean	Austria
Religious fragmentation:			
Largest group (%)	46	45	39
Index of fragmentation (*F*)	.62	.63	.66
Party system fragmentation:			
Largest party (%)	51.3	50.9	45.4
Index of fragmentation (*F*)	.58	.58	.59
Crosscutting of			
Religion and parties:			
Index (*XC*)	.40	.40	.39
Angle	20°	16°	14°
Class and parties:			
Index (*XC*)	.44	.44	.45
Angle	40°	36°	37°
Religion and class:			
Index (*XC*)	.50	.50	.50
Angle	70°	64°	70°

SOURCE: Calculated from 1967 survey data supplied by the Institut für Empirische Sozialforschung in Vienna and the 1962 national election results.

segmental autonomy only takes the form of what Dahl calls "sociological" or nonterritorial federalism.[83] Similarly, the unitary Netherlands may be described as sociologically federal.

TRADITIONS OF ELITE ACCOMMODATION

Plural societies may enjoy stable democratic government if the political leaders engage in coalescent rather than adversarial

83. Quoted in Sidney Verba, "Some Dilemmas in Comparative Research," *World Politics* 20, no. 1 (October 1967): 126.

decision-making. Elite coalescence may be motivated by an awareness of the dangers inherent in segmental cleavages and a desire to avert them. The theory that plural societies cannot sustain stable democratic regimes then becomes a self-negating prophecy: elites cooperate in spite of the segmental differences dividing them because to do otherwise would mean to call forth the prophesied consequences of the plural character of the society. An alternative or additional factor predisposing political leaders to be moderate and cooperative is the prior existence of a tradition of elite accommodation.

Daalder, in particular, has forcefully called attention to the importance of such traditions. In his analysis of the historical process of nation-building in the Netherlands and Switzerland, he argues that in both countries "traditions of pluralism and political accommodation long preceded the processes of political modernization." Consequently, Dutch and Swiss consociationalism should be regarded not as a "response to the perils of subcultural splits, but [as] the prior reason why subcultural divisions never did become perilous."[84] A predemocratic historical tendency toward moderation and compromise can indeed be an independent factor that can appreciably strengthen the chances of consociational democracy. Switzerland and the Netherlands never experienced any substantial period of absolutism, and preabsolutist traditions of diffuse and dispersed power relationships remained strong. Straight majority rule—the democratic equivalent of royal absolutism—therefore never had a strong appeal.

Lehmbruch discerns similar conciliar traditions not only in the development of the Netherlands and Switzerland, but also in Belgian and, to an important extent, Austrian history. Both in Austria and in Switzerland, grand coalition government in the Länder and cantons preceded the national grand coalitions. During the First Republic, all of the Länder had proportional all-party executives either by constitutional prescription or, as in Vorarlberg, on a voluntary basis. The proportional "magic for-

84. Hans Daalder, "On Building Consociational Nations: The Cases of the Netherlands and Switzerland," *International Social Science Journal* 23, no. 3 (1971): 367–68.

mula" for the composition of the Swiss Federal Council was not adopted until 1959, but the cantons adopted similar practices at a much earlier date. The canton of Berne set the example in 1854 when the conservative majority admitted the Radical opposition into the cantonal executive.[85] Kenneth D. McRae points out that all four countries that later developed into consociational democracies

> lay at one period or another within the boundaries of the Holy Roman Empire, and all four escaped in varying degrees the long, gradual centralization of authority that was characteristic of France, Spain, England, Scotland and other national monarchies from the twelfth to the sixteenth centuries. Further, all four felt to a greater or lesser degree the impact of the Thirty Years' War and the religious settlement of the Treaty of Westphalia [which] provided explicitly for resolving differences between the Protestant and Catholic members of the Empire by mutual agreement rather than by majority vote.[86]

Among the four consociational democracies, the inheritance of accommodationist traditions has been very important in the Netherlands and Switzerland, less so in Belgium, and the least in Austria; Daalder and McRae also agree on this ranking.[87] In none of these countries, however, can the explanation of elite coalescence in terms of traditional conflict-managing practices entirely replace the self-negating prophecy. The latter element was clearly present in the settlement of the schools conflict in the Netherlands in 1917 and is shown by the prime minister's words when he proposed the establishment of a special ad hoc grand coalition of top party leaders to settle the issue. He described the conflict as "a wedge . . . driven into our national life and splitting our nation into two nations," and he argued that "our nation cannot develop vigorously and cannot release the energy which we must have at our disposal, unless this wedge is removed from our national life." And at the first meeting of the commission, he

85. Gerhard Lehmbruch, *Proporzdemokratie: Politisches System und politische Kultur in der Schweiz und in Österreich* (Tübingen: Mohr, 1967), pp. 8, 17.

86. McRae, *Consociational Democracy,* p. 11.

87. Daalder, "Consociational Democracy Theme," p. 618; McRae, *Consociational Democracy,* pp. 25–27.

appealed to the members to abandon their uncompromising attitudes: "In the struggle that has dominated our politics for many years, you have tried to win a victory for those goals which, if you had absolute power, you would consider to agree most closely with your own opinions. . . . You are now confronted with the fact that your respective opinions set bounds to each other."[88] Moreover, the nature of the Pacification of 1917, which also included the solution of the suffrage issue, indicates that the influence of old traditions of elite cooperation cannot account for the outcome all by itself: the settlement was not incrementalist, but comprehensive and far-reaching, and it was forged within a relatively short period of time. Lorwin's apt characterization of the Catholic-Liberal coalition in the predemocratic era of the birth of independent Belgium as a "remarkable and self-conscious 'union of the oppositions' " also fits the later Pacification in Holland quite well.[89]

Austria is a better example of the operation of the self-negating prophecy. Although it is hazardous to conclude from the absence of serious civil strife in the Netherlands in the early twentieth century that the issues were not explosive and that civil war was an impossibility, the Austrian case leaves no uncertainty in this respect because the First Republic did end in civil war and dictatorship. And all observers agree on the overriding importance of the desire among the major leaders to avoid a repetition of these tragic events as a motive for setting up the grand coalition in 1945. For instance, although Lehmbruch is emphatic about the historical precedents of the Austrian grand coalition, he nevertheless states that it was the experience of civil war in the First Republic that provided the main thrust.[90] According to Frederick C. Engelmann, "critics and objective observers agree with Austria's leading politicians in the assessment that the coali-

88. Quoted in P. J. Oud, *Honderd jaren, 1840–1940: Een eeuw van staatkundige vormgeving in Nederland* (Assen: Van Gorcum, 1954), p. 237; and in J. A. A. H. de Beaufort, *Vijftig jaren uit onze geschiedenis: 1868–1918*, 2 vols. (Amsterdam: Van Kampen, 1928), 2: 212.

89. Val R. Lorwin, "Constitutionalism and Controlled Violence in the Modern State: The Case of Belgium," paper presented at the annual meeting of the American Historical Association, San Francisco, 1965, p. 4 (italics added).

90. Lehmbruch, *Proporzdemokratie*, p. 25.

tion was a response to the civil-war tension of the First Republic."[91] And Otto Kirchheimer also specifically attributes Austria's "carefully pre-arranged system of collaboration" to its "historical record of political frustration and abiding suspicion."[92]

The most outspoken and revealing statement on the origin of the Austrian grand coalition is by Bluhm, who uses the idea of the Hobbesian social contract to describe it. The "state of nature" that the Catholic and Socialist leaders experienced from 1918 to 1945 led them to the conclusion of a rational social contract: "By 1945 Austrians had had enough and were ready to 'contract out' of their desperate situation."[93]

A prior tradition of elite accommodation is—like the other conditions discussed in this chapter—a favorable condition for consociational democracy. It may even be of greater importance than the other factors, but it is not a prerequisite. An accommodationist inheritance and the occurrence of a self-negating prophecy are complementary rather than mutually exclusive. It is particularly important to stress the voluntary, rational, purposive, and contractual elements of consociational democracy because the discussion of the consociational model as a normative model in later chapters presupposes that consociationalism is an example that can be freely and deliberately followed. As we shall see, cooperative traditions that predispose toward consociational decision-making are by no means rare in the plural societies of the Third World. But, in addition, one should not rule out the possibility that leaders in plural societies are capable of a creative and constructive act of free will.

91. Frederick C. Engelmann, "Haggling for the Equilibrium: The Renegotiation of the Austrian Coalition, 1959," *American Political Science Review* 56, no. 3 (September 1962): 651.

92. Otto Kirchheimer, "The Waning of Opposition in Parliamentary Regimes," *Social Research* 24, no. 2 (summer 1957): 137. See also Rudolf Steininger, *Polarisierung und Integration: Eine vergleichende Untersuchung der strukturellen Versäulung der Gesellschaft in den Niederlanden und in Österreich* (Meisenheim am Glan: Hain, 1975), p. 215.

93. Bluhm, *Building an Austrian Nation,* p. 46.

4 Consociational Elements in Nonconsociational Democracies

The four consociational democracies differ considerably in the degree to which they approximate the pure consociational model, as has already been pointed out in passing in the previous chapters.[1] As far as the strength of segmentation is concerned, Switzerland is less clearly a plural society than the other three countries. Its segments cannot be as easily defined as those in Austria, Belgium, and the Netherlands, and it ranks only in Val R. Lorwin's medium category of segmented pluralism compared with the high ranking of the other three consociational democracies. Lorwin has also ranked fourteen spheres of activity in the four countries (such as education, mass media, political and socioeconomic organizations, and leisure activities) by their degree of segmented pluralism, that is, the degree to which these spheres are organized along the lines of segmental cleavages. Belgium receives a "high" rating eleven times, the Netherlands eight times, and Austria seven times. Switzerland is judged to be significantly less segmented according to this method of measurement, too: only three spheres of activity receive a "high" rating.[2] With regard to elite coalescence, Austria and Switzerland are more thoroughly consociational than Belgium and the Netherlands, and the Belgian case is complicated by the fact that consociational solutions were for many years applied much more frequently and consistently to problems concerning the religious-ideological cleavages than to those concerning the language division.

In addition, there have been changes over time. Since the high point of consociational development in the late 1950s, the sa-

1. See above, esp. pp. 15, 31–33, 60–61.

2. Val R. Lorwin, "Segmented Pluralism: Ideological Cleavages and Political Cohesion in the Smaller European Democracies," *Comparative Politics* 3, no. 2 (January 1971): 155. At an earlier point, he states that only in Austria "has segmentation approached completeness" (p. 144).

lience and intensity of the segmental cleavages in all four countries have declined, with the sole exception of the feelings aroused by the Belgian linguistic question. At the same time, the last problem is increasingly being handled by consociational, especially semifederal, arrangements. But in most other respects, elite coalescence has declined. The Austrian grand coalition was succeeded in 1966 by a one-party Catholic cabinet which in turn gave way to a Socialist cabinet in 1970. And in the Netherlands the Socialists and their smaller left-wing allies adopted an explicit anticonsociational attitude. They advocated a radical return to majority rule and followed the decidedly unconsociational strategy of forming a British-style "shadow cabinet" to oppose the incumbent coalition in the election campaigns of 1971 and 1972.[3]

The closest approximation to the ideal type of consociational democracy is the case of Austria during the era of grand coalition cabinets from 1945 to 1966. The other three cases, even at their apogee in the late 1950s, deviated in some significant respects from the pure model, although they come sufficiently close to be classified as consociational democracies. Conversely, some of the nonconsociational democracies have a number of significant consociational elements.

A TYPOLOGY OF DEMOCRATIC REGIMES

Consociational democracy is one type of a fourfold typology that results from the cross-tabulation of the structure of society—plural or homogeneous—and the behavior of the political elites—coalescent or adversarial (see figure 2). It corresponds partly to Gabriel A. Almond's typology of democratic systems. The centrifugal and centripetal types are by and large the same as the Continental European and Anglo-American types respectively. The terms "centrifugal" and "centripetal" are used here instead of Almond's terminology in order to avoid any unintended geographical connotations.

3. For a fuller discussion of the postconsociational phase of Dutch politics, see Arend Lijphart, *The Politics of Accommodation: Pluralism and Democracy in the Netherlands*, 2d ed. (Berkeley: University of California Press, 1975), pp. 196–219.

FIG. 2. A Typology of Democratic Regimes

Elite Behavior	Structure of Society: Homogeneous	Structure of Society: Plural
Coalescent	Depoliticized Democracy	Consociational Democracy
Adversarial	Centripetal Democracy	Centrifugal Democracy

The depoliticized type represents the kind of democratic regime toward which the Western democracies appeared to be moving in the early 1960s, according to a number of eminent scholars who observed the major political developments at that time. It is described by such terms as the "New Europe," "interest-group liberalism," and the "democratic Leviathan." The trend seemed to be toward a lessening of ideological and religious tensions and a simultaneous increase in coalescent decision-making. For instance, Ernst B. Haas argued that the "clustering of affections and expectations" within separate segments of populations "seems to be a thing of the past." At the same time he saw the typical democracy of the New Europe ruled in the grand coalition fashion. Especially in the economic realm, the trend was toward "democratic planning," featuring, in Haas's words, "the continuous participation of *all major voluntary groups* in European society through elaborate systems of committees and councils. . . . Permanent negotiation and occasional conciliation tend to replace active confrontation, doctrinaire discussion and class warfare."[4] The Norwegian style of decision-making, as described by Stein Rokkan, may serve as an example. The crucial economic decisions are made in "yearly rounds of negotiations" among all interested groups: "the government authorities meet directly with the trade union leaders, the representatives of the farmers, the smallholders, and the fishermen, and the delegates of the Employers' Association" around the bargaining table.[5]

The equivalent of this trend in American democracy is what Theodore Lowi has termed "interest-group liberalism." The essence of this philosophy, favored especially during the Kennedy Administration, is succinctly stated by Arthur Schlesinger, Jr.: "The leading interests in society are all represented in the interior processes of policy formation—which can be done only if members or advocates of these interests are included in key positions of government."[6] This "New America" idea is strikingly similar to the typical pattern of grand coalition politics in the New Europe.

The four types in the typology of figure 2 represent not only different combinations of social pluralism and elite behavior but also different degrees of political stability. The centrifugal type of democracy is unstable, whereas the centripetal and consociational types are stable democracies. Because depoliticized democracy combines the stabilizing features of both the centripetal and consociational types, it should have the greatest stability. But this is not the case, mainly as a result of the destabilizing effects of the opposition to the insufficiently democratic quality of this type of regime. Most of the criticisms of consociational democracy apply to the depoliticized type, while the latter lacks the

4. Ernst B. Haas, "Technocracy, Pluralism and the New Europe," in *A New Europe?* ed. Stephen R. Graubard (Boston: Houghton Mifflin, 1964), pp. 68, 70 (italics added).

5. Stein Rokkan, "Norway: Numerical Democracy and Corporate Pluralism," in *Political Oppositions in Western Democracies,* ed. Robert A. Dahl (New Haven: Yale University Press, 1966), p. 107.

6. Quoted by Theodore Lowi, "The Public Philosophy: Interest-Group Liberalism," *American Political Science Review* 61, no. 1 (March 1967): 15.

justification that coalescent behavior is indispensable in order to manage the severe cleavages of a plural society. For instance, Lowi condemns interest-group liberalism on a number of grounds, including its tendency to result in "an oligopolistic situation" and in "the atrophy of institutions of popular control."[7] Robert A. Dahl, in a study published in 1966, speculates with great foresight that an increasingly important source of conflict in Western democracies will be the nature of the democratic Leviathan. There are already signs, he argues, "that many young people, intellectuals, and academics reject the democratic Leviathan . . . because, in their view, it is not democratic enough: this new Leviathan is too remote and bureaucratized, too addicted to bargaining and compromise, too much an instrument of political elites and technicians with whom they feel slight identification."[8]

The neodemocratic opposition to the depoliticized democratic regime may cause political instability in several ways. It may spur the search for ways to reintroduce an adversarial pattern of politics, which means a shift from the depoliticized type to the centripetal type of democracy. Because this change maintains the democratic nature of the regime, it is a favorable outcome. But the neodemocratic opposition may also take the form of radical demands for participatory democracy, or of direct extraparliamentary action. These may lead to the overloading of the decision-making system and consequently to a reduction in governmental effectiveness.[9] Moreover, they may result in antidemocratic attitudes and actions either among the frustrated minority championing the ideal of participatory democracy or among their opponents as a conservative reaction to the aims and methods of the neodemocrats.

It should be emphasized that, contrary to the view of some critics, the fourfold typology of democratic regimes is neither static nor purely descriptive.[10] It links the independent variables

7. Ibid., pp. 18, 23.
8. Dahl, *Political Oppositions*, pp. 399–400.
9. See Samuel P. Huntington, "Postindustrial Politics: How Benign Will It Be?" *Comparative Politics* 6, no. 2 (January 1974): 172–77.
10. See Jeffrey Obler, Jürg Steiner, and Guido Dierickx, *The "Burden" of*

of the plural or nonplural character of society and of elite behavior to the dependent variable of political stability. Any change in the independent variables will therefore affect the degree of stability of the democracy under consideration. Furthermore, because one of the variables in the relationship is political stability, the typology indicates which types are inherently more likely to last—the centripetal and consociational regimes—and which are more likely to be short-lived—the centrifugal and depoliticized regimes. For instance, the fact that the trend toward depoliticized democracy that appeared so irresistible in the early 1960s was halted and even reversed can be explained both by the unexpectedly slow disappearance of old cleavages and the emergence of new ones (that is, the horizontal movement toward the left side of the typology was stopped and reversed) and by the inherent instability of the depoliticized regime. Finally, the typology, in conjunction with the earlier discussion of the favorable conditions for consociational democracy, says something about the direction in which the unstable centrifugal type is likely to develop: into consociational democracy if the conditions are favorable, and into a nondemocratic regime otherwise.

CENTRIPETAL DEMOCRACIES

The typology of figure 2 can be looked at not only as a classificatory system for a set of interrelated ideal types but also as a scheme for the classification of empirical political systems. The latter view allows us to try to place the several Western democracies into the categories of the typology. The main purpose of this exercise will be to determine how well they fit these categories, which two or more categories are overlapped by cases that do not have a perfect fit, and, in particular, to what extent and in which ways the mainly nonconsociational democracies do have consociational features. Such a classification requires that the time span under consideration be clearly specified, because

---

Consociational Decision-Making: A Review Essay of Austria, Belgium, the Netherlands, and Switzerland, Sage Professional Papers in Comparative Politics (Beverly Hills: Sage, 1977).

the structure of societies and elite behavior, as well as the regimes defined by these two factors, are all subject to change—although there are few instances of dramatic shifts like the ones experienced by Austria: from the centrifugal democracy of the First Republic to an autocratic interlude and then to the consociationalism of the grand coalition period of the Second Republic, followed in 1966 by a regime with both centripetal and depoliticized characteristics.[11] For the less changeable cases, the "average" situation in the post-World War II era will be considered.

The category of centripetal democracies is equivalent to that of Almond's Anglo-American political systems, but it also includes the three Scandinavian countries, Finland, and Iceland. In Almond's original formulation, Scandinavia is considered to be in an intermediate position between the Anglo-American and Continental European systems, but he later includes them with Britain and the United States in the group of countries with homogeneous political cultures. This is also in line with Dankwart A. Rustow's assessment of the Scandinavian countries as a "highly homogeneous group of societies."[12] The description applies to Finland and Iceland as well, although there are differences among the five Nordic countries with regard to their political cultures: Norway, Finland, and Iceland are relatively less homogeneous. In fact, Harry Eckstein argues that Norway is characterized by "segmental cleavages" which he also describes as "astonishingly great, sharp, and persistent divisions." Norway's divisions may indeed be somewhat deeper than those in neighboring Denmark and Sweden, but they seem relatively minor and inconsequential compared with the cleavages one encounters when one travels farther south in Continental Europe—a comparison that Eckstein does not make. Also, to the extent that there are significant divisions, they are counterbalanced by what Eckstein himself describes as an overarching

11. See Kurt Steiner, *Politics in Austria* (Boston: Little, Brown, 1972), pp. 409–26.

12. Dankwart A. Rustow, "Scandinavia: Working Multiparty Systems," in *Modern Political Parties: Approaches to Comparative Politics,* ed. Sigmund Neumann (Chicago: University of Chicago Press, 1956), p. 191.

"profound sense of community" and a "social and political homogeneity that cuts across all divisions."[13] On balance, therefore, Norway can be safely grouped with the other basically homogeneous Scandinavian countries. Finland has a stronger claim to the status of plural society because of its small Swedish-speaking minority and, like Iceland, because of the presence of a large Communist party.

As far as the second dimension of the typology—elite behavior—is concerned, the Scandinavian countries have generally followed the government-versus-opposition pattern but this has not meant an extreme adversarial style. For instance, in Denmark one finds a far-reaching search for compromise not at the level of the cabinet—Denmark is known for its long periods of government by minority cabinets—but in the legislature. The rule of the parliamentary game prescribes that the top leaders of all four major parties do their utmost to reach a consensus. This is *glidningspolitik,* which Gerald R. McDaniel translates as the "politics of smoothness,"[14] an apt characterization of coalescent decision-making. In the field of socioeconomic planning and administration, the coalescent style has become quite pervasive in the Scandinavian countries, probably more so than elsewhere in the Western world. Of all Western democracies, therefore, the Scandinavian countries appear to have moved the farthest in the direction of the depoliticized type.[15]

Of the Anglo-American countries themselves, Great Britain, Australia, and New Zealand are basically homogeneous and have adversarial elites; the same can be said about the Republic of Ireland. These countries can therefore be classified as centripetal democracies without difficulty. It should be noted, however, that in practice politics is not consistently played in the adversarial style. Even in Britain, the government consults the

13. Harry Eckstein, *Division and Cohesion in Democracy: A Study of Norway* (Princeton: Princeton University Press, 1966), pp. 61, 67, 78, 121.

14. Gerald R. McDaniel, "The Danish Unicameral Parliament" (Ph.D. diss., University of California, Berkeley, 1963), p. iv.

15. See Martin O. Heisler and Robert B. Kvavik, "Patterns of European Politics: The 'European Polity' Model," in *Politics in Europe: Structures and Processes in Some Postindustrial Democracies,* ed. Martin O. Heisler (New York: McKay, 1974), pp. 46–48.

leaders of the opposition on critical issues instead of simply outvoting the minority; this means that even Britain does not follow the *pure* "British model." A second qualification is in order with regard to the British case. The usual description of Britain as highly homogeneous pays insufficient attention to the distinction between England, Great Britain, and the United Kingdom. England may indeed be highly homogeneous, but the addition of Scotland and Wales makes Britain a multinational country—a fact that has become increasingly important for British political life in recent years.[16] Further, the United Kingdom unites Northern Ireland to Great Britain, and Northern Ireland is clearly a plural society and a centrifugal democracy. Another Anglo-American country, Canada, is also a plural society. Canada, which has developed a number of consociational devices to deal with its English-French cleavage, and Northern Ireland, which the British government has recently been trying to turn into a consociational democracy, will be discussed at greater length later in this chapter.

Almond's linking of the United States with Britain in his Anglo-American type implies that he would classify the United States in the centripetal category. Despite the signs of growing divisiveness and declining political stability in the 1960s and 1970s, this placement most likely still expresses the consensus of students of comparative politics. However, it ignores American deviations on both of the dimensions that define the centripetal type. Instead of being highly homogeneous, American political culture is fragmented or plural to a significant degree. As Dahl states, "the South has for nearly two centuries formed a distinctive regional subculture."[17] In the years prior to the secession of the South and the Civil War, the United States should be regarded as a centrifugal democracy. After the Civil War, a consociational arrangement developed that gave to the Southern segment a high degree of autonomy and to its leaders a crucial position in federal decision-making by such means as chairman-

16. See Richard Rose's analysis, "The United Kingdom as a Multi-National Regime," in his *Governing Without Consensus: An Irish Perspective* (London: Faber and Faber, 1971), pp. 42–73.

17. Dahl, *Political Oppositions;* p. 358.

ships of key congressional committees and the filibuster. The slow progress of civil rights legislation was to a large extent caused by these consociational features that added up to an informal but effective Southern veto power.

There is, of course, a second sense in which the United States is a plural rather than a homogeneous society: it is divided not only into Southern and non-Southern but also into black and white segments. Irene Tinker adopts this perspective when she calls the American Negroes an "unassimilated minority in a plural society" and argues that "America is not now, nor likely to become for sometime, a country with a homogeneous population."[18] It is worth noting that the ideology of black power, although it is far from a uniform and consistent program, has several striking consociational features. There is, first of all, the idea of emphasizing the separateness of the black segment and the need to organize segmental political parties and segmental interest organizations. The representatives of the segment can then contemplate the formation of coalitions with different groups and parties. Stokely Carmichael and Charles V. Hamilton state: "It is absolutely imperative that black people strive to form an independent base of political power *first*. . . . The blacks will [then] have the mobilized ability to grant or withhold from coalition." A directly related notion is that of segmental autonomy: "We must begin to think of the black community as a base of organization to control institutions in that community."[19] The assumption is also that segmental organization and autonomy will foster greater equality: not just "separate *but* equal" but "separate and *thus* equal." Whether or not such an at least partly consociational program can have any chance of success—the weak numerical and socioeconomic position of the black segment and its lack of a clear territorial base are unfavorable

18. Irene Tinker, "Nationalism in a Plural Society: The Case of the American Negro," *Western Political Quarterly* 19, no. 1 (March 1966): 112, 122. See also S. J. Makielski, Jr., "The United States as a Plural Society," *Plural Societies* 3, no. 3 (Autumn 1972): 29–34.

19. Stokely Carmichael and Charles V. Hamilton, *Black Power: The Politics of Liberation in America* (New York: Random House, 1967), pp. 96, 166. See also Donald J. McCormack, "Stokely Carmichael and Pan-Africanism: Back to Black Power," *Journal of Politics* 35, no. 2 (May 1973): 386–409.

factors—the experience of the European consociational democracies shows that separateness does not inherently spell inequality.

CENTRIFUGAL DEMOCRACIES

The centrifugal democracies correspond to Almond's unstable Continental European political systems. The examples that Almond gives are the French Third and Fourth Republics, the Weimar Republic, and postwar Italy. The same regimes exemplify the centrifugal type, and additional instances of it are the Austrian First Republic and the short-lived Spanish Republic of the early 1930s. The French, German, and Italian cases require a brief elaboration and clarification because, especially as far as France and Germany are concerned, their classification as centrifugal can be and has been challenged.

The French Fourth Republic is often regarded as the outstanding example of unstable, ineffective, and immobilist democracy, but the explanation of its political instability in terms of cultural fragmentation has been criticized on two grounds. In the first place, Eric A. Nordlinger rejects the argument that the "ideological inundation of French politics" and its "fragmented party system" were responsible for its chronic instability; he states that this explanation conveniently overlooks "the way in which the game of politics is actually played in France. Although ideologism pervades the parties' electoral and propaganda efforts, this public ideological posturing of French politicians does not prevent them from playing out their game of compromise in the Assembly and its *couloirs.* In fact, the political class thinks of compromise as a positive principle of action, with parliamentary activity largely revolving around nonideological squabbles."[20] However, this description fits only the center parties and not the Communists and Gaullists, who in the Fourth Republic were adversarial to such an extent that they rejected the regime.

In addition, although the elites of the center parties that supported the Republic were largely nonideological, this did not

20. Eric A. Nordlinger, "Democratic Stability and Instability: The French Case," *World Politics* 18, no. 1 (October 1965): 143.

contribute much to the system's stability because, as Nathan Leites points out, a cardinal rule of the parliamentary political game in France was the politicians' "well-developed capacity for avoiding their responsibility."[21] They played the political game in the same fashion as the game of *boules* was played in Laurence Wylie's village in the Vaucluse: both players and audience were more interested in the game itself than in its outcome, and most of the fun and excitement arose out of the players' arguments, designed to maneuver themselves out of the responsibility for making decisions.[22] In other words, they were nonideological but not constructively pragmatic. Also, it is incorrect to assume that, because the elites were not divided by irreconcilable ideological differences, mass politics was not ideologically fragmented.

The second criticism of the cultural fragmentation thesis alleges, on the basis of independent evidence, that not only at the elite level but also at the mass level, ideology played a negligible role in France. Philip E. Converse and Georges Dupeux demonstrate that the French electorate was not highly politicized and felt little allegiance to the political parties.[23] But the lack of stable partisan attachments does not necessarily indicate that the political culture was not fragmented. Duncan MacRae argues persuasively that political divisions did extend to the electorate as a whole in spite of the apparent "lack of involvement of the average voter." Even though political allegiances were diffuse, there were "relatively fixed and non-overlapping *social* groupings" to which "separate leaders and separate media of communication had access."[24] The combination of fragmentation into subcultures and low politicization can in turn be explained

21. Nathan Leites, *On the Game of Politics in France* (Stanford: Stanford University Press, 1959), p. 2; see also the chapter entitled "The Struggle against Responsibility," pp. 35–75.

22. Laurence Wylie, *Village in the Vaucluse: An Account of Life in a French Village*, rev. ed. (New York: Harper and Row, 1964), pp. 250–59.

23. Philip E. Converse and Georges Dupeux, "Politicization of the Electorate in France and the United States," *Public Opinion Quarterly* 26, no. 1 (spring 1962): 1–23. See also David R. Cameron, "Stability and Change in Patterns of French Partisanship," *Public Opinion Quarterly* 36, no. 1 (spring 1972): 19–30.

24. Duncan MacRae, Jr., *Parliament, Parties, and Society in France: 1946–1958* (New York: St. Martin's Press, 1967), p. 333.

by the negative French attitude toward authority. Stanley Hoffmann speaks of "potential insurrection against authority," and Michel Crozier observes that this attitude makes it "impossible for an individual of the group to become its leader."[25] Strong cohesion within subcultural segments is an important condition for successful consociational democracy; the lack of it in France can explain both how the French people were fragmented but at the same time not politically involved, and why the political elites did not have the advantage of strong support from the rank and file for constructive cooperation.

On the other hand, the example of France also illustrates that the lack of problem-solving ability as a cause of political instability must not be overstated. After all, as Maurice Duverger points out, in spite of all of the Fourth Republic's flaws and weaknesses, it "would have continued to exist if it had not been for the Algerian war."[26] The critical factor was the heavy burden of an essentially external problem on the political system. Similarly, the fragmented Weimar Republic might have survived, too, if it had not been for the unusually difficult problems it was faced with.

Finally, if the Fourth Republic was unstable because it belonged to the centrifugal type, can the greater stability of the Fifth Republic be explained according to the same theoretical framework? The stability of a centrifugal democracy increases if its society becomes less plural and/or if the behavior of its elites becomes less adversarial. Both developments can be discerned in French politics since 1958.[27] Ideology has become a less prominent force among the French populace and French political culture has become more homogeneous. At the elite level, the

25. Stanley Hoffmann, *In Search of France* (Cambridge, Mass.: Harvard University Press, 1963), p. 8 (italics omitted); Michel Crozier, *The Bureaucratic Phenomenon: An Examination of Bureaucracy in Modern Organizations and Its Cultural Setting in France* (Chicago: University of Chicago Press, 1964), p. 220.

26. Maurice Duverger, "The Development of Democracy in France," in *Democracy in a Changing Society*, ed. Henry W. Ehrmann (New York: Praeger, 1964), p. 77.

27. See P. G. Cerny, "Cleavage, Aggregation, and Change in French Politics," *British Journal of Political Science* 2, no. 4 (October 1972): 443–55; and John Frears, "Conflict in France: The Decline and Fall of a Stereotype," *Political Studies* 20, no. 1 (March 1972): 31–41.

changes have been smaller. But the effect of the less adversarial style, especially among the governing elites of the Right, has been "artificially" but nonetheless effectively reinforced by institutional changes giving them the advantages of large legislative majorities and control of the presidency. The overall movement of the French regime has been mainly in the direction of the centripetal rather than of the consociational type.

Germany's experience with democracy also appears to throw some doubt on the typology of democratic regimes and the theory on which it is based. Weimar Germany was a centrifugal democracy, but the Bonn Republic must undoubtedly be grouped with the centripetal democracies. This is an extraordinary shift because great and rapid changes in a country's political culture can normally not be expected. There are three reasons that can plausibly account for the change from the fragmented political culture of the unstable Weimar Republic to the much more homogeneous culture of the Bonn regime. In the first place, life in Germany was far from "normal" in the period from the end of Weimar to the early days of the new institutions of Bonn. The traumatic experiences of totalitarian rule, war, defeat, and occupation strongly accelerated developments that would normally occur at a much slower pace. Second, under the auspices of the allied powers "a conscious manipulative change of fundamental political attitudes" took place. In Sidney Verba's words, this added up to a "remaking of political culture."[28] Third, Bonn and Weimar are fundamentally different not only with regard to their governmental institutions and their stability and effectiveness, but also in the geographical sense: Bonn Germany is a much smaller country than Weimar Germany. And the loss of the eastern territories has meant that, as Seymour Martin Lipset argues, "the greater homogeneity of western Germany now became a national homogeneity."[29]

28. Sidney Verba, "Germany: The Remaking of Political Culture," in *Political Culture and Political Development*, ed. Lucian W. Pye and Sidney Verba (Princeton: Princeton University Press, 1965), p. 133. See also David P. Conradt, "West Germany: A Remade Political Culture?" *Comparative Political Studies* 7, no. 2 (July 1974): 222–38.

29. Seymour Martin Lipset, *The First New Nation: The United States in Historical and Comparative Perspective* (New York: Basic Books, 1963), p. 292.

Another question that must be answered with regard to the classification of the Bonn Republic as a centripetal regime concerns the nature of the "grand coalition" of Christian Democrats and Socialists under the chancellorship of Kurt Georg Kiesinger from 1966 to 1969: did the formation of this cabinet entail a move toward either a consociational or a depoliticized regime? There is some evidence that points in this direction. Some advocates of the coalition, as Gerhard Lehmbruch argues, were motivated by "traditions of proportional participation which date back to a situation when alternative government was a notion alien to German political thought." A different motive for banding together, not unfamiliar in consociational regimes, was the rise of an extremist challenge to the system in the form of the neo-Nazi National Democratic Party. On the other hand, the coalition was not really a grand one because it excluded the Liberals—a small but significant political force in Germany, unlike in neighboring Austria. It was also intended from the beginning to be a purely temporary arrangement. Moreover, it was repeatedly emphasized that the German arrangement would not be a duplicate of the Austrian grand coalition which had a generally unfavorable reputation in Germany. And the most important motives behind the Kiesinger coalition appear to have been of a pragmatic and short-run nature: the Christian Democrats' reluctance to be too dependent on the Liberals as a coalition partner and the Socialists' eagerness to enter the cabinet and thus to prove themselves a responsible and reliable party. The two parties also envisaged the disappearance of the Liberals; instead of a permanent shift to grand coalition government, spokesmen of the two large parties emphasized, their cooperation represented a provisional arrangement aimed at—but, as it turned out, not successful in—"creating the conditions of an authentic two-party system."[30]

The Italian case remains a clear example of centrifugal democracy, but even here a few qualifications are in order. At the local level, one often finds cordial relations and fruitful cooperation

30. Gerhard Lehmbruch, "The Ambiguous Coalition in West Germany," *Government and Opposition* 3, no. 2 (spring 1968): 181–204, esp. 185, 187.

among Christian Democratic, Socialist, and Communist party and government officials.[31] At the national level, the "opening to the left" represented the bridging of the segmental cleavage between Christian Democrats and Socialists. The next step toward a grand coalition spanning the political spectrum from Christian Democrats to Communists—the "historic compromise" proposed by Communist leader Enrico Berlinguer in 1973—would entail the introduction of the principal element of consociational democracy.[32]

SEMICONSOCIATIONAL DEMOCRACY: CANADA

Canada is a deviant case in the Anglo-American world in that it is partly French-speaking. This is also the main characteristic that makes it a plural society. Using Almond's terminology, Robert Presthus calls the Canadian political culture "dual" and "deeply fragmented," primarily along the anglophone-francophone axis.[33] Similarly, Canada can be regarded as a binational state.[34] As in the European plural societies, there are also significant religious and class divisions; these partly crosscut and partly coincide with the linguistic cleavage (see figure 3).[35] The angle at which religion and class cut across each other does not deviate much from a right angle, but the deviation that is present reflects the generally lower socioeconomic status of the Roman Catholics.

A more important deviation from crosscutting is the intersection of religion and language: French speakers, who are in the

31. Sidney Tarrow, *Partisanship and Political Exchange in French and Italian Local Politics: A Contribution to the Typology of Party Systems,* Professional Papers in Contemporary Political Sociology, no. 06-004 (London: Sage, 1974).

32. See Luciano Pellicani, "Verso il superamento del pluralismo polarizzato," *Rivista italiana di scienza politica* 4, no. 3 (December 1974): 645–73.

33. Robert Presthus, *Elite Accommodation in Canadian Politics* (Cambridge, Cambridge University Press, 1973), pp. 18, 20.

34. See, for instance, Richard Pious, "Canada and the Crisis of Quebec," *Journal of International Affairs* 27, no. 1 (1973): 53.

35. Figure 3 is based on data from the 1965 Canadian election survey by John Meisel and his collaborators. The indices (*XC*) and angles of crosscutting are as follows: religion and class, 0.49 and 66°; religion and language, 0.27 and 1°; and language and class, 0.50 and 72°.

FIG. 3. Crosscutting Cleavages: Canada

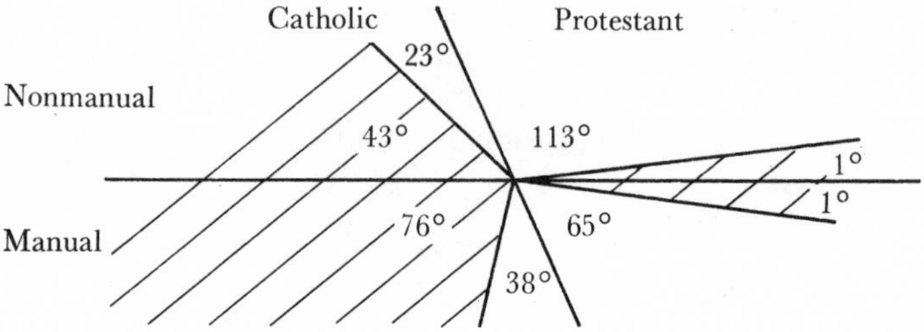

shaded area of figure 3, are virtually absent on the Protestant side. Almost all francophones are Catholic. The coincidence of these two divisions is reinforced by the regional factor, which is of great importance in Canada: the French speakers are concentrated in the province of Quebec and in the areas contiguous to it. As a minority of about 30 percent of the total Canadian population, religiously homogeneous, and largely concentrated in one province, the French speakers are more clearly a segment in a plural society or a political subculture than the religiously heterogeneous English speakers, who are spread out over the remaining nine provinces. In this respect, Canada is similar to the United States, where the South constitutes a distinct subculture but the non-South is an internally much less homogeneous group and can be called a subculture only in the residual sense. Consequently, the province of Quebec plays a special role in Canadian politics. Although, as Kenneth McRae argues, "the image of a *famille spirituelle* can no longer do justice to Quebec's diversity, the image of a *Lager,* a defensive complex in a hostile environment, is not inappropriate."[36]

36. Kenneth D. McRae, "Consociationalism and the Canadian Political System," in *Consociational Democracy: Political Accommodation in Segmented Societies,* ed. Kenneth D. McRae (Toronto: McClelland and Stewart, 1974), p. 240.

McRae has also estimated, following Lorwin's example, the extent to which the most important spheres of activity are organized along the lines of the linguistic cleavage.[37] The results show a lower degree of segmented pluralism in Canada than in Austria, Belgium, and the Netherlands, but a slightly higher degree than in Switzerland. The spheres of activity with a high degree of pluralism are education and the media of communication, which are obvious candidates for linguistically separate organization.[38] Education is a provincial responsibility. This points up the significant fact that the Canadian linguistic cleavage is mainly institutionalized by the federal system, as in Belgium after 1970 and in Switzerland, and that political parties and interest organizations contribute very little in this respect. John Meisel writes:

> Canada's most serious cleavage by far, that between the French and English cultures, although spilling over provincial boundaries, has very largely (but not entirely) become a matter for provincial-federal and inter-provincial negotiations in which the government of Quebec, of whatever stripe, speaks most loudly for the interests of French Canada. Canada's primary cleavage is thus institutionalised to a very high degree outside the party system or, at best, in a manner only indirectly related to it.[39]

The consequences of Canada's federal division into ten provinces (the two sparsely populated territories will be disregarded) for the structure of cleavages is shown in table 8. For the purpose of this table, the 1965 election survey data and the aggregate election results were used. Only English speakers and French speakers, only Protestants and Catholics, only manual and nonmanual workers, and only the four largest parties were included. Where the parties had to be dichotomized for the purpose of calculating the angle of crosscutting, the New Demo-

37. Lorwin restricted his classification to religious and ideological pluralism and did not take the Belgian and Swiss linguistic cleavages into account.

38. McRae, "Consociationalism and the Canadian Political System," pp. 245–47.

39. John Meisel, *Cleavages, Parties and Values in Canada,* Professional Papers in Contemporary Political Sociology, no. 06–003 (London: Sage, 1974), pp. 11, 13.

TABLE 8. Fragmentation and Crosscutting in Canada: Provincial Averages and National Totals (1965)

	Provinces Mean	Provinces Weighted Mean	Canada
Religious fragmentation:			
Largest group (%)	72	78	53
Index of fragmentation (*F*)	.38	.32	.50
Linguistic fragmentation:			
Largest group (%)	93	92	72
Index of fragmentation (*F*)	.11	.13	.41
Religious and linguistic fragmentation:			
Largest group (%)	72	78	53
Index of fragmentation (*F*)	.40	.35	.60
Party system fragmentation:			
Largest party (%)	47	45	40
Index of fragmentation (*F*)	.62	.66	.70
Crosscutting of			
Religion and language:			
Index (*XC*)	.32	.27	.27
Angle	1°	1°	1°
Religion and class:			
Index (*XC*)	.48	.49	.49
Angle	50°	55°	64°
Language and class:			
Index (*XC*)	.49	.49	.50
Angle	22°	40°	72°
Religion and parties:			
Index (*XC*)	.49	.48	.45
Angle	51°	39°	33°
Class and parties:			
Index (*XC*)	.49	.49	.50
Angle	67°	59°	85°
Language and parties:			
Index (*XC*)	.57	.58	.54
Angle	30°	40°	45°

SOURCE: Calculated from the 1965 election survey data collected by John Meisel et al., and the 1965 parliamentary election results.

cratic party was grouped with the Liberals and the Social Credit party with the Conservatives.

The angles of crosscutting should be interpreted with caution because this measure is not a completely satisfactory instrument in cases like the Canadian relationship between language and religion; in summarizing a fourfold division created by two dichotomous cleavages, it does not distinguish between a situation in which one cell is nearly empty (the Canadian case) and a situation in which two diagonal cells are nearly empty (the case of almost perfectly coinciding cleavages). The indices of crosscutting (*XC*) show that religion and language coincide rather than crosscut to a considerable extent, and that the party system follows the religious cleavage more closely than the linguistic cleavage. Unlike the situation in Switzerland (see table 6 above), the weighted average of religious and linguistic crosscutting in the provinces is not lower than the index for Canada as a whole: six of the provinces have values of crosscutting for religion and language that exceed the national value of *XC* (0.27).

However, Canada is quite similar to Switzerland with regard to the much greater homogeneity of the provinces than of the country as a whole. A comparison of the weighted means of fragmentation in the Canadian provinces and the Swiss cantons with the total national fragmentation in the two countries shows that, in both cases, religious fragmentation is cut by about one-third (from 0.50 to 0.32 in Canada and from 0.49 to 0.34 in Switzerland), linguistic fragmentation by more than one-half (in fact, as much as about two-thirds, from 0.41 to 0.13, in the Canadian case, and from 0.40 to 0.17 in Switzerland), and the two types of fragmentation combined by more than one-third (from 0.60 to 0.35 and from 0.68 to 0.43 respectively). Canada's federal system therefore has the effect of creating an appreciably more homogeneous country of provinces. It is also worth recalling that Canada and Switzerland are the most decentralized of the West European and North American federal states: the percentage of all government revenues spent by the central government was only 61 percent in Switzerland and 65 percent in Canada in 1959, considerably lower than the corresponding figures for the United States, the German Federal Republic, and Austria.[40]

Segmental autonomy, embodied in the federal system, is also the strongest consociational feature of Canadian democracy. Since the 1950s, the powers of the provinces have increased a great deal, and Quebec in particular has become almost semisovereign. A recent study concludes that the Quebec government has secured "a greater range of powers and resources than is exploited by any other provincial government."[41]

The federal aspect of Canadian government was already strongly present at the time of the United Province of Canada from 1840 to 1867, although this regime was formally unitary and was set up by the British with the avowed purpose, following the recommendations of the Durham Report, of assimilating the francophones into British culture. The single legislature of the United Province had equal numbers of representatives from each of its two sections, Upper Canada (Ontario) and Lower Canada (Quebec). Assimilation was soon recognized to be impossible and was abandoned in favor of a consociational type of cultural coexistence. Canadian historian William Ormsby writes: "Paradoxically, the union, which had been designed for precisely the opposite purpose, left considerable room for the development of federal characteristics. Once assimilation was rejected, equal representation assumed the guise of a political guarantee for the continued existence of two distinct cultures." And he summarizes the experience of the United Province in the following words: "For more than a quarter of a century the union managed to function as a *quasi-federal system,* but eventually the forces of dualism came into direct conflict with the unitary character of the constitution."[42] The British North America Act of 1867 then established a formal federal system.

40. Bruce M. Russett et al., *World Handbook of Political and Social Indicators* (New Haven: Yale University Press, 1964), pp. 64–65.

41. Kenneth McRoberts and Dale Posgate, *Quebec: Social Change and Political Crisis* (Toronto: McClelland and Stewart, 1976), p. 205.

42. William Ormsby, "The Province of Canada: The Emergence of Consociational Politics," in McRae, *Consociational Democracy,* pp. 271, 272–73 (italics added). See also Douglas V. Verney and Diana M. Verney, "A Canadian Political Community? The Case for Tripartite Confederalism," *Journal of Commonwealth and Comparative Studies* 12, no. 1 (March 1974): 11–14.

Another consociational device in the United Province was the "double majority" principle. Under this informal rule, which was often but not invariably applied, legislation that especially concerned one of the sections of the province could be passed only if it received the votes of the majority of that section in addition to an overall majority in the legislature. The "double majority" rule is, of course, the equivalent of the mutual veto and of Calhoun's principle of concurrent majority. It did not survive the end of the union in an explicit form, but the province of Quebec, to which as the representative of a minority segment the veto power is of great importance, can still be said to have a largely effective informal veto over decisions that concern its vital interests.

Two other consociational methods are much weaker but by no means completely absent in Canada: the rules of proportionality and grand coalition. Both federal elections and cabinet formations are conducted in accordance with majority rule: the electoral method is the plurality and single-member constituency system, and cabinets are one-party cabinets—which sometimes means minority cabinets—instead of either narrowly or broadly based coalition governments. McRae calls the majoritarian philosophy "the Achilles heel of the Canadian political system" and "the *damnosa hereditas* of Anglo-American democracy."[43] There are, however, a few proportional and coalescent elements in Canadian politics that temper majority and adversarial rule. In the first place, proportional representation as an electoral method is not a crucial ingredient of consociational democracy when the segments are geographically concentrated. If the boundaries of the electoral districts faithfully follow segmental boundaries and if the districts are equal in size, even the plurality and single-member constitutuency method will produce proportional representation of the segments. The Canadian ridings are not completely homogeneous, but less than one-fourth of them have English or French minorities of over 10 percent. Second, although the francophones have lagged behind in civil service appointments, since the passage of the Official Lan-

43. Kenneth D. McRae, "Epilogue," in McRae, *Consociational Democracy,* p. 301.

guages Act of 1969 their proportion has increased, especially in the higher positions. And even earlier, at least some attempt was made not to deviate from proportionality too far. For instance, John Porter cites the statement of a member of the federal cabinet to the effect that "there are two principles to be observed, the efficiency of the service and the promotion of national unity."[44] A third example of the proportionality principle is the Supreme Court Act of 1949 which states that at least three of the nine justices must be appointed from the superior courts or the bar of Quebec.

Furthermore, although Canada does not have grand coalition cabinets, it does have several coalescent elements both inside and outside the federal cabinet. The interprovincial bodies such as the Council of Ministers of Education, the federal-provincial conferences, the numerous federal boards, councils, and commissions with provincial representation as their basis of membership, and the meetings and consultations among high provincial civil servants all may be regarded as grand coalitions.[45] In the federal cabinet, both segments are usually well represented, but this depends on the extent to which the governing party itself is a kind of grand coalition instead of a segmental party. Because the Liberal party has strong support from both anglophones and francophones, Liberal cabinets have been intraparty grand coalitions of the segments. Because the Conservative party usually has little support in Quebec and among French speakers elsewhere, it is in a much weaker position in this respect. For instance, S. J. R. Noel argues that "the inability of the [Conservative] Diefenbaker government to involve a Quebec political élite in a process of accommodation at the federal level was surely one of the major factors contributing to its downfall. Its policies and decisions were not anti-Quebec; its failure to appreciate the importance of élite accommodation was."[46] On the whole, however, "longstanding and firm traditions require

44. John Porter, *The Vertical Mosaic: An Analysis of Social Class and Power in Canada* (Toronto: University of Toronto Press, 1965), p. 441.

45. S. J. R. Noel, "Consociational Democracy and Canadian Federalism," *Canadian Journal of Political Science* 4, no. 1 (March 1971): 16.

46. Ibid., p. 17.

the Cabinet to be faithfully representative not only of provinces but also of religion and language, even to the extent of some sacrifice of efficiency."[47]

The application of the grand coalition principle along the temporal dimension to the most important government positions also deserves attention. There has been a rotation between anglophones and francophones in the leadership of the Liberal party and consequently in the prime ministership in Liberal cabinets, in the office of governor general since the appointment of the first Canadian, in the speakership of the House of Commons, and in the position of chief justice of the Supreme Court.

In the period of the United Province of Canada, which was more strongly consociational than the confederation that succeeded it, each section developed a two-party system and the four parliamentary groups worked in two loose coalitions across the segmental cleavage: Upper Canada Conservatives with Lower Canada Bleus and Upper Canada Reformers with Lower Canada Rouges. After the establishment of responsible government in 1848, an informal system of double prime ministerships and twinned ministerial portfolios was set up in order to give exactly equal weight to both segments.[48] This arrangement was reinforced by the concurrent majority rule. A final striking consociational feature of the United Province was that its capital rotated between the two sections until Ottawa was made the permanent seat of government.

The extent to which consociationalism has developed in Canada is quite remarkable because the conditions for it have generally not been encouraging. The only clearly favorable factor is segmental isolation: the two Canadian segments are often referred to as the "two solitudes." The distribution of power was dual and unequal in the United Province, with the French speakers at first in the majority, but the two segments had equal representation in the legislature. In federal Canada, the balance has become dual and unequal with an anglophone majority in terms of both popular votes and parliamentary seats. The "mul-

47. McRae, "Consociationalism and the Canadian Political System," p. 251.
48. Ibid., pp. 255–56.

ticulturalism" policy announced in 1971 was only a feeble attempt to pay greater attention to the cultural interests of Canadians of neither British nor French extraction; it did not represent a significant step in the direction of dividing the English-speaking majority of about 70 percent into separate Anglo-Celtic and "other" minority cultures of about 45 and 25 percent respectively. Moreover, the francophones have tended to interpret multiculturalism more as a potential danger to the status of French as one of the two dominant languages and cultures than as a welcome move toward a multiple balance of power. Canada is a middle rather than a small power, and no serious external threats strengthen its weak national loyalties. As Meisel writes, "Canada is almost totally lacking in a genuinely shared set of symbols, heroes, historical incidents, enemies, or even ambitions."[49] The data on crosscutting of language and class in table 8 show that the two segments are not economic equals, although the disparity is not extreme.

Moreover, not even a trace of prior consociational traditions can be detected. The European powers that colonized Canada were centralizing nation-states with political traditions that were sharply different from those prevalent in the Holy Roman Empire and its successor states. McRae argues that the British and French traditions were reinforced because their Canadian "colonial experiments represented a selective fragmentation from the parent society. . . . New France was a projection of the France of Louis XIV and Colbert, but it lacked the counterbalance of older feudalism. British North America after the loss of the American colonies was dominated by Imperial governors and British military garrisons, and until the 1840s it lacked an effective political counterforce to this strong executive influence."[50] Moreover, the British influence at the formative stage of Canadian representative institutions was dominant and

49. John Meisel, "Canadian Parties and Politics," in *Contemporary Canada*, ed. R. H. Leach (Durham: Duke University Press, 1968), p. 135.

50. McRae, "Consociationalism and the Canadian Political System," pp. 254–55. See also Juan Linz's evaluation of the conditions for consociational democracy in Canada: "Early State-Building and Late Peripheral Nationalisms against the State: The Case of Spain," in *Building States and Nations: Analyses by Region*, ed. S. N. Eisenstadt and Stein Rokkan (Beverly Hills: Sage, 1973), pp. 92–94.

pervasive. Thus the spontaneous development of a series of key consociational devices arising from the necessity of ruling a plural society in the United Province serves as a strong reminder that prior traditions of elite accommodation are a favorable but not a necessary condition for consociational democracy.

Writers on Canadian politics disagree on how the country should be classified in the typology of democratic regimes. Presthus states that it "fits nicely" into the consociational category.[51] But McRae thinks that "the existing Canadian political system, even at its best, must be viewed as a very imperfect example of consociational democracy."[52] An "average" of these two views is probably the most nearly correct interpretation: Canada fits approximately in between the centrifugal and consociational types. The future of the Canadian political system will depend to a large extent on whether it moves in the direction of greater consociationalism and, as a result, greater stability and unity, or in the direction of a more centrifugal regime with a partition of the country as its most likely outcome.

SEMICONSOCIATIONAL DEMOCRACY: ISRAEL

The second Western democracy with sufficient consociational features to be called a semiconsociational regime is Israel. Although its major cleavage, that between Jews and Arabs, theoretically makes it a binational state, the Jews are an overwhelming majority and hence it is primarily a Jewish state. Within the Jewish community, there is an increasingly important division between Jews of Western and those of Eastern origin, but the principal segmental cleavages among the Jews that make Israel a plural society are of a religious and ideological nature. There are three segments: socialists, secular nonsocialists, and religious Jews. Their strength can be estimated on the basis of the results of the Knesset elections, in which the socialist parties collectively

51. Presthus, *Elite Accommodation,* p. 7.

52. McRae, "Epilogue," p. 300. See also F. C. Engelmann and M. A. Schwartz, *Canadian Political Parties: Origins, Character, Impact* (Scarborough: Prentice-Hall of Canada, 1975), pp. 289–93.

(excluding the communists) received around 50 percent of the total vote until the 1973 elections, the nonsocialist parties more than 25 percent, and the religious parties about 15 percent.

These three segments are very similar to the subcultures of Austria, Belgium, and Holland with regard to both the religious-ideological nature of the cleavages and the degree to which political and social life is organized along the lines of cleavage. Each segment has a major political party as well as a varying number of smaller parties. Furthermore, as K. Z. Paltiel writes, "individually and as blocs Israeli parties stand at the apex of sets and networks of collective and cooperative agricultural settlements; trade unions and trade union-owned industries; industrial, marketing, purchasing, transportation and artisan cooperatives; housing and commercial contracting companies; health, welfare, leisure time and sports institutions; newspaper, weekly, periodical and book-publishing companies; vocational, educational, ideological and religious institutions; women's and youth movements." The encompassing and self-sufficient character of the segments amply justifies their description as *familles spirituelles* in a system of segmented pluralism.[53] The common Hebrew term that is applied to the subcultures is *mahane* or "camp," the equivalent of the Austrian *Lager.*[54]

The most striking consociational element of Israeli democracy is segmental autonomy. The national political system respects and is built upon the separate and self-contained camps with their extensive organizational networks. This phenomenon can be characterized as "federalism in a unitary state," and it justifies the description of Israel as "quasi-federal."[55] It is strengthened by a geographical element: as Emanuel Gutmann points out, the members of the religious camp increasingly tend to segregate themselves into separate neighborhoods in almost all cities and towns.[56]

53. K. Z. Paltiel, "The Israeli Coalition System," *Government and Opposition* 10, no. 4 (autumn 1975): 398.

54. Emanuel Gutmann, "Religion and National Integration in Israel," paper presented at the Round Table on Political Integration of the International Political Science Association, Jerusalem, 1974, p. 15.

55. Leonard J. Fein, *Politics in Israel* (Boston: Little, Brown, 1967), p. 100; Paltiel, "Israeli Coalition System," p. 405.

56. Gutmann, "Religion and National Integration," p. 19.

Two other consociational principles that are very strong in Israel are proportionality and the mutual veto. The electoral system is one of the two most proportional systems in the world: as in the Netherlands, the other example of an extreme PR system, the whole country serves as a single constituency. The effect is that even very small parties can enter the Knesset, as long as their share of the total vote is at least 1 percent. The so-called party key approach to appointments and financial allocations ensures the faithful application of the proportionality principle in these areas as well.

A particularly important instrument in the hands of the religious camp is the veto power, which it uses with regard to the most deeply contentious issue among Israelis (especially between religious and secular Jews), the role of religion in the state. By means of its veto, the religious minority has succeeded in preventing any significant changes in the system of religious state-supported education, which enrolls between a third and a quarter of the school-age children, and in the jurisdiction of the religious authorities over personal law. As Alan Arian writes, "the religious issue is neutralized by deferring it."[57] The mutual veto has also been responsible for the immobilism on the drafting of an Israeli constitution. Because no compromise appears to be possible between the advocates of a liberal constitutional state and those desiring a theocracy, Israel has a few "basic laws" but not a full-fledged constitution, and the Knesset enjoys legislative sovereignty.

In contrast to the strongly consociational nature of Israeli democracy with respect to the three important but secondary principles of autonomy, veto, and proportionality, it only weakly approximates the primary consociational principle of grand coalition. The cabinet has almost always included the main parties of both the socialist and the religious camps and frequently also the Progressives or Independent Liberals, a minor party in the nonsocialist camp. And the cabinet coalitions have usually been larger than minimum winning size.[58] However, with the excep-

57. Alan Arian, *Consensus in Israel* (New York: General Learning Press, 1971), p. 21; see also pp. 3–4, 13–15.

58. David Nachmias, "Coalition Politics in Israel," *Comparative Political Studies* 7, no. 3 (October 1974): 317–20.

tion of the grand coalitions in the 1967–70 period, the principal nonsocialist party has not participated in the cabinet. As far as the main segmental parties are concerned, there is no pattern of shifting coalitions either—the socialist Mapai and its successors have always been in the cabinet—and there is little support for a move in this direction or for a grand coalition on a more permanent basis. "It is quite surprising," Gutmann writes, "to what extent adherence to the classical parliamentary pattern of government-opposition confrontation is taken as the norm in a country in which no change of government has yet occurred."[59] With regard to the composition of its cabinets, Israel is less a consociational democracy than a dominant-party system, similar to the Italian one in which the presence of a dominant ruling party has long given a modicum of stability to an essentially centrifugal regime.[60]

Israel fulfills almost all of the conditions that are conducive to consociational democracy; in fact, these are so strongly favorable that they should have been able to sustain a much higher degree of consociationalism than has actually been developed. The only dubious factor is the balance of power, because the socialist camp consists of a narrow majority or a near-majority of the population. But its political strength is reduced by the division into several parties and the fact that the main socialist segmental party has never won a majority of the seats in the Knesset. Its minority position has forced it to form cabinet coalitions with smaller parties which have been willing to cooperate for the same reason: as Peter Y. Medding states, "there exists less fear of absolute power in a coalition situation."[61] Conversely, the political strength of the religious camp is actually greater than that expressed by the number of Knesset seats it wins, since it is generally assumed that the basic sentiments underlying its programs are supported by many more people than those voting for

59. Gutmann, "Religion and National Integration," p. 25.

60. See Alan Arian and Samuel H. Barnes, "The Dominant Party System: A Neglected Model of Democratic Stability," *Journal of Politics* 36, no. 3 (August 1974): 592–614.

61. Peter Y. Medding, *Mapai in Israel: Political Organisation and Government in a New Society* (London: Cambridge University Press, 1972), p. 306.

the religious parties. The balance of power can therefore be described as a moderately multiple one.

A highly favorable factor is the existence of strong overarching loyalties that counteract the division into separate segments. It should be recognized, first of all, that religion both divides and unites: "Although it is also a source of disaffection within Israeli (Jewish) society, religion as a *common primordial sentiment* creates common attachments and serves as a fusionary element."[62] The commitment to the survival of the Jewish people and of Israel as a Jewish state further contributes to the overarching national consensus. In fact, the national sentiments are so strong that Leonard J. Fein argues: "It would be too much to say that Israel is a fragmented society, or that there is no unifying political culture."[63] In addition, the economic inequality of the segments, especially the difference between the socialist and secular non-socialist camps, is of slight consequence because of the overall highly egalitarian nature of Israeli society.

Israel's small size and the very serious threats to its existence are conspicuously favorable factors for producing internal unity. Fein does not exaggerate when he states that the foreign threat "provides to Israel an undoubted source of unity, an issue so preeminent and so undisputed as to make all other cleavages seem trivial." And he speculates that "it may well be that Israel's is an example of a nonworking multiparty system which works, which works because of factors extraneous to the system itself."[64] Arian also forcefully points to the enormous influence of Israel's fragile security: "There is in Israel a very high degree of consensus on the need for the existence of consensus."[65] It is significant that the one period of grand coalition cabinets began on the eve of the Six-Day War in 1967, but it lasted only three years.

Finally, Israel also has the advantage of strong traditions of accommodation developed in the Zionist movement and in the

62. Gutmann, "Religion and National Integration," p. 4 (italics added). See also Ervin Birnbaum, *The Politics of Compromise: State and Religion in Israel* (Rutherford, N. J.: Fairleigh Dickinson University Press, 1970).

63. Fein, *Politics in Israel,* p. 57.

64. Ibid., p. 209.

65. Arian, *Consensus in Israel*, p. 3.

Yishuv, the preindependence Jewish community in Palestine. Because these were both voluntary arrangements without any of the coercive powers of a sovereign state, the adoption of proportionality, a federal-type structure, and a coalescent style of decision-making was the logical answer to the need for cooperation and compromise. It is safe to conclude that "the accommodative processes were well-developed when the State emerged in 1948."[66]

The two authors who have written about Israel from the point of view of the consociational model are cautious in their judgment as to how well the country fits the model. Paltiel merely states that "the consociational approach provides a fruitful framework for analysing political integration and the nature of democracy in Israel."[67] And Gutmann concludes that, "although not a consociationalism in the accepted sense of the term, the Israeli ruling coalition is based on some of its elements."[68] Like Canada, Israel may be regarded as a combination of consociational and centrifugal democracy. Unlike Canada, however, the conditions for consociationalism in Israel have been extremely favorable. The Canadian example, especially the case of the strongly consociational United Province, shows that such favorable conditions are not necessary conditions, the Israeli case that they are not sufficient conditions.

THE LIMITS OF CONSOCIATIONALISM: NORTHERN IRELAND

The most unambiguous instance of a plural society and a centrifugal democracy in the Western world is Northern Ireland. Although it is not a sovereign state, it may be considered on a par with independent countries because from 1921 until the imposition of direct rule from London in 1972 the powers of the Stormont (the Northern Ireland parliament) were so generously interpreted that they far exceeded the usual powers of

66. Paltiel, "Israeli Coalition System," p. 406. See also S. N. Eisenstadt, *Israeli Society* (London: Weidenfeld and Nicolson, 1967), pp. 408–12.

67. Paltiel, "Israeli Coalition System," p. 414.

68. Gutmann, "Religion and National Integration," p. 27.

subnational governmental units even in federal states. A good characterization is by Ian Budge and Cornelius O'Leary: "a self-governing province with some of the trappings of sovereignty."[69]

The Protestants and Catholics of Northern Ireland form two quite distinct and separate segments with their own social, educational, and recreational organizations. The degree of social segregation is also indicated by the extremely low frequency of intermarriage. Rosemary Harris states that "Protestants and Catholics form two endogamous groups probably more separated from each other in sexual matters than most white and negro groups in societies which supposedly abhor miscegenation."[70] Religious and political allegiances are particularly closely intertwined. On the basis of Richard Rose's 1968 survey findings concerning the degree of support given by Protestants to the Unionist party and by Catholics to the Nationalist and Northern Ireland Labour parties, the angle and index of crosscutting between religious and party system cleavages can be calculated: these are a very low 2° and 0.21 respectively.[71] Conor Cruise O'Brien even claims that, in the few instances of incompatible allegiances, a person's political affiliation is decisive for his assignment to one of the two communities: "In Northern Ireland a person who adheres to the politics of the other religion—a Protestant Nationalist, or Catholic Unionist—is for most practical purposes deemed, by the group he left, to have gone over to the other religion: which of course is worse than having been born in it."[72] The aims pursued by the segmental Unionist and Nationalist parties, which were the principal political parties before 1972, were also completely incompatible: the Unionists

69. Ian Budge and Cornelius O'Leary, *Belfast: Approach to Crisis—A Study of Belfast Politics, 1613–1970* (London: Macmillan, 1973), p. 143.

70. Rosemary Harris, *Prejudice and Tolerance in Ulster: A Study of Neighbours and "Strangers" in a Border Community* (Manchester: Manchester University Press, 1972), p. x. See also David E. Schmitt, *Violence in Northern Ireland: Ethnic Conflict and Radicalization in an International Setting* (Morristown, N. J.: General Learning Press, 1974), pp. 12–14.

71. Rose, *Governing Without Consensus*. See also Richard Rose, *Northern Ireland: A Time of Choice* (London: Macmillan, 1976).

72. Conor Cruise O'Brien, *States of Ireland* (London: Hutchinson, 1972), p. 13.

insisted on the retention of autonomy within the United Kingdom, and the Nationalists desired union with the Republic of Ireland. The Northern Ireland Labour party and the new Alliance party have been more moderate and have attempted to appeal to both religious segments, but they have not succeeded in becoming major political forces.

The extremely plural nature of Northern Ireland society was complemented by an uncompromisingly adversarial style of governance. The Unionists representing the Protestant majority of about two-thirds of the population formed a one-party government during the entire period from 1921 to 1972. This government was, in the words of the first Unionist prime minister of Northern Ireland, "a Protestant government."[73] Protestant strength was exaggerated in the Stormont and in the local councils by the abolition of proportional representation and the return to the plurality system first for local elections and then also for parliamentary elections in the 1920s. In communities with Catholic majorities, Protestant politicians still generally held power as the result of gerrymandering, malapportionment, the restricted franchise, and plural voting. The showcase of the Northern Ireland gerrymander and malapportionment was its second largest city, Londonderry, with a Catholic and Nationalist majority among both voters and the total population but a comfortable Unionist majority on the council. Majority rule was therefore not alleviated by any minority veto or autonomy. There was also considerable discrimination against Catholics with regard to civil service appointments.

The solution to which the British governments, both Conservative and Labour, became committed after the outbreak of widespread violence in 1968 is the essentially consociational one of a power-sharing executive, despite the fact that such a grand coalition is alien to the British political tradition—another indication that prior traditions are not always of decisive importance. They also reinstituted proportional representation—the single transferable vote, which, it should be noted, is not as

73. Lord Craigavon, quoted in Liam de Paor, *Divided Ulster*, 2d ed. (Harmondsworth: Penguin Books, 1971), p. 105.

suitable a consociational method as the list systems used in the continental European consociational democracies, because it maximizes the voters' choice and consequently diminishes the power and flexibility of the segmental leaders—and abolished the electoral abuses that had disadvantaged the Catholic minority. The constitutional convention elected by proportional representation in 1975 was told in advance that its proposals had to incorporate the idea of power-sharing.

The problem with a consociational solution for Northern Ireland is not that it is theoretically inapplicable—in fact, it is the only logical solution short of partition—but that it cannot be imposed against the will of one of the segments, especially if it is a majority segment. Most of the Protestant leaders as well as the rank and file remain opposed to sharing power with the Catholics. And they showed their power by the 1974 general strike of Protestant workers that paralyzed Northern Ireland and brought down the partly power-sharing executive of Catholics and moderate Protestants that had been in office for only a few months.

The conditions for consociational democracy in Northern Ireland, whether mandatory or voluntary, are overwhelmingly unfavorable. Northern Ireland exemplifies the least favorable balance of power situation: a dual division without equilibrium and with one segment capable of exercising hegemonic power. This permanent majority-minority relationship is exacerbated by the numerical strengths of Protestants and Catholics in the island of Ireland as a whole. As O'Brien shows, a double imbalance appears when we look beyond Northern Ireland as a separate system: the Protestants have a two to one majority in the North, but their "fear and suspicion of Catholics in Northern Ireland do not correspond to these proportions, but to the proportions between Catholic and Protestant in the *entire island of Ireland,* in which Protestants are outnumbered by Catholics by more than three to one. And Catholics in Northern Ireland are also strongly conscious of this proportion, and of rights which they believe it to imply."[74]

74. O'Brien, *States of Ireland,* p. 11.

The dual Protestant-Catholic imbalance within Northern Ireland further means that proportional representation cannot contribute much to the formation of a grand coalition government. It mirrors rather than exaggerates the popular majority, but a majority remains a majority. This is also the problem with Brian Barry's suggestion that, because compulsory power-sharing is unworkable, a system of "cooperation without co-optation" should be attempted, such as a more tolerant majority and the acceptance by the minority of the role of "loyal opposition."[75] Such an arrangement is a good alternative if it means a pattern of shifting coalitions, but the loyalty of a "loyal opposition" is bound to be severely strained by a permanent oppositional role.

A number of other factors are equally negative. Northern Ireland is not a nation and there are no overarching solidarities that can offset the centrifugal effects of the segmental cleavages. In fact, national solidarities deepen the cleavages of Northern Ireland: historically, most Catholics have tended to feel allegiance to the Republic whereas the Protestants have been loyal to the British Crown. The political traditions of the Protestant majority do not provide a fertile basis for consociational democracy either: the British model sets the standards of governmental organization. And both power-sharing and proportional representation (even in the "British" form of the single transferable vote rather than the continental varieties of list systems) are decidedly un-British. The British effort to introduce these consociational methods in Northern Ireland contrasts sharply with the steadfast refusal of British governments to consider them for Great Britain itself. The economic inequality of the two segments is an unfavorable condition, too, although this factor should not be exaggerated. The angle of crosscutting between religion and social class is 68° and *XC* equals 0.50. Indeed, as Rose emphasizes, "given their larger numbers in the population . . . there are *more poor Protestants than poor Catholics* in Northern Ireland."[76] But the Catholic self-image of an economically sup-

75. Brian Barry, "The Consociational Model and Its Dangers," *European Journal of Political Research* 3, no. 4 (December 1975): 405–06.

76. Rose, *Governing Without Consensus*, p. 289.

pressed minority may be more important than the less stark reality.

Three favorable conditions appear to be present in Northern Ireland, but upon closer analysis they prove to be either ambivalent or largely negative. The first is the factor of size. Northern Ireland appears to be in a particularly propitious situation because it is an extremely small country with a population of only about 1.5 million, and because it does not conduct its own foreign policy. On the other hand, the small size of the population also means that the supply of political talent is likely to be small. Northern Ireland's potential with respect to capable leadership is well illustrated by the examples that Rose gives: "In so far as ability is proportionate to numbers, then Northern Ireland . . . might have the political talent of an English county such as Durham, Cheshire or Hampshire, or of an American state such as Nebraska, Oregon or West Virginia." And if Northern Ireland did not have its semi-independent status, "it might provide an occasional Cabinet minister for a United Kingdom government, but no more, judging by the record of Scotland and Wales."[77] Smallness is conducive to consociational democracy only to a certain limit, and Northern Ireland may well be below the threshold.

A closely related factor is the presence of external threats. The proposition that foreign threats may produce an impetus toward consociationalism is based on the idea that such threats stimulate internal feelings of solidarity and demonstrate the urgent necessity of united and cooperative action to both the segmental leaders and their followers. The Northern Ireland regime has been under the continuous external threat—albeit not a grave one—of the Republic's constitutional claim to the province, but this irredentist demand has not produced cooperative attitudes. The obvious modification which the proposition needs, and which has already been mentioned earlier, is that an external threat must be perceived as a common danger by all of the segments in order to have a unifying effect. Otherwise, as in the case of Northern Ireland, it will serve only to widen the differences between segments.

77. Ibid., p. 179.

The third only partially favorable factor is segmental isolation. Rival segments may coexist peacefully if there is little contact between them and consequently little occasion for conflict. The Protestant-Catholic cleavage in Northern Ireland is extremely sharp, and this does appear to have the function of the good fences that make good neighbors. Rosemary Harris reports in her anthropological study of the small rural community of Ballybeg that there were few contacts across the religious divide, and that when a meeting did occur "the greatest efforts were made to prevent any controversial topic from being discussed." And she suggests that it was because of the deep religious cleavage that such cross-religious individual contacts were particularly "neighbourly."[78] On the other hand, segmental isolation is only social and not geographical: although the cities have become increasingly ghettoized since 1968, the two populations are highly interspersed territorially. As table 9 shows, the six counties are almost as fragmented as Northern Ireland as a whole:

TABLE 9. Religious Fragmentation in Northern Ireland; County Averages and Country Totals (1961)

	Counties		Northern Ireland
	Mean	Weighted Mean	
Largest group (%)	59.3	66.3	65.1
Index of fragmentation (*F*)	.46	.43	.45

SOURCE: Calculated from data in Richard Rose, *Governing Without Consensus: An Irish Perspective* (London: Faber and Faber, 1971), p. 90.

the means indicate an even greater heterogeneity of the counties than of the whole country, and the weighted means show only a slightly lower degree of heterogeneity. The physical proximity of the two populations has been an important factor in outbreaks of violence.

78. Harris, *Prejudice and Tolerance*, pp. 146, 199.

The territorial mingling of the two segments is not only a negative (though not necessarily insuperable) condition for the establishment of a consociational arrangement; it is also a serious obstacle to the partition of the country. Partition would require an exchange and resettlement of populations—the human and material costs of which would be huge—but some form of partition may be the only solution, if consociational democracy should ultimately prove to be unattainable or unworkable. In fact, only the very recognition that partition is the sole realistic but highly undesirable alternative to power-sharing, combined with a firm and steady British insistence of the goal of a power-sharing executive, may still lead to a grudging acceptance of a consociational solution in the basically unfavorable environment of Northern Ireland.

5 Consociational Democracy in the Third World

The theoretical literature on political development and nation-building has the tendency, as discussed in the introductory chapter, to draw a superficial dichotomous contrast between the plural societies of the Third World and the supposedly homogeneous societies of the First World, to overlook the existence and relevance of the several significantly plural Western societies, to ignore the fact that a few of these societies have been able to sustain a stable democratic regime of the consociational type, and to disregard the normative lessons of the consociational example. It would not be accurate, however, to portray the entire body of political development theories as uniformly indifferent or hostile to the possibilities of consociational democracy. There are hints and suggestions to be found throughout this literature, but they are usually not elaborated. For instance, Robert Melson and Howard Wolpe conclude their analysis of the politics of communalism, that is, segmented pluralism, in the developing countries with the following exhortation: "Political arrangements must be found which accord to all communal groups a meaningful role in national life and which are able to keep communal conflict within manageable bounds. The stability of culturally plural societies is threatened not by communalism, per se, but by the failure of national institutions explicitly to recognize and accommodate existing communal divisions and interests."[1] This advice is sound and the diagnosis on

1. Robert Melson and Howard Wolpe, "Modernization and the Politics of Communalism: A Theoretical Perspective," *American Political Science Review* 64, no. 4 (December 1970): 1130. See also Charles W. Anderson, Fred R. von der Mehden, and Crawford Young, *Issues of Political Development* (Englewood Cliffs, N. J.: Prentice-Hall, 1967), pp. 75–79; and Robert A. Dahl, *Regimes and Oppositions* (New Haven: Yale University Press, 1973), pp. 22–25. An exceptional treatment of political development which explicitly does not equate this process with ethnic assimilation and centralization is Cynthia H. Enloe, *Ethnic Conflict and Political Development* (Boston: Little, Brown, 1973).

which it rests is correct, but the authors do not specify the nature of the arrangements that can accommodate segmental cleavages.

There are also a few evident and striking exceptions to the general tendency to neglect the potential value of either consociational or similar solutions to the political problems of plural societies. One of these is Eric A. Nordlinger's construction of a new democratic model that is specifically applicable to both Western and non-Western deeply divided societies. Several of the "conflict-regulating practices" typical of his model are identical with or similar to consociational methods: a stable governing coalition patterned after the Austrian example, proportionality, the mutual veto, and the package deal.[2] Another example is Claude Ake's study of political integration in the developing countries. He argues that "the ultimate cure for the inherent instability of the new states lies mainly in the modification of the political behavior of its elites." And he recommends that the government be in the hands of an "elite coalition," that is, a coalition of all of the leaders of "the major social, religious, professional, and ethnic groups. . . . Consensus is sought not at the grass-roots level but at the leadership level by enlisting the support of leading personalities from all major social groups."[3]

THE LEWIS MODEL

The most interesting, specific, and detailed proposal of this kind is made by Sir Arthur Lewis—not a political scientist but, like J. S. Furnivall, an economist.[4] Lewis discusses the politics of thir-

2. Eric A. Nordlinger, *Conflict Regulation in Divided Societies,* Occasional Papers in International Affairs, no. 29 (Cambridge, Mass.: Center for International Affairs, Harvard University, 1972), pp. 17, 20–31.

3. Claude Ake, *A Theory of Political Integration* (Homewood, Ill.: Dorsey Press, 1967), pp. 79, 112–13.

4. W. Arthur Lewis, *Politics in West Africa* (London: Allen and Unwin, 1965), esp. ch. 3. For a vigorous endorsement of Lewis's approach, see William G. Fleming, "American Political Science and African Politics," *Journal of Modern African Studies* 7, no. 3 (October 1969): 495–511. See also Sidney Verba, "Some Dilemmas in Comparative Research," *World Politics* 20, no. 1 (October 1967): 125–27; Donald Rothchild, "Ethnicity and Conflict Resolution," *World Politics*

teen West African states: Liberia, the former British colonies of Ghana, Nigeria, and Sierra Leone, and the former French colonies of Mauritania, Senegal, Mali, Guinea, Upper Volta, Ivory Coast, Togo, Dahomey, and Niger. His prescription for these countries, and by implication for other plural societies as well, is an essentially consociational one. His initial assumptions are similar to those of Furnivall and other development theorists. He distinguishes between the plural societies of West Africa and "class societies" like Britain and France. Plural societies are divided by tribal, religious, linguistic, cultural, economic, and regional differences. Class societies are the essentially homogeneous societies of the West, in which social class is the major source of political identification but is not a deep cleavage. Lewis makes the usual mistake of attributing a too high degree of homogeneity and consensus to the countries of the West. France is culturally fragmented along religious and ideological dimensions and should have been classified, according to Lewis's own definitions, as a plural society; his homogeneous class society is mainly derived from the British example. But this lapse does not affect the remainder of his argument. The democratic forms of government that he examines are those of Britain and France, the former colonial rulers in West Africa, and he does not mention alternative forms occurring in the Western world. In fact, his Western model of government approximates the British case more closely than the French case: its characteristic features are a two-party system, a clear government-versus-opposition pattern, plurality or majority electoral systems, and a unitary and centralized government.

Lewis attributes the failure of democracy and the rise of one-party regimes in West Africa to the fact that this kind of democracy is not viable in plural societies. Up to this point, his argument has followed conventional lines, but now he diverges sharply from the hypothesis that a plural society cannot sustain democratic government: it is not democracy that is inappro-

---

22. no. 4 (July 1970): 611–16: and Robert P. van den Helm, "Aspects of the Study of State Formation and Nation-Building," *International Journal of Politics* 4, no. 1–2 (spring-summer 1974): 22–24.

priate for plural societies, he argues, but only a particular kind of it, namely, British-style democracy. He then proceeds to construct an alternative model based on his analysis of the political needs of the West African plural systems: "Britain and France are class societies, and their institutions and conventions are designed to cope with this fact. West Africa is not a class society; its problem is that it is a plural society. What is good for a class society is bad for a plural society. Hence to create good political institutions in West Africa one has to think their problem through from the foundations up."[5]

What plural societies need, Lewis states, is coalition government rather than polarization into government and opposition. This is demanded by the primary meaning of democracy: citizens must have the opportunity to participate, directly or indirectly, in decision-making. The second meaning of democracy, that the will of the majority must prevail, violates the primary rule if representatives are grouped into a government and an opposition, because it excludes the minority from the decision-making process for an extended period of time. Nevertheless, majority rule may be acceptable in consensual societies, but in plural societies "it is totally immoral, inconsistent with the primary meaning of democracy, and destructive of any prospect of building a nation in which different peoples might live together in harmony." The governing coalition should consist of all the major parties, and the minor parties should also be free to join. Lewis suggests that it may be helpful to include such a rule in the constitution: "Instead of the President sending for the leader of the largest party to form a Cabinet, the rule may tell him to send for the leader of every party which has received more than 20 per cent of the votes, and divide the Cabinet seats between them, or such of them as will co-operate."[6]

Second, each segment in a plural society should be fairly represented; this means, according to Lewis, that they should be proportionally represented. In a plural society the primary meaning of democracy "leads to proportional representation,

5. Lewis, *Politics in West Africa,* p. 64.
6. Ibid., pp. 64–66, 83.

with all parties offered seats in all decision-making bodies, including the Cabinet itself." Third, the best party system is not necessarily a two-party system. The crucial requirement is that each segment be represented by its own party. This results in a national system of two, three, or four substantial parties in the West African countries. Finally, Lewis recommends a federal division of powers or at least "a reasonable degree of provincial devolution." A country with significant regional differences "needs to give its provinces the opportunity to look after their own affairs, if they are to feel content with the political union." Federalism will also ensure, if there are wide economic differences among the regions, that "the richer areas [will] not be taxed heavily to subsidize the poorer."[7]

All of Lewis's recommendations bear a close resemblance to the principles of consociational democracy. This is particularly remarkable because they are products of his creative imagination; at no point does he show an awareness of the empirical precedents provided by some or all of the European consociational democracies. The only difference between Lewis's scheme and the normative rules of consociationalism is that Lewis tends to be rather more specific than the latter would require. For instance, grand coalition is a consociational principle but the 20 percent rule may not suit particular situations. Consociational theory emphasizes the importance of a high degree of autonomy for each of the separate segments; federalism or provincial devolution is one way in which this rule can be implemented if each segment is geographically concentrated. Proportionality is a principle that should be applied not only to representation in the legislative and executive bodies but also to administrative appointments and to the allocation of public funds.

Lewis also has a preference for a specific kind of proportional representation method: the single transferable vote instead of the list system.[8] The former increases the influence of the voters and reduces that of the party leaders. As a result, it makes the task of forging compromises at the elite level somewhat more

7. Ibid., pp. 51, 55, 63, 71, 81.
8. Ibid., pp. 73–74.

difficult. All four of the European consociational democracies use list systems; the single transferable vote is the PR method preferred in the Anglo-American countries. This is not a matter of great consequence, but it does suggest the strength of the British normative model: even Lewis is not completely free of its bias.

Although Lewis does not mention the European consociational democracies, his arguments and proposals are strengthened considerably by the empirical evidence they provide. The relevance and applicability of his ideas—and, in general, of the consociational model as a normative example—would be strengthened further, if (1) several empirical instances of the application of the consociational model in non-Western plural societies could be adduced, (2) consociational democracy were found to be successful in all of these instances, and (3) in all other cases, the conditions for its possible application were found to be favorable. The actual record is mixed on these three counts and is therefore not fully convincing. Nevertheless, there are three clear examples (Lebanon, Malaysia, and Cyprus) and one more doubtful case (Nigeria) where consociational democracy was instituted in the Third World. In two of these cases, moreover, consociationalism was reasonably successful for an extended period of time (that is, at least ten years). And the conditions for consociational democracy, derived from both its Western and non-Western applications, are by no means overwhelmingly unfavorable elsewhere in the Third World.

CONSOCIATIONAL DEMOCRACY IN LEBANON, 1943–1975

Lebanon is a plural society with a large number of rigidly self-contained religious segments. The main sects are the Maronite Christians (about 30 percent of the population in the mid-1950s), the Sunni Moslems (20 percent), Shiite Moslems (18 percent), and Greek Orthodox (11 percent). In addition, there are about ten smaller sects most of which are either Christian or Moslem. The two groups of sects, Christian and Moslem, are almost evenly balanced in numbers. The Lebanese sects may be likened to the religious-ideological segments of the European consociational democracies; President Charles Helou referred to them as "spiritual families" in his inaugural address in 1964.[9]

Lebanon was a consociational democracy from its independence in 1943 until the fatal civil war that broke out in 1975. The informal and unwritten "national pact" concluded at the time of independence prescribed government by a kind of grand coalition of top officeholders in what Pierre Rondot calls a "quasi-presidential system": a Maronite president, a Sunni prime minister, a Shiite chairman of the legislature, and a Greek Orthodox deputy chairman and deputy prime minister.[10] The numerical strength of the sects was reflected in the relative importance of these offices. The cabinet, in which the sects were proportionally represented, was also a part of the ruling grand coalition. The methods used for the election of the president and the members of parliament do not belong to the usual proportional representation systems but were proportional in their effects. The president was chosen by parliament by majority vote, but, since it was predetermined that he be a Maronite, this majority method did not entail a contest among the different sects. Parliamentary elections were conducted according to the plurality and multimember constituency system. In each constituency slates of candidates were nominated in such a way that each slate reflected the segmental composition of the constituency, and the voters chose among these different proportionally constituted slates. The number and size of the constituencies and the total number of legislators varied over the years, but an overall ratio of six Christian to five Moslem members of the legislature remained the same.

This electoral arrangement can therefore be characterized, in Michael W. Suleiman's words, as a "preset proportional representation system on a communal or religious basis."[11] It has

9. Quoted in Michael C. Hudson, "Democracy and Social Mobilization in Lebanese Politics," *Comparative Politics* 1, no. 2 (January 1969): 245.

10. Pierre Rondot, "The Political Institutions of Lebanese Democracy," in *Politics in Lebanon,* ed. Leonard Binder (New York: Wiley, 1966), p. 135.

11. Michael W. Suleiman, *Political Parties in Lebanon: The Challenge of a Fragmented Political Culture* (Ithaca: Cornell University Press, 1967), p. 45. See also Riad Younes, *Politik und Proporzsystem in einer südlibanesischen Dorfgemeinschaft: Eine empirisch sozio-politische Untersuchung* (Munich: Weltforum Verlag, 1975).

also often been praised as a proportional system that produced compromise and harmony because in order to be elected a candidate needed the votes of members of both his own and other sects. This was a drawback, however, from the consociational point of view because it did not bring together the real segmental spokesmen at a site suitable for political accommodation: "The typical champions of each community run the risk . . . of being passed over in favor of tamer individuals." But the result was not fatal for consociational democracy: because the legislature was rather ineffectual, the more important issues were moved up to the cabinet for decision, and the cabinet was "a true Parliament on a small scale" with a proportional composition and with the further advantage of conducting its deliberations in secret.[12] Proportionality was also strictly observed with regard to appointments to the civil service.

Segmental autonomy was another strong consociational feature of Lebanese democracy. Leonard Binder writes that it was an integral, although unwritten, part of the constitution that "the regime will not interfere in the area of intra-confessional social relationships."[13] Each sect has its own schools and social, recreational, and welfare organizations. Furthermore, the personal status laws (concerning such matters as marriage, divorce, and inheritance) differ from sect to sect and are administered in separate sectarian courts. The mutual veto was an equally basic, but again unwritten, provision of the political system. Suleiman writes that "Calhoun's thesis of 'concurrent majority' can be seen in operation" in the Lebanese case.[14]

On the whole, consociational democracy in Lebanon must be judged to have performed satisfactorily for more than thirty years. Its main weakness was the inflexible institutionalization of consociational principles. The segmental allocation of the highest offices and the "preset" electoral proportionality, both of which favored the Christian sects that constituted a majority in the 1932 census, were incapable of allowing a smooth adjustment to the gradual loss of majority status by the Christians to

12. Rondot, "Political Institutions of Lebanese Democracy," pp. 133–34.

13. Leonard Binder, "Political Change in Lebanon," in Binder, *Politics in Lebanon,* p. 295.

14. Suleiman, *Political Parties in Lebanon,* p. 54.

the Moslems. In other respects, too, there was a tendency toward immobilism, but it is surely an exaggeration to state, as Edward Shils did, that Lebanon was "a country which must be kept *completely still* politically in order to prevent communal self-centeredness and mutual distrust from turning into active and angry contention." Before 1975, the regime was challenged by several other outbreaks of civil strife, but it survived these and kept their damage limited; for instance, the civil war of 1958 was, in Shils's words, an "unusually pacific civil war."[15] Compared with the frequent revolutionary upheavals to which other Middle Eastern countries have been prone, and in spite of the flaws in its consociational institutions, the Lebanese consociational regime established a remarkable—although obviously far from perfect—record of democratic stability.

CONSOCIATIONAL DEMOCRACY IN MALAYSIA, 1955–1969

The case of Malaysia provides the second example of reasonably successful consociational democracy in the Third World, although the nature of its plural society and the kind of consociational institutions it developed differ considerably both from Lebanon and from the European cases. The segments of Malaysian plural society are fewer in number but more different from each other than the Lebanese sects. The largest segment is the Malay one, comprising about 53 percent of the population of Malaya (West Malaysia); the Chinese form 35 percent, and the Indians and Pakistanis 11 percent of this population. In Malaysia as a whole, that is, including the East Malaysian states of Sarawak and Sabah, all of these percentages are somewhat lower, and the Malays do not have majority status. The segments are separated from each other by the mutually reinforcing cleavages of language, religion, culture, and race.

15. Edward Shils, "The Prospects for Lebanese Civility," in *Politics in Lebanon*, pp. 2, 4 (italics added). See also the conclusions of Theodor Hanf, *Erziehungswesen in Gesellschaft und Politik des Libanon* (Bielefeld: Bertelsmann Universitätsverlag, 1969), pp. 43–52; and of David R. Smock and Audrey C. Smock, *The Politics of Pluralism: A Comparative Study of Lebanon and Ghana* (New York: Elsevier, 1975), pp. 152–92.

The all-important consociational device of Malaysia is the Alliance, a grand coalition of the principal Malay, Chinese, and Indian political parties. The Alliance was set up in the early 1950s by Malay and Chinese leaders, soon joined by the Indians, and won more than four-fifths of the vote and all but one of the parliamentary seats in the first federal elections in 1955. It then formed a cabinet in which all three segmental parties were represented. The grand coalition pattern was therefore already established when Malaya became independent in 1957, and it held together through two more federal elections in 1959 and 1964, through the change from Malaya to Malaysia by the addition of Singapore, Sarawak, and Sabah in 1963, and through the departure of Singapore from the federation in 1965, until a temporary breakdown in 1969. The Alliance arrangement entailed a high degree of freedom for the segments in the conduct of their internal social and cultural affairs. It should be noted that this autonomy is not a function of the federal setup of Malaysia, because the segmental boundaries are not geographical and do not coincide with the state boundaries, and because the federation is a highly centralized one with the exception of the special status enjoyed by the two East Malaysian states.

The Alliance can be said to have adhered to the rule of proportionality only if the political and economic spheres are considered together. The original agreement that created the Alliance regime was a trade-off: political and governmental superiority for the Malays and continued economic hegemony for the Chinese. This bargain was advantageous to both parties; as Milton J. Esman states, "the Malays gained political independence, control of government, and a polity which was to be Malay in style and in its system of symbols. In return the Chinese gained more than overseas Chinese in Southeast Asia had dreamed of—equal citizenship, political participation and officeholding, unimpaired economic opportunity, and tolerance for their language, religion, and cultural institutions."[16]

In politics and government, the Malay party in the Alliance

16. Milton J. Esman, *Administration and Development in Malaysia: Institution-Building and Reform in a Plural Society* (Ithaca: Cornell University Press, 1972), p. 25.

was clearly the senior and dominant partner and the Chinese and Indian parties the junior partners. The electoral system was not proportional but followed the British rule of plurality vote and single-member districts. This method favored the Malays as the largest group, and it was tilted even more in their favor by the malapportionment of the constituencies to the advantage of the rural areas with Malay majorities. The Alliance partners negotiated the assignment of candidates of the three parties to the constituencies and invariably settled on a ratio which disproportionately favored the Malays. The ratio of recruitment to the top civil service positions was four Malays to one non-Malay, and in many other respects the Malays were granted "special rights." Nevertheless, Esman estimates that non-Malays still held some two-thirds of the professional and managerial posts in the civil service in 1972 as a result of their educational superiority.[17] The generally dominant position of the Malays in politics also meant that the minority veto could operate only weakly. It is extremely difficult to evaluate—and impossible to measure exactly—whether the economic superiority of the non-Malays adequately balanced Malay political hegemony, but R. S. Milne concludes that "when the whole scene is surveyed, in its social, economic, and political aspects, it becomes clear that a kind of short-term rough justice between the claims of the communities [was] in fact . . . attained."[18]

Even if we accept Milne's judgment, Malaysian consociational democracy still cannot be judged an unqualified success, because it did not achieve long-term stability. It broke down after the 1969 elections in which the Alliance parties lost much of their popular support, although not their parliamentary majority, to a number of anti-Alliance communal parties. Rioting and civil disorder broke out, and parliament was suspended. A Malay-

17. Milton J. Esman, "Malaysia: Communal Coexistence and Mutual Deterence," in *Racial Tensions and National Identity*, ed. Ernest Q. Campbell (Nashville: Vanderbilt University Press, 1972), p. 235; Gordon P. Means, " 'Special Rights' as a Strategy for Development: The Case of Malaysia," *Comparative Politics* 5, no. 1 (October 1972): 29–61.

18. R. S. Milne, *Government and Politics in Malaysia* (Boston: Houghton Mifflin, 1967), p. 41.

dominated emergency council ruled until 1971, when parliamentary government was restored, but only after the parliament first voted to entrench the privileged position of the Malays in the constitution and to ban all further public as well as parliamentary discussion of these sensitive provisions. The Alliance leaders resumed their efforts to build grand coalitions both by co-opting communal parties into the Alliance and by entering into postelection coalitions. Because of the limitation of the freedom of expression and the increasing political and economic discrimination in favor of the Malays, it is doubtful that Malaysia after 1971 can be regarded as either fully democratic or fully consociational, but before 1969 it certainly was, in Karl von Vorys's words, a viable "democracy without consensus," and hence an inspiring example to those who believe that "it is altogether too early to give up hope about democracy in Asia and Africa."[19]

LEBANON AND MALAYSIA: FAVORABLE AND UNFAVORABLE CONDITIONS

The examples of Lebanon from 1943 to 1975 and of Malaysia between 1955 and 1969 strengthen the case for consociational democracy as a normative model not only because they provide concrete evidence of its applicability and feasibility in two plural societies in the Third World but also because the conditions for consociationalism in these countries were not uniformly favorable.

The main differences between them concern their domestic power configurations, their size, and the effects of external threats. Lebanon's plural society contains numerous segments, but they are all minorities and the four largest ones together comprise about 80 percent of the population. The situation is therefore close to the most favorable condition of a moderately multiple balance of power. Malaysia, on the other hand, approximates the other extreme. The Malay segment has majority

19. Karl von Vorys, *Democracy Without Consensus: Communalism and Political Stability in Malaysia* (Princeton: Princeton University Press, 1975), p. 12.

status in Malaya and a near-majority in Malaysia as a whole. Their numerical superiority was reduced during the brief period of political union with Singapore, and one of the motives behind the decision to force Singapore out of the federation in 1965 was the desire to restore their former dominance. The numerical imbalance between the near-majority Malays and the minority segments also accounts for the politically dominant role of the Malays in the Alliance and in Malaysian government—a feature that throws some doubt on the consociational character of the Malaysian regime even in the 1955–69 period.

Both Lebanon and Malaysia are small countries, but Malaysia's population of about eleven million is of the same order of magnitude as those of the European consociational democracies, whereas Lebanon's population of about two million is similar to the very small size of Northern Ireland. An important contribution to the establishment of consociational democracy in Lebanon was the struggle for independence that united the religious communities against the external control of the French mandatory power in 1943. Hassan Saab writes: "All other deeper problems of Lebanese life and society were subordinated to this overwhelming concern. Deep social issues could divide and the pressing need was for unity behind the overall goal of national liberation."[20] But after independence the conflicts in the Middle East became more and more dysfunctional because they pitted the Christian segments against the pro-Arab Moslems on many issues and imposed the burden of harboring large numbers of Palestinian refugees and guerrilla forces. In fact, it is primarily to Lebanon's increasingly unfavorable international environment—combined with the internal flaw of consociational rigidity—that the 1975 breakdown of the democratic regime must be attributed.

Malaysian independence was achieved without a struggle, but the consociational system was aided considerably at one point of its existence by an external threat. In the 1964 elections, the voters rallied behind the Alliance parties in response to the military danger posed by the Indonesian "confrontation."

20. Hassan Saab, "The Rationalist School in Lebanese Politics," in *Politics in Lebanon,* p. 276.

Prior traditions conducive to consociational democracy have played a role in both countries but an especially prominent one in Lebanon. The Lebanese pattern of segmental autonomy has its roots in the "millet" system of the Ottoman Empire: the minority religious communities were accorded an inferior but internally autonomous status. It should also be mentioned that the French-inspired constitution of 1926 already embodied the principle of proportionality for civil service appointments, and that the trend toward the allotment of the highest offices to specific sects was gradually set in the 1930s. The only similar precursor to consociational practices in Malaysia was the formation by the colonial authorities of the Communities Liaison Committee consisting of six Malays, six Chinese, one Indian, and three other minority representatives. The committee was not set up until 1949 and therefore hardly qualifies as a traditional precedent, but it provided valuable experience for the intersegmental bargaining of the Alliance a few years later. "While the committee never developed a genuine non-communal approach to the problems confronting Malaya," Gordon P. Means states, "it did demonstrate that significant communal compromise was more likely to emerge from semi-secret and 'off-the-record' negotiations conducted by communal leaders."[21]

The remaining conditions were largely negative in both cases. There is a Malay nationalism and all of the official symbols of the Malaysian state derive from Malay culture, but these are either meaningless or repugnant to the other segments. As Esman states, "seldom have . . . peoples with so little in common been fated to share the same territory and participate in the same political system."[22] The Lebanese segments share one important cultural element—the Arabic language—but lack truly overarching loyalties. One can find segmental nationalisms, for instance among the Maronites and the Druze, and Arab nationalism in Lebanon, but no real Lebanese national sentiments. Lebanon is

21. Gordon P. Means, *Malaysian Politics* (London: University of London Press, 1970), p. 124.

22. Esman, "Malaysia," p. 228. See also Nancy L. Snider, "Is National Integration Necessary? The Malaysian Case," *Journal of International Affairs* 27, no. 1 (1973): 80–89.

not, as Leila Meo's book title indicates, an "improbable nation" but a multinational "improbable state."[23]

Among the mutually reinforcing cleavages in the two countries is, significantly, the economic one. Except for their privileged position in the civil service, the Malays are mainly subsistence farmers and unskilled workers, whereas the Chinese dominate all other sectors of the economy and earn more than twice or three times the average income of the Malays. In Lebanon, there is a similar but narrower difference between the more well-to-do Christians and the generally poorer Moslems, and each of the sects "has generally tended to specialize in one or two occupations"—a situation that can be characterized as an "ethnic division of labor."[24]

Finally, both countries have a high degree of segmental isolation. There is hardly any social communication or interaction among the Malaysian segments, and, although a "high degree of civility" accompanies the contacts that do occur, "the underlying social distance approaches infinity."[25] In Lebanon, likewise, "interconfessional links are found only at the top of each confessional structure."[26] But this mutual isolation is only social and not territorial. Although, especially in Lebanon, each segment has its traditional strongholds, neither country is a "federal society." Table 10 shows the fragmentation of Lebanon into fourteen sects and of Malaysia into its Malay, Chinese, and Indian segments both for the two countries as a whole and for the five Lebanese provinces and thirteen Malaysian states. The index of fragmentation is especially high in the Lebanese case, and in both cases the reduction of fragmentation in the geographical subdivisions as measured by the weighted means is minimal: from 0.81 to 0.70 in Lebanon and from 0.58 to 0.51 in Malaysia.

The general conclusion has to be that the development and

23. Leila M. T. Meo, *Lebanon: Improbable Nation* (Bloomington: Indiana University Press, 1965).

24. Charles Issawi, "Economic and Social Foundations of Democracy in the Middle East," *International Affairs* 32, no. 1 (January 1956): 37.

25. Esman, "Malaysia," p. 228.

26. Binder, "Political Change in Lebanon," p. 303.

TABLE 10. Segmental Fragmentation in Four Non-Western Plural Societies: Subnational Averages and National Totals

	States/Provinces/Districts Mean	States/Provinces/Districts Weighted Mean	Whole Country
Lebanon (1956)			
Largest group (%)	43.0	44.9	30.3
Index of fragmentation (*F*)	.72	.70	.81
Malaysia (1967)			
Largest group (%)	61.9	57.7	50.6
Index of fragmentation (*F*)	.47	.51	.58
Cyprus (1960)			
Largest group (%)	81.0	80.9	80.9
Index of fragmentation (*F*)	.30	.31	.31
Nigeria (1952–53)			
Largest group (%)	72.5	64.4	23.9
Index of fragmentation (*F*)	.42	.51	.82

SOURCES: Calculated from data in Michael W. Suleiman, *Political Parties in Lebanon: The Challenge of a Fragmented Political Culture* (Ithaca: Cornell University Press, 1967), p. 27; Milton J. Esman, *Administration and Development in Malaysia: Institution-Building and Reform in a Plural Society* (Ithaca: Cornell University Press, 1972), p. 18; C. J. Visser, *Cyprus: Mislukte republiek* (The Hague: Nederlands Instituut voor Vredesvraagstukken, 1975), app.; and James S. Coleman, *Nigeria: Background to Nationalism* (Berkeley: University of California Press, 1958), p. 15.

maintenance of consociational democracy in these non-Western plural societies was certainly favored by a few propitious factors, but that a number of other factors were clearly negative. Because the conditions were by no means overwhelmingly favorable, the considerable success of both consociational experiments cannot be considered inevitable in any way. This conclusion strengthens the theoretical and normative significance of the two cases.

CONSOCIATIONAL FAILURE IN CYPRUS, 1960–1963

Cyprus began its existence as an independent state in 1960 with a thoroughly consociational constitution, drafted by representatives of the Greek and Turkish governments and of the Greek and Turkish communities in Cyprus. Although it did not prove successful, it was a valiant attempt to set up a system of political accommodation for the highly plural Cypriot society. The two segments into which it is divided are the Greeks, comprising about 78 percent of the population, and the Turks with 18 percent, according to the 1960 census. The remaining 4 percent are politically insignificant minorities. There is a perfect coincidence of linguistic, religious, and cultural cleavages. The Greek Cypriots speak Greek, belong to the Greek Orthodox church, and are strongly oriented toward the cultural tradition of Greece. The Turks in Cyprus speak Turkish, are Moslems, and feel strongly related to Turkey's culture. These cleavages permeate the island's organizational structures, too. Adamantia Pollis describes the two educational systems of Cyprus, faithfully patterned after those of Greece and Turkey, as follows: "The curriculum of the Greek schools, taught in Greek of course, extols Greek national history and 'proves' the Greekness of Cyprus, while the curriculum in the Turkish schools is similarly structured in terms of Turkish nationalism." Voluntary organizations are exclusively segmental and completely segregated: "Political parties, trade unions, professional and agricultural associations are divided along ethnic lines. . . . No organization exists, to the author's knowledge, that includes both Greeks and Turks."[27]

All of the principles of consociational democracy—grand coalition, proportionality, autonomy, and veto—were elaborately embodied in the 1960 constitution.[28] It provided for a presiden-

27. Adamantia Pollis, "Intergroup Conflict and British Colonial Policy: The Case of Cyprus," *Comparative Politics* 5, no. 4 (July 1973): 596–97.

28. See Stanley Kyriakides, *Cyprus: Constitutionalism and Crisis Government* (Philadelphia: University of Pennsylvania Press, 1968), pp. 53–71; and T. W. Adams, "The First Republic of Cyprus: A Review of an Unworkable Constitution," *Western Political Quarterly* 19, no. 3 (September 1966): 475–90.

tial regime with a Greek president elected by the Greek community and a Turkish vice-president, with almost co-equal powers, elected by the Turkish community. The grand coalition arrangement was completed by the provision that the cabinet had to consist of seven Greek ministers designated by the president and three Turkish ministers designated by the vice-president. The seven-to-three ratio entailed a deliberate over-representation of the Turkish minority rather than strict proportionality. The same ratio was applied to the composition of the legislature—35 members were elected by the Greeks and 15 by the Turks—and to civil service appointments. A six-to-four ratio, which was an even greater deviation from strict proportionality but still ensured a Greek majority, was set for the army and the police.

The constitution also guaranteed a great deal of autonomy for the two ethnic segments by setting up two separately elected communal chambers with exclusive legislative powers over religious, educational, cultural, and personal status matters, and by prescribing separate municipal councils in the five largest towns of the island. These provisions went far toward setting up a "federal" system without actual territorial federalism, which was thwarted by the highly interspersed residential patterns of the two populations: table 10 shows that the average ethnic composition of Cyprus's six districts was a virtual mirror image of that of the island as a whole. Finally, the 1960 constitution gave both the president and the vice-president jointly or separately an absolute veto power over decisions by the cabinet or the legislature in the fields of foreign affairs, defense, and security. And all legislative decisions on taxes, the municipalities, and the electoral system could be reached only by concurrent majorities of the two segmental groups in the legislature.

The constitutional system operated, albeit far from satisfactorily, from 1960 until December 1963, when civil war broke out and the government fell apart into two separate systems: the Greeks under the formal but truncated governmental machinery and the Turks under their vice-president, the fifteen Turkish members of the legislature, and the Turkish communal chamber. A United Nations peace-keeping force was sent to the island in 1964 to maintain a fragile ceasefire. The trend has meanwhile been toward increasing physical separation. After the civil war broke out, the Turks fled into urban enclaves, and Turkey's armed invasion of 1974 produced a territorial partition; most of the Greeks who lived in the Turkish-occupied northern part of the island have fled to the south, and the Turks in the south have succeeded in migrating in large numbers to the area under Turkish military control.

Cyprus's consociational constitution failed to work because the Greek majority only reluctantly accepted it in 1960 and viewed its main provisions with increasing distaste in the following years, while the Turkish minority insisted on the faithful adherence to every consociational provision and overused their veto power. For instance, the Turkish members of the legislature denied their concurrent majority to tax legislation not only because of its intrinsically objectionable features but also as a weapon to compel more rapid and thorough implementation of the seven-to-three ratio in the civil service. In November 1963, Archbishop Makarios, the Greek president of Cyprus, proposed a series of constitutional amendments designed to eliminate the most distasteful consociational devices: the presidential and vice-presidential vetoes, the concurrent majority in the legislature, the separate municipal governments, and the Turkish overrepresentation in the civil service, the police, and the armed forces. These proposals were rejected both by the Turkish Cypriot leaders and by the government of Turkey, and the entire consociational experiment ended in the civil war that started a few days later.[29]

The main reason why consociationalism failed in Cyprus is that it cannot be imposed against the wishes of one or more segments in a plural society and, in particular, against the resistance of a majority segment. In this respect, the Cypriot case parallels that of Northern Ireland. The dual imbalance of power constituted the crucially unfavorable factor. Moreover, almost all other conditions in Cyprus were distinctly less favorable

29. See Thomas Ehrlich, *Cyprus: 1958–1967* (London: Oxford University Press, 1974), pp. 36–60.

than those in Lebanon and Malaysia, and militated against the success of consociational democracy. Its population of slightly over half a million is considerably smaller than even those of Lebanon and Northern Ireland. External threats and interventions emanated mainly from Turkey and Greece and consequently hurt rather than helped internal unity. The anticolonial movement against the British was a struggle not for independence but for *enosis*, or integration with Greece, a goal to which the Turkish Cypriots were bitterly opposed. There was no Cypriot nationalism nor any other overarching loyalty to counteract the divergent Greek and Turkish nationalisms dividing the islanders. The economic inequality between the segments, though not very severe, added another negative factor: the Turkish segment was both numerically and economically inferior to the Greeks. Until 1963, segmental isolation was social and not, or only very weakly, territorial (see table 10). The only mildly favorable element was Cyprus's historical experience, shared with Lebanon, of being ruled under the Ottoman millet system. The Cypriot example again shows that such prior traditions are not of decisive importance.

DEMOCRATIC FAILURE IN NIGERIA, 1957–1966

The degeneration of Nigeria's democracy into military rule, the Biafran secession, and civil war may be regarded as another failure of consociational democracy. Nigeria is clearly a plural society; its population, numbering about 45 million in the early 1960s, is segmented into literally hundreds of ethnic groups, but the eight largest comprise more than three-fourths of the total population and the three largest more than half. All ethnic groups are geographically concentrated; the three largest ones were dominant in the three original states of the Nigerian federation—the Hausas in the North, the Ibos in the East, and the Yorubas in the West—and dominated the major political parties in these states. David E. Apter, the first modern author to use the term "consociational," uses Nigeria as his main example of a consociational system. He defines this kind of regime as "a joining together of constituent units which do not lose their identity when merging in some form of union," and he adds that it "may range from a relatively loose confederation of groups and states to federal arrangements with a recognized structure." Among its other characteristics are its willingness "to accommodate a variety of groups of divergent ideas in order to achieve a goal of unity," its "collective or corporate leadership," and the necessity of forging compromises that constitute "a minimal program acceptable to all."[30] Apter's concept of consociationalism is similar to but considerably broader than that used in this book: the elements of grand coalition, autonomy, and veto can be detected in it but are not stated explicitly.

When we examine the Nigerian case, it becomes clear that it hardly fits the narrower definition of consociational democracy at all. The coalition of the three main parties in the preindependence federal cabinet from 1957 to 1959 undoubtedly influenced Apter's characterization of Nigeria as consociational: his book was published shortly afterward, in 1961. But no more grand coalitions were formed after the federal elections of 1959 and Nigeria's independence in 1960. The cabinet in power from 1959 to 1964 was a coalition of the largest Nigerian party, with its political base in the Northern state, and the party that was dominant in the East. The political party from the Western state became the principal opposition party. And instead of any movement toward a more inclusive cabinet, the trend was toward one-party majority rule. A crisis in the Western state was used to suspend its state government, destroy the main Western party, and imprison several of its leaders. Meanwhile, the large Northern party achieved an absolute majority in the lower house of the federal parliament as a result of the defection of members of other parties and a number of by-elections, and its attitude toward its junior partner in the cabinet became that of a "firm master."[31] In the next cabinet, formed after the 1964 elections

30. David E. Apter, *The Political Kingdom in Uganda: A Study in Bureaucratic Nationalism* (Princeton: Princeton University Press, 1961), pp. 24–25 (italics omitted).

31. John P. Mackintosh, *Nigerian Government and Politics* (London: Allen and Unwin, 1966), p. 547.

and brought down by a military takeover in 1966, the Northerners were even more strongly predominant.

The 1960 constitution contained a weak provision of veto power in the form of a senate with equal representation from the three states. This gave the Eastern and Western senators an opportunity to block decisions by the lower house with its absolute majority of Northern members. But this "veto" was only a power to delay legislation for six months, and it was never effective in practice. Neither was proportionality a norm of any consequence. In particular, the adoption of the British electoral system led to the domination of the three largest segments over the smaller ethnic groups in their respective states.

Nigeria's only possible claim to consociational status must be based on its federal system, which gave a high degree of autonomy to its state governments. From the consociational point of view, however, the federation appears to have been designed in such a way as to virtually guarantee its failure. The federal boundaries did not follow ethnic boundaries, and the smaller but still sizable segments were not given their own states. The Nigerian lawyer Ben O. Nwabueze writes: "Federalism in Nigeria failed in its objective of building governmental units upon fairly homogeneous social groupings in order that they should manage their internal affairs within the unity of the whole." Instead, the states in the federation "were structured, unhappily, upon the nucleus of a major tribe, commanding about two-thirds of the population of the [state], with a number of minority tribes clustered around it."[32] Table 10 shows the ethnic fragmentation of Nigeria as a whole and the averages for the three states and the small federal capital territory of Lagos, based on the 1952–53 census data (the census conducted a decade later was of questionable accuracy and politically very controversial). Although only the ten largest ethnic segments are taken into consideration, the index of fragmentation is an extremely high 0.82. It is significant that the weighted average of the federal units (0.51) is much lower than the national total but still quite high.

32. Ben O. Nwabueze, *Constitutionalism in the Emergent States* (London: Hurst, 1973), p. 113.

An even greater flaw in Nigeria's federalism was that it turned a multiple ethnic balance of power, with no ethnic segment coming even close to majority status, into a federal imbalance with one state, the North, comprising 60 percent of the total population and 75 percent of the total land area. Nigeria's problem, as Ulf Himmelstrand points out, was not ethnicity as such but "the interplay among ethnic affiliation, size of ethnic groups, and administrative boundaries."[33] The creation of the Midwestern state in 1963 was a slight improvement, but it was carved out of the West and did not affect Northern dominance. A major improvement was the transformation of the entire federal structure into a twelve-state federation, entailing the division of the North into six states, by the military rulers in 1967—too late to save Nigerian democracy.

The chances for the survival of democracy in Nigeria might have been better if a consociational pattern had been adopted. The multiple ethnic balance of power and the geographic concentration of the ethnic segments were favorable factors. But the large size of the country, especially by African standards, as well as most of the other conditions were distinctly less favorable. At any rate, the actual experience of Nigeria in the 1957–66 period must be considered that of democratic failure—not consociational failure.

THIRD WORLD CONDITIONS: A GENERAL APPRAISAL

The cases of Lebanon and Malaysia as well as the close correspondence between the Lewis model for West Africa and the consociational model lend considerable support to the suggestion that the consociational model should be given serious consideration as an alternative to the British model of democracy in the plural societies of the Third World. On the other hand, the example of Cyprus shows that an effort to establish consociational democracy can fail, and even one negative instance is

33. Ulf Himmelstrand, " 'Tribalism,' Regionalism, Nationalism, and Secession in Nigeria," in *Building States and Nations: Analyses by Region,* ed. S. N. Eisenstadt and Stein Rokkan (Beverly Hills: Sage, 1973), p. 432.

sufficient to prove that consociationalism is not always a workable solution. In order to reach a general conclusion about its feasibility in the Third World, the next step is to attempt a review of the conditions that increase or decrease the likelihood that it will succeed. Such a general appraisal has its dangers because Third World countries obviously differ from each other in many respects, and my generalizations therefore do not necessarily apply to any specific country. The conditions that are generally or frequently—not always and not without exception—favorable will be reviewed first. Malaysia and Lebanon will serve as the bases of comparison. Both cases show—as do the European examples—that consociational democracy is possible even when several conditions are unfavorable, and their characteristics will be the yardstick against which other countries can be compared: are the conditions in the plural societies of the Third World generally at least as favorable as those in Lebanon and Malaysia, significantly less favorable, or perhaps even overwhelmingly unfavorable, as in the Cypriot case?

It is worth reiterating that these conditions should be regarded as *helpful* factors; as was pointed out earlier, particularly on the basis of an examination of the Canadian and Israeli experiences, they are neither necessary nor sufficient conditions. In line with this empirical finding, consociational democracy as a normative model also entails a rejection of social determinism. It assumes that political elites enjoy a high degree of freedom of choice, and that they may resort to consociational methods of decision-making as a result of a rational recognition of the centrifugal tendencies inherent in plural societies and a deliberate effort to counteract these dangers. This notion of the crucial role of the leadership is similar to Machiavelli's conviction that the *virtù* and prudence of the leaders are decisive since "time brings with it all things, and may produce *indifferently* either good or evil."[34]

In our earlier discussion of protoconsociational traditions as a

34. Niccolò Machiavelli, *The Prince*, trans. Luigi Ricci, in *The Prince and the Discourses* (New York: Modern Library, 1950), p. 11 (italics added). See also Taketsugu Tsurutani, "Machiavelli and the Problem of Political Development," *Review of Politics* 30, no. 3 (July 1968): esp. 318–19.

favorable factor for consociational democracy, Hans Daalder's criticism of the notions of free choice and purposive political engineering by political elites was cited. He argues that strong traditions of political accommodation and coalescent decision-making existed in Switzerland and the Netherlands before the advent of political modernization and nation-building. Similarly, he argues that these processes in the developing countries are highly dependent on prior elite experiences but notes that the "prevailing ideological outlooks in the new States are not favourable for consociationalist choices," even though older traditions of coalescent decision-making and segmental autonomy are strong, because these traditions are usually regarded by the present leaders as "obstacles which should be cleared away, rather than as building-stones from which a new, pluralist nation might be constructed."[35] These remarks concede that there is room for free choice after all: if the elites have anticonsociational attitudes in spite of prior traditions favorable to consociationalism, they are dynamic and autonomous agents who are able not only to deviate from but presumably also to decide to revert to these older political traditions.

A more significant implication of Daalder's remarks is that many of the new states have precolonial traditions that can serve as a firm foundation for consociational democracy. By comparison, the British model of majority rule, government-versus-opposition politics, and unitary government is quite alien to non-Western traditions. Many other observers support this contention. Rupert Emerson states that "the Western assumption [i.e., the assumption of the British model] of the majority's right to overrule a dissident minority after a period of debate does violence to conceptions basic to non-Western peoples." There are vast differences among the traditions of Asian and African societies, of course, but "their native inclination is generally toward extensive and unhurried deliberation aimed at ultimate consensus. The gradual discovery of areas of agreement is the

35. Hans Daalder, "On Building Consociational Nations: The Cases of the Netherlands and Switzerland," *International Social Science Journal* 23, no. 3 (1971): 368. See also Hans Daalder, "Government and Opposition in the New States," *Government and Opposition* 1, no. 2 (January 1966): 205–26.

significant feature and not the ability to come to a speedy resolution of issues by counting heads."[36] Michael Haas argues that there is a typical "Asian way" of decision-making based on such ideas as *mufakat,* a Malay term for the "principle of unanimity built through discussion rather than voting," and *mushawarah,* the "traditional Indonesian method of coming to agreement not through majority decision but by a search for something like the Quaker 'sense of the meeting.' "[37] Julius Nyerere quotes with approval the following description of government in the typical African village community: "The Elders sit under the big tree, and talk until they agree."[38] Similarly, Lewis points out that the West African tribes have strong democratic traditions that deviate from the British model: "The tribe has made its decision by discussion, in much the way that coalitions function; this kind of democratic procedure is at the heart of the original institutions of the people."[39]

A particularly convincing testimony in this respect is the conclusion reached by M. G. Smith after his analysis of precolonial societies in Africa. His original conception of plural societies, discussed in chapter 1, entailed the proposition that domination by one of the cultural segments was a necessary and unavoidable consequence of pluralism. However, after "reviewing ethnographic materials on precolonial African societies for evidence of pluralism" in order to test the initial hypothesis that domination was invariably linked with pluralism, he arrived at an "unanticipated result": the discovery of a type of plural society which he labeled a "consociation," that is, an association of "separately constituted corporate collectivities as equal and internally au-

36. Rupert Emerson, *From Empire to Nation: The Rise to Self-Assertion of Asian and African Peoples* (Cambridge, Mass.: Harvard University Press, 1960), p. 284.

37. Michael Haas, "The 'Asian Way' to Peace," *Pacific Community* 4, no. 4 (July 1973): 503–05. The definition of *mushawarah* is from Herbert Feith, "Indonesia," in *Governments and Politics of Southeast Asia,* ed. George McTurnan Kahin (Ithaca: Cornell University Press, 1959), p. 192.

38. Julius Nyerere, "Democracy and the Party System," in *The Ideologies of the Developing Nations,* ed. Paul E. Sigmund, rev. ed. (New York: Praeger, 1967), p. 294. See also Ahmed Mohiddin, "The Basic Unit of African Ideal Society in Nyerere's Thought," *Africa* 25, no. 1 (March 1970): 3–24.

39. Lewis, *Politics in West Africa,* p. 86.

tonomous partners in a common society."[40] This definition is quite similar to that of a consociational system as used in this book, but the fact that the same term is used is a coincidence.

In addition to prior traditions of coalescent decision-making and segmental autonomy, there are a number of other factors that are generally favorable to consociationalism in the plural societies of the Third World. Primordial loyalties are strong and nationalism tends to be weak in plural societies, but to the extent that some national feeling exists at the elite and mass levels, the chances of consociational democracy are enhanced. In most of the new states, national attachments are feeble but are not, as in Lebanon and Malaysia, entirely absent. In those countries that had to struggle for independence, the colonial power supplied the external threat that increased internal unity.

Moreover, cooperation at the elite level is facilitated to the extent that the leaders' motivation is provided not only by a perception of common interests but also by a common background and outlook. In this respect, the situation is generally more favorable in the new states than in Lebanon and Malaysia. Especially during the struggle for independence and in the immediate postindependence years, the political leaders were often an unusually homogeneous group. William J. Foltz observes that most of the new states have had "the good fortune to possess a narrowly constricted and homogeneous set of politically relevant strata." Their leaders have been "united by ties of personal friendship, frequently reinforced by common educational and agitational experiences and by dedication to the nationalist cause."[41] An especially significant unifying element at the elite level in most African states is the adoption of English or French as the official language. Because these are not the languages of any ethnic segment, they are ethnically neutral. But, as Pierre L. van den Berghe points out, such an official but still

40. M. G. Smith, "Pluralism in Precolonial African Societies," and "Some Developments in the Analytic Framework of Pluralism," in *Pluralism in Africa*, ed. Leo Kuper and M. G. Smith (Berkeley: University of California Press, 1969), pp. 94, 439.

41. William J. Foltz, "Building the Newest Nations: Short-Run Strategies and Long-Run Problems," in *Nation-Building*, ed. Karl W. Deutsch and William J. Foltz (New York: Atherton, 1963), pp. 118, 121.

foreign language is an "esoteric prestige medium" that creates "an important bond across ethnic lines at the top of the social pyramid."[42]

A final generally favorable condition is a high degree of segmental isolation. The primordial cleavage lines are usually very sharply drawn—a tendency strengthened by the frequent practice of indirect rule by the former colonial powers—and politics tends to be organized, if permitted, on a segmental basis. This feature is somewhat less characteristic of the African than of the Asian plural societies. Van den Berghe generalizes about the African situation in the following words: "The important characteristic of ethnicity in the African context is both its complexity and fluidity, compared to more crystallized situations such as in Belgium or Switzerland where the basic cleavages are fewer, more stable, and less ambiguous."[43] Lebanon and Malaysia are in this respect probably closer to the two European countries than to the typical African plural society. On the other hand, the lower degree of sharpness of the segmental cleavages in Africa is compensated by the fact that segmental isolation in Africa is usually reinforced by the geographical concentration of the segments—a feature that Lebanon and Malaysia lack.

Both in Africa and elsewhere in the Third World segmental isolation entails a strengthening of the political inertness of the nonelite public and of their deferential attitudes to the segmental leaders. This is a pervasive characteristic of the non-Western political process, according to Lucian Pye's general description of this type of politics: "The communal framework of politics . . . means that political loyalty is governed more by a sense of identification with the concrete group than by identification with the professed policy goals of the group. . . . So long as the leaders appear to be working in the interests of the group as a whole, they usually do not have to be concerned that the loyalties of the members will be tested by current decisions."[44]

42. Pierre L. van den Berghe, "Ethnicity: The African Experience," *International Social Science Journal* 23, no. 4 (1971): 516.

43. Ibid., p. 513.

44. Lucian W. Pye, "The Non-Western Political Process," *Journal of Politics* 20, no. 3 (August 1958): 472–73.

Particularly in the short run, this kind of political loyalty gives the political leaders the great advantage of a high degree of freedom in their relations with the leaders of other groups. The non-Western leaders generally enjoy this advantage to an even greater extent than the leaders in the European consociational democracies. In the longer run, however, there is a danger that the leaders will concentrate too much on elite-level politics and lose touch with the rank and file. The social and psychological distance between elite and mass in the non-Western countries is regarded by much of the political development literature as so great that the concept of national integration is often employed in a dual sense to mean not only surmounting ethnic and other segmental loyalties but also closing the elite-mass gap. Simultaneously searching for political accommodations at the elite level and maintaining close relations with the rank and file is a difficult but, as the European consociational experience shows, not impossible balancing act.

The role of the political leadership will also be of paramount importance in any decision to adopt the consociational model of government or particular features of it. Lewis expects, rather unrealistically, that a shift toward grand coalition government can originate at the mass level: "The prospect of stable coalition government depends in the last analysis not on the politicians but on the decision of the public that this is what it wants." And he appeals to a new generation of West Africans to "rewrite the rules of the political game" in order to force the politicians into coalescent instead of adversarial behavior.[45] If the consociational model is to be accepted, it will have to be introduced by the elites. It is useless and probably counterproductive to appeal over their heads to the mass public.

AMBIVALENT FACTORS

The condition found to be of crucial importance for successful consociationalism in all of the cases examined so far is the balance of power among the segments. The non-Western plural

45. Lewis, *Politics in West Africa,* pp. 84–85.

societies vary widely in this respect—from an unfavorable dual imbalance as in Cyprus and Ceylon, to a slightly more favorable triple imbalance with a near-majority segment as in Malaysia, and to a favorable multiple balance without majority dominance as in Lebanon. Most African plural societies as well as Papua New Guinea also have multiple power configurations but suffer the disadvantage of fragmentation into a relatively large number of segments.

An unfavorable domestic balance of power may, however, be improved by counterbalancing external forces in a few cases. Clifford Geertz points out, for instance, that in Malaysia the Chinese and Malays have been held together at least partly by "the fear on the part of either group that should the Federation dissolve they may become a clearly submerged minority in some other political framework: the Malays through the turn of the Chinese to Singapore and China; the Chinese through the turn of the Malays to Indonesia." This external counterbalance is even more important in the Ceylonese situation of dual imbalance. Here, "both the Tamils and Sinhalese manage to see themselves as minorities: the Tamils because 70 percent of the Ceylonese are Sinhalese; the Sinhalese because the eight million of them in Ceylon are all there are, while in addition to the two million Tamils on the island there are 28 million more in South India."[46] But such a propitious combination of internal and external power balances is not inevitable. For instance, the two Northern Ireland segments do not regard themselves as minorities—a Protestant minority in all of Ireland and a Catholic minority in the North—but as two majorities, an actual and a potential one. And probably the worst situation is that of a majority segment that is afraid of being turned into a minority.

The extreme fragmentation found in many African countries usually entails the absence of a majority segment, but the division into very many segments also presents an obstacle to consociational democracy. The extent of fragmentation must not be

46. Clifford Geertz, "The Integrative Revolution: Primordial Sentiments and Civil Politics in the New States," in *Old Societies and New States: The Quest for Modernity in Asia and Africa,* ed. Clifford Geertz (New York: Free Press, 1963), pp. 115–16.

exaggerated, however. Usually, as Karl W. Deutsch points out, half of the total population is made up of no more than about six separate segments, and no more than ten to fifteen of such groups make up 90 percent of the population.[47] Nigeria is a good example of this. The colonial rulers were often guilty of presenting an overdrawn picture of extreme ethnic complexity in their dependencies, at least partly as an excuse for the delay in introducing self-government. Actually, the advent of independence and political modernization has tended to reduce fragmentation to some extent. Samuel P. Huntington points out that one of the most striking aspects of modernization is "the increased consciousness, coherence, organization, and action which it produces in many social forces which existed on a much lower level of conscious identity and organization in traditional society."[48] In Nigeria, for instance, the concepts Yoruba and Ibo are notions that have acquired significant meaning and content only recently. In other countries, such aggregation has taken place along racial, linguistic, religious, and regional lines. Geertz argues that this is a general tendency in the non-Western plural societies: "Whether it involves becoming an Outer Islander in addition to a Minangkabau, a Kachin over and above a Duleng, a Christian as well as a Maronite, or a Yoruba rather than only an Egna, the process . . . is general. It is a progressive extension of the sense of primordial similarity and difference generated from the direct and protracted encounter of culturally diverse groups in local contexts to more broadly defined groups of a similar sort interacting within the framework of the entire national society."[49] By combining small units into larger meaningful ethnic groups, this process provides the building blocks for consociationalism.

The only parallel in the European consociational experience is the Swiss case. Austria, Belgium, and the Netherlands have only

47. Karl W. Deutsch, "Nation-Building and National Development: Some Issues for Political Research," in Deutsch and Foltz, *Nation-Building,* pp. 5–6.

48. Samuel P. Huntington, *Political Order in Changing Societies* (New Haven: Yale University Press, 1968), pp. 38–39.

49. Geertz, "Integrative Revolution," pp. 153–54. See also Richard L. Sklar, "The Contribution of Tribalism to Nationalism in Western Nigeria," *Journal of Human Relations* 8, no. 3–4 (spring-summer 1960): 407–18.

a few major segments, but Switzerland is fragmented by a complex pattern of crosscutting linguistic, regional, religious, and ideological cleavages into a large number of groups. This multiplicity of small groups has not prevented effective negotiation and cooperation because these small units have been aggregated into larger linguistic-regional segments by the federal system and into larger religious-ideological segments by the party system.

The second ambivalent factor—favorable in some countries but unfavorable in others—as far as the chances of consociational democracy are concerned, is size. The population sizes of the non-Western states differ a great deal, from a few extremely large countries with populations exceeding a hundred million like India and Indonesia to some small countries like Cyprus, Gabon, and Gambia with populations well below the one million mark. Most African states are in the favorable range with regard to size: their populations number at least a few millions and are therefore larger than those of Lebanon and Northern Ireland but smaller than the Malaysian population. Nigeria is an exceptional giant by African standards. Hence it is especially for the smaller African countries that the consociational model may be a useful normative example.

The final ambivalent factor concerns the economic equality of the segments. On the one hand, the primordial segments of the non-Western plural societies generally are, like the European religious and linguistic segments, "vertical" groupings that are crosscut by the horizontal socioeconomic divisions. This is especially true when the segments are geographically concentrated. Such a structure of what Donald L. Horowitz calls "parallel groups" does not suffer from the kind of illegitimacy characteristic of systems in which ethnic and class divisions completely or nearly coincide: "This does not mean, of course, that each group has proportionate numbers of its members in all social strata or that mobility opportunities are proportioned to the demand. Discrepancies in these proportions typically constitute an irritant in the relations of parallel groups. . . . The point is that each group has its own elite strata—perhaps traditional, perhaps modern, probably both, [and that] the groups do not stand in a generalized hierarchical relation to each other."[50] In Africa, Van den Berghe states, "class and ethnicity . . . are largely independent and often conflicting principles of social solidarity and organization." In this respect, Lebanon and Malaysia with their geographically mixed segments and ethnic division of labor represent unfavorable exceptions. On the other hand, the regional—and therefore frequently also the segmental—differences in economic development may be very large. In Africa, "differences in *per capita* income, literacy rates, kilometres of road and many other indices of development may be as great as one to ten or even one to a hundred."[51] Compared with inequalities of this magnitude, the differences between the Lebanese and Malaysian segments seem relatively minor.

UNFAVORABLE FACTORS

A set of unfavorable factors appears upon examination of the developmental dynamics of Third World societies: the political consequences of economic and social modernization for plural societies. Political development often stagnates and may turn into political decay, but social and economic development moves inexorably, though sometimes slowly, forward. After rejecting a series of other hypotheses linking nonelite characteristics to the likelihood of conflict regulation along consociational lines, Nordlinger argues that the only significant factor of this kind is the process of socioeconomic modernization, and that its impact is uniformly unfavorable: it "detracts from the realization of regulatory outcomes in societies deeply divided along communal lines by further increasing the number of nonelite individuals who manifest hostile beliefs, feelings and jealousies toward the opposing segment, by further intensifying such attitudes among individuals who already hold them, and by placing individuals in situations which allow or encourage them to act out their antagonistic beliefs and feelings."[52]

50. Donald L. Horowitz, "Three Dimensions of Ethnic Politics," *World Politics* 23, no. 2 (January 1971): 236–37.
51. Van den Berghe, "Ethnicity," pp. 510, 514.
52. Nordlinger, *Conflict Regulation,* p. 112 (italics omitted).

This factor is obviously of great importance. It means that a number of the characteristics of non-Western societies that were listed earlier as favorable are becoming unfavorable. In particular, deferential attitudes toward the political elites are weakening and interelite negotiations are thus rendered more difficult; this trend is offset to some extent, however, by the persistence of patron-client relations in the Third World, which can serve as a substitute for elite predominance and mass deference and which are far more characteristic of non-Western than of Western societies.[53] The relative isolation of the segments which was conducive to peaceful coexistence among them is increasingly being challenged by the processes of urbanization, geographical mobility, and nationwide trade. And, although material standards of living may be improving only slowly, expectations concerning prosperity are rising rapidly, placing a heavy burden on governmental decision-making. Another unfavorable trend is that in those countries that had to struggle to gain their independence—a struggle that had a strong unifying effect—independence was won many years ago and the memories of the common effort are fading.

Nevertheless, the consequences of modernization are not totally negative. As was indicated earlier, modernization has resulted in the growth of larger ethnic groupings in societies that were originally very severely fragmented and has thus laid the basis for greater manageability of conflicts. Also, as economic development proceeds, extreme regional and segmental inequalities are likely to be reduced: "One of the great ironies of underdevelopment is that, the less developed a country is, the greater its internal inequalities."[54] Finally, there is—somewhat paradoxically—an element of hope in the fact that the political development of many newly independent countries has actually been political decay and lapse into dictatorship. This means that there is now a pervasive disenchantment with Western democratic ideals and practices. Because the "Western" model is actually most often synonymous with the British model, the time may be ripe for the consideration of the alternative consociational example.

53. Ibid., pp. 81–82, 86.
54. Van den Berghe, "Ethnicity," p. 514.

The last point calls attention to another generally unfavorable condition for consociational democracy in the Third World. Although the premodern native traditions tend to be strongly conducive to consociational democracy—as noted at the beginning of this general appraisal of Third World conditions—the traditions introduced by the colonial rulers were largely unfavorable. Most of the now independent plural societies in the Third World are former colonies, and the models of democracy that they tended to follow when they tried to institute democratic institutions of their own were those of their former masters: the British model or models closely resembling the British one rather than the consociational example. Raoul Narroll points out that, in general, there are strong correlations between "former colonial empire affiliation . . . and many substantive political and economic indicators."[55] It seems especially plausible to expect a relationship between former colonial ruler and the type of democracy adopted, and further, in plural societies, between these two factors and the success or failure of democracy. This hypothesis will be explored in the next chapter.

55. Raoul Naroll, "A Holonational Bibliography," *Comparative Political Studies* 5, no. 2 (July 1972): 212. See also William B. Moul, "On Getting Something for Nothing: A Note on Causal Models of Political Development," *Comparative Political Studies* 7, no. 2 (July 1974): 150–52.

6 The Consociational Example As Colonial Heritage

That the profoundly undemocratic institution of colonialism could become, in Rupert Emerson's words, a "school for democracy," entails a double paradox. First, it is paradoxical that the principal and most effective colonizers in the modern world were democracies: Great Britain, France, the United States, the Netherlands, and Belgium. Second, the standards of independent democratic government to which the political leaders in the colonies aspired were, paradoxically, set by these colonialists. This was done by their political performance at home rather than by the elements of democratic representation that they introduced into their colonies, although the influence of the latter should not be disregarded entirely.[1] The indigenous leaders consequently tended to opt for democratic government as they advanced toward independence. This goal, as W. J. M. Mackenzie points out, meshed with the sentiment among the Europeans that, if they had to leave, "it must be with honour, honour defined by European standards of good government and democracy."[2]

THE COLONIZERS' DEMOCRATIC MODELS

It may be possible to abstract a general "European" or "Western" model of democracy, but the most directly relevant examples for the newly independent countries were those of the particular colonial power: British, French, American, Dutch, or Belgian democracy. The British model had the greatest influence be-

1. Rupert Emerson, *From Empire to Nation: The Rise to Self-Assertion of Asian and African Peoples* (Cambridge, Mass.: Harvard University Press, 1960), pp. 227–28.
2. W. J. M. Mackenzie, "Some Conclusions," in *Five Elections in Africa: A Group of Electoral Studies,* ed. W. J. M. Mackenzie and Kenneth Robinson (Oxford: Clarendon Press, 1960), p. 465.

cause the British colonial empire was the largest by far, dwarfing the Dutch and Belgian empires. Moreover, the French and American models differ from the British one, but they are closer to the British than to the consociational example. As shown in chapter 4, France belongs to the centrifugal and the United States to the centripetal type of democratic regime; both of these types are characterized by an adversarial elite style. Unlike the British model, the French model includes a multiparty system, but like the British it is characterized by adversarial rather than coalescent elite behavior, a unitary instead of a federal government, and a majority electoral system which is closer to the British plurality system than to the proportional representation method of consociational democracy (although the French experimented briefly with a form of PR during the Fourth Republic). The United States has had great influence as a normative model in Latin America, but not in Africa or Asia, with the exception of the Philippines. It differs from the British model mainly because it is federal. For this reason, W. Arthur Lewis remarks that the new states of West Africa would have fared better if they had had an American instead of the British or French constitutional heritage: then "they would have taken the federal idea for granted, and it would have been the centralizers who were arguing an unpopular case."[3] But the American model resembles the British one in most other respects. Although certain consociational arrangements can be discerned in American political history, the American model is primarily an adversarial one. In fact, because presidential government concentrates a great deal of power in the hands of one man, it is not conducive to either the idea or the implementation of government by grand coalition—unless such extraordinary arrangements are made as the Colombian rule of alternation of the presidency between the two major parties or the Lebanese method of a "grand coalition" composed of the president, the prime minister, and other incumbents of the highest offices.

The degree to which democracy is identified with the British—or, more generally, the adversarial—model in the

3. W. Arthur Lewis, *Politics in West Africa* (London: Allen and Unwin, 1965), p. 55.

minds of both non-Western politicians and scholarly observers is shown in the following comment by Edward Shils: "There are no new states in Asia or Africa . . . in which the elites who demanded independence did not, at the moment just prior to their success, believe that self-government and democratic government were identical." And these elites believed for the most part that "democratic self-government entailed the full paraphernalia of the modern polity," including "a legislative body *under the dominance of the majority party*."[4] The complete hypothesis linking former colonial rule to the type of democracy adopted upon independence and to the success or failure of the new democratic regime is stated by Lewis. After reviewing a series of possible explanations for the failure of democracy and the rise of one-party regimes in West Africa, he concludes that "democracy was set back . . . mainly because the ideas and institutions of democracy inherited from Europe were inappropriate" to these plural societies. And before their leaders can grasp the fact that there exists a suitable model of democracy for them, Lewis says, they will need "much un-brainwashing."[5] It is undoubtedly an exaggeration to state that the influence of the European—that is, the adversarial British or French—model was the principal culprit, and "brainwashing" may be too strong a term to describe the intellectual bias imposed by the model. After all, the two countries that are examples of reasonably successful consociationalism in the Third World emerged from British and French control: Malaya, Sabah, and Sarawak were British colonies and Lebanon a French mandate. It is worth noting also that even when the British themselves have been directly or indirectly instrumental in drafting constitutions for territories under their control, they have not unalterably adhered to their own democratic model: they have tried to impose the consociational model on Northern Ireland, and they encouraged and approved of the ill-fated consociational experiment for their former colony of Cyprus.

4. Edward Shils, "The Fortunes of Constitutional Government in the Political Development of the New States," in *Development: For What?* ed. John H. Hallowell (Durham: Duke University Press, 1964), p. 103 (italics added).

5. Lewis, *Politics in West Africa,* pp. 55, 86.

FIG. 4. Former Colonial Rule, Type of Democracy, and Democratic Performance in Plural Societies

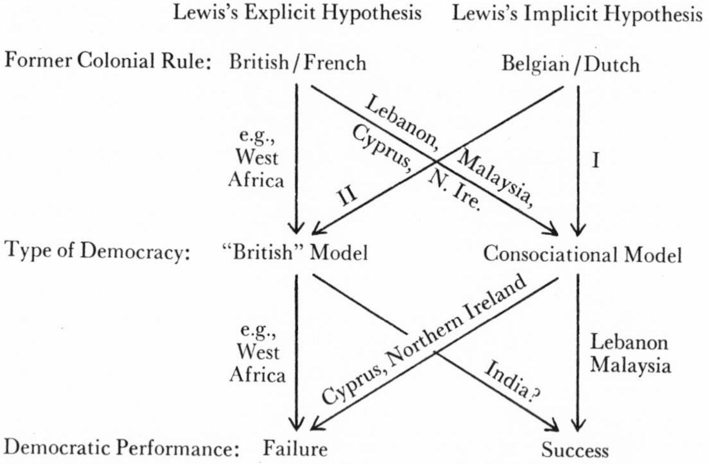

These four examples are indicated in figure 4, which juxtaposes Lewis's hypothesis and its logical complement. The complementary hypothesis is only implicit in Lewis's work, because he does not mention any Western or non-Western cases of his preferred democratic model, which is essentially equivalent to the consociational model. The West African states bear out his explicit hypothesis, and many other examples can be found. In fact, most other former British and French colonies that are plural societies fit the hypothesis. The only clear exceptions to the first part of the hypothesized relationship are Lebanon, Malaysia, Cyprus, and Northern Ireland: the last case is included here for the sake of completeness, although it is not in the same ex-colonial category as the other examples. The major counterexample to the second part of Lewis's hypothesis appears to be India, a plural society with a democratic regime that was reasonably stable and successful at least until 1975. Some legitimate doubts may be raised, however, about the extent to which Indian democracy is an undiluted application of the British model. Decision-making in New Delhi has not been conducted according to grand coalition principles: the Congress party has dominated the political process (until the 1977 election), and it is a broadly aggregative party rather than a party of ethnic representation. But, in Rajni Kothari's words, the Indian system is "not just a system providing means of competition and conflict but also a *coalitional arena* in which both ruling and oppositional groups can enter their diverse claims."[6] In addition, India's federal structure was specifically designed to provide autonomy for the linguistic segments, and their geographical concentration ensures their just representation in the federal legislature in spite of the plurality method of election.

So far, then, Lewis's hypothesis stands up quite well. The only complete exceptions are Cyprus and Northern Ireland: there is a relationship between a British heritage and the failure of democracy in these cases, but the hypothesized intervening factor of the exclusive application of the British model of democracy is absent. Lebanon and Malaysia do not fit the first part of the hypothesis either but are in accord with its implicit second part. The crucial test, however, entails an examination of the entire logical but implicit complement to Lewis's hypothesis, and the crucial cases are those with a consociational instead of a British, French, or American colonial heritage: the former Dutch colonies—Indonesia, Surinam, and the Netherlands Antilles—the former Belgian Congo (now Zaire), and Rwanda and Burundi, formerly constituting the Belgian trust territory of Ruanda-Urundi. Switzerland and republican Austria have not been colonial powers, but some attention should be paid to the case of Uruguay for which Swiss democracy served as a model during two periods of the country's political history. To what extent do these cases show the relationship labeled as I in figure 4 or instead relationship II, and what has been their fate in terms of democratic success or failure?

THE BELGIAN AND DUTCH MODELS IN SIX NEW STATES

The latter question will be answered first: of the six countries that enjoyed the advantage of the consociational example as part of their colonial heritage, only two have compiled reasonably

6. Rajni Kothari, *Politics in India* (Boston: Little, Brown, 1970), p. 421 (italics added).

successful democratic records. In the Congo, democracy collapsed almost immediately after independence. Under the provisional constitution hurriedly drafted after consultations between the Belgian government and several Congolese delegations, parliamentary elections were held in May 1960, a prime minister and a cabinet were installed, and a president was chosen. The Congo became independent under this new democratic government on July 1, and then quickly plunged into chaos. During July, the Congolese army mutinied, the province of Katanga seceded, Belgian troops intervened, and the United Nations began its involvement in the Congo. In August, the Baluba ethnic segment's stronghold of South Kasai seceded, and the forcible attempt to reconquer it turned into a massacre of the Baluba civilian population which, according to U.N. Secretary-General Dag Hammarskjöld, had "the characteristics of the crime of genocide."[7] A constitutional crisis developed in early September over the president's dismissal of the prime minister, and the army decided to "neutralize" these two incumbents of the highest offices and to appoint a nonparliamentary caretaker government. This first and somewhat tentative military coup ended the Congolese democratic experiment. In the turbulent years that followed, there were a few attempts to return to democratic and parliamentary processes, but a final army takeover in 1965 ushered in a long period of nondemocratic rule under General Joseph Mobutu.

Rwanda and Burundi achieved independence in 1962, two years after the Congo. The process of decolonization in Rwanda coincided with a social revolution in which the Hutu majority overthrew the traditionally dominant Tutsi minority. The U.N. Commission for Ruanda-Urundi described the situation in early 1961 as a Hutu "racial dictatorship,"[8] and the first national elections held later in the same year resulted, as expected, in an overwhelming victory of the main Hutu party. Two years later, when some of the Tutsis who had fled to neighboring countries

7. J. Gérard-Libois and Benoit Verhaegen, *Congo 1960*, 2 vols. (Brussels: Centre de Recherche et d'Information Socio-Politiques, 1961), 2: 806.

8. René Lemarchand, *Rwanda and Burundi* (London: Pall Mall Press, 1970), p. 194.

attempted to invade Rwanda, more than ten thousand Tutsis still living in Rwanda were killed in what René Lemarchand calls an "unprecedented orgy of violence and murder," and the Vatican Radio characterized as "the most terrible and systematic genocide since the genocide of the Jews by Hitler."[9] Many more Tutsis became refugees, and only a small fraction of the Tutsi ethnic segment that comprised about 15 percent of the approximately three million Rwandese in 1960 remained in the country. Rwanda now became an unabashed Hutu-dominated one-party state.

In Burundi—very similar to Rwanda in geographical size, population, and numerical ratio between Hutus and Tutsis—events took a different but also nondemocratic turn. A constitutional monarchy was established and, although a legislature was elected by universal suffrage in 1961, the Tutsi king in practice retained considerable political power. After the Hutu electoral victory of 1965 and the subsequent swing to royal absolutism, Hutu army officers staged an abortive coup against the monarchy in the aftermath of which between 2,500 and 5,000 Hutus were killed. Two further coups, now mainly by Tutsi officers, abolished the monarchy and established a Tutsi-dominated one-party regime.

Democracy also failed in Indonesia, but it lasted longer than in the former Belgian dependencies. Following the unilateral declaration of independence in 1945 and a four-year revolutionary struggle against the Dutch, sovereignty was formally transferred to the federal government of Indonesia in 1949. Federalism was abolished after a short interlude, and 1950 saw the beginning of a period of reasonably stable constitutional rule with cabinets responsible at first to a nonelected but broadly representative parliament and after 1955 to a popularly elected legislature. From 1957 on, however, President Soekarno and the army rapidly gained power at the expense of parliamentary government. Martial law was imposed in 1957; the Outer Islands rebellion against Javanese predominance broke out in 1958; the 1950 constitution was abolished in 1959; and the elected parliament

9. Ibid., pp. 216, 224. See also Aaron Segal, *Massacre in Rwanda,* Fabian Research Series, no. 240 (London: Fabian Society, 1964).

was dissolved in 1960. Constitutional democracy was replaced by a nondemocratic regime euphemistically called "guided democracy."

Democratic government has proved more viable in the two small Dutch ex-colonies in South America, Surinam and the Netherlands Antilles, with populations of less than half a million and about a quarter million respectively. The first parliamentary elections with universal suffrage were held in 1949 while the two countries were still ruled as colonies. Five years later, they attained full internal self-government within the Kingdom of the Netherlands as equal partners with the European Netherlands. This ended their colonial status, as the General Assembly of the United Nations formally acknowledged after a thorough examination of the provisions of the new charter of the tripartite kingdom by the Committee on Information from Non-Self-Governing Territories.[10] The relations between Surinam's ethnic segments deteriorated after the late 1960s, and one of the issues dividing them was the question of whether to secede from the kingdom. Nevertheless, when Surinam severed its ties with the kingdom and established a sovereign republic in 1975, this was done not only with the blessing of its Dutch and Netherlands Antilles partners but also with the preservation of domestic peace and democracy. The Netherlands Antilles, too, has maintained both its democratic regime and its unity so far, but the latter is quite precarious as a result of the fierce rivalry between the two main islands of Curaçao and Aruba and the ever-present possibility of an Aruban attempt to become a sovereign ministate.

These brief sketches of the fate of democratic government in the six Belgian and Dutch ex-colonies show that the relationship between the consociational colonial heritage and successful democracy in these newly independent states is extremely weak—contrary to Lewis's implicit hypothesis shown in figure 4 above. It is therefore especially important to investigate the intervening variable of the type of democracy that was adopted:

10. Albert L. Gastmann, *The Politics of Surinam and the Netherlands Antilles* (Rio Piedras: Institute of Caribbean Studies, University of Puerto Rico, 1968), pp. 100–04.

to what extent was *consociational* democracy instituted at the time of independence? As we shall see, Lewis's assertion concerning the great influence exerted by the models of goverance that the colonial rulers provided remains valid when tested against the six empirical cases under discussion here, but at the same time it must be pointed out that this influence had definite limits: the consociational model was transplanted with varying degrees of fidelity and never perfectly from Belgium and Holland to their dependencies.

There are four main reasons for this imperfect transmission: First of all, as has been pointed out earlier, the concrete Belgian and Dutch cases are only imperfect instances of consociational democracy and approximate the ideal type of consociational decision-making less closely than Austria and Switzerland. Particularly with regard to the principles of grand coalition and mutual veto, the Belgian and Dutch models were weak because in neither country has the grand coalition method been consistently applied to the cabinet. Second, the Belgian and Dutch political systems were specific implementations of the consociational model, and the example that was transmitted to the colonies sometimes represented the implementation of a consociational principle that was suitable to Belgium and Holland but inappropriate for the colony, instead of the general principle itself. In particular, segmental autonomy has mainly taken a nonterritorial form in the mother-countries, and the model that was presented to the colonial dependencies—some of which were obvious candidates for a federal arrangement because of the geographical concentration of their ethnic segments—was that of a unitary and not a federal government. Belgium's move to a semifederal solution of its linguistic problem came too late to serve as an example to its African territories.

Third, it was obviously easier to copy formal constitutional and legal rules than informal political practices. For instance, proportionality as an electoral method was a much more conspicuous and straightforward example to follow than the coalescent style of decision-making that was not anchored in any law or constitution; linguistic parity in the Belgian cabinet was not introduced in the constitution until 1970. Fourth, of the five

Western democracies that were significant colonial powers, Belgium did the least to train its dependencies for self-government, and the Dutch performance in Indonesia was also far from outstanding. These difficulties with regard to the transplantation of the consociational example will be examined in greater detail in the remainder of this chapter.

CONSOCIATIONALISM AND FORMAL CONSTITUTIONAL RULES

As far as the formal, written constitutional arrangements are concerned, the strength of the Belgian and Dutch examples was overwhelming in all but one of the cases. Many of the authors who have analyzed the transition to independence or autonomy of the Belgian and Dutch colonies emphasize the close resemblance of the new constitutions to those of Belgium and the Netherlands. The 1960 Congolese constitution is described as "virtually a replica of the Belgian constitution," establishing a regime "closely resembling in its formal exterior the metropolitan model."[11] The provisional 1961 constitution of Burundi was "greatly inspired by the Belgian constitution" and is also characterized as "a barely modified copy of the Belgian constitution"; the new constitution adopted after independence in 1962 again borrowed "most of the provisions of the Belgian constitution."[12] The Indonesian constitution of 1950 was for the most part "an unimaginative, rigid, and doctrinaire adaptation of the constitution of the Netherlands."[13] The 1955 constitution of the Netherlands Antilles—scarcely distinguishable from that of Surinam of

11. Crawford Young, *Politics in the Congo: Decolonization and Independence* (Princeton: Princeton University Press, 1965), pp. 56, 182. See also René Lemarchand, *Political Awakening in the Belgian Congo* (Berkeley: University of California Press, 1964), pp. 214–15; and Walter Geerts, *Binza 10: De eerste tien onafhankelijkheidsjaren van de Democratische Republiek Kongo* (Ghent: Story-Scientia, 1970), p. 57.

12. Gabriel Mpozagara, *La République du Burundi* (Paris: Berger-Levrault, 1971), p. 27; and Raymond Rozier, *Le Burundi: Pays de la vache et du tambour* (Paris: Presses du Palais Royal, 1973), pp. 318, 374.

13. George McT. Kahin, "Indonesia," in *Major Governments of Asia*, ed. George McT. Kahin, 2d ed. (Ithaca: Cornell University Press, 1963), p. 627.

the same year—was "clearly modeled after the Dutch constitution," and the 1951 basic law on the island governments "extensively used the provisions of the Dutch municipal government law as examples."[14]

Formal constitutional rules play only a limited part in consociational democracy, of course. Many of the articles borrowed from the Belgian and Dutch constitutions have no direct relevance to consociationalism and are neutral as between the consociational and British models. Other provisions can be considered indirectly helpful to consociational democracy. In particular, the fact that Belgium and the Netherlands have parliamentary systems, in which grand coalitions can be arranged more easily and flexible than in presidential systems, was a favorable factor. The only clear exception to the adoption of the parliamentary model is Rwanda. Its provisional constitution of 1961 prescribed a parliamentary regime, but in the 1962 constitution—which in most other respects, too, differed from the Belgian model—a kind of presidential system was introduced.[15] As we shall see later, however, the literal adoption of constitutional provisions applicable to the Belgian and Dutch monarchs without adaptation to the similar but not identical position of heads of state in the Congolese and Indonesian republics interfered with both parliamentary and consociational arrangements in the two new states.

A direct and positive contribution of constitutional borrowing to consociational democracy was the adoption of list systems of proportional representation, prescribed by both the Belgian and Dutch constitutions, by all of the ex-colonies with the partial exception of Surinam. The law by which the Dutch parliament introduced elections by universal suffrage for the Surinam legislature merely stipulated that Surinam's capital and only major city of Paramaribo elect ten representatives and the other dis-

14. A. J. M. Kunst, *Receptie en concordantie van recht: De invloed van het Nederlandse recht op dat van de Nederlandse Antillen* (Willemstad: Rechtshogeschool van de Nederlandse Antillen, 1973), p. 21.

15. See F. Nkundabagenzi, *Rwanda politique, 1958–1960* (Brussels: Centre de Recherche et d'Information Socio-Politiques, 1961), pp. 391–97; and J. Vanderlinden, *La République Rwandaise* (Paris: Berger-Levrault, 1970), pp. 28–56.

tricts a total of eleven. This apportionment of seats entailed an overrepresentation of Paramaribo: with only slightly more than a third of the eligible voters in the first universal suffrage elections of 1949, it was given almost half of the seats. The principal motive for this deviation from proportionality was the desire to weight the votes of the better-educated urban population more heavily than those of the rural voters. Proportional representation was not prescribed, but the division of the country into one or more Paramaribo and several rural districts guaranteed, according to the Dutch government, "an equitable distribution of the seats and an adequate representation of all groups," given the considerable degree of geographical concentration of the ethnic segments.[16]

The originally dominant Creole segment (those with some degree of Negro ancestry but including, in the early years, a few whites among their political leaders) succeeded in implementing these electoral privisions to their own advantage by adopting the British plurality method and making Paramaribo into a single district. Thus the main Creole party captured all ten Paramaribo seats, and the East Indian (Hindustani) party, which in a proportional system would have been entitled to at least two seats, did not win any. The combination of the overrepresentation of Paramaribo voters and the use of the plurality vote in this ten-member district gave the Creoles—the largest ethnic segment but not a majority—an absolute majority of thirteen seats in the legislature; the East Indians won six seats, and the Javanese two.[17] A fully proportional method would have made the distribution of seats among the three principal ethnic segments of Surinam about 9 to 8 to 4 instead of 13 to 6 to 2.

In 1963 and 1966, during a period of close collaboration between Creoles and East Indians, three fundamental changes were made in the electoral law: (1) the overrepresentation of Paramaribo was eliminated; (2) proportional representation

16. W. H. van Helsdingen, *De Staatsregeling van Suriname van 1955: Historische toelichting en praktijk* (The Hague: Staatsdrukkerij- en Uitgeverijbedrijf, 1957), pp. 178, 186.

17. F. E. M. Mitrasing, *Tien jaar Suriname: Van afhankelijkheid tot gelijkgerechtigdheid* (Leiden: Luctor et Emergo, 1959), pp. 152–53, 159, 169–70, 176.

was adopted for the Paramaribo district and one other large district; and (3) the voters were given a second ballot for electing about a third of the enlarged 39-member legislature by proportional representation in a single nationwide district. These amendments made the electoral law rather complicated but highly proportional in its effects. It is also worth noting that the details of the new proportional representation rules—the list system, the d'Hondt method, an electoral threshold that equals the electoral quotient, and the possibility of casting a preferential vote for a specific candidate on the list—were all borrowed without change from the Dutch election law.[18] During the same period, the composition of the civil service became more proportional as more East Indians were hired and Creole predominance was attenuated.

In the other Belgian and Dutch ex-colonies, too, proportional representation successfully fulfilled its purpose of producing legislatures that faithfully reflected the strengths of the different population segments. The 1960 elections in the Congo thus became, as Crawford Young writes, "largely an ethnic census."[19] George McT. Kahin criticizes the Dutch-inspired proportional representation method used in the 1955 Indonesian elections and concludes: "Had the elections been based upon single-member constituencies, different political mechanics might well have been set in motion, and conceivably the electoral process might then, as in Great Britain, have served to bridge differences rather than to increase them."[20] This conclusion is completely at variance, of course, with consociational theory. In addition, it should be pointed out that, in spite of the extreme Indonesian system of proportional representation which was, like the Dutch model, highly advantageous for small parties, and in spite of Indonesia's large and diverse population, the 1955 elections did not result in an unmanageable proliferation of parties; in fact, the elected parliament was less fragmented than its

18. See C. D. Ooft, *Kort begrip van de Staatsinrichting van Suriname* (Paramaribo, 1967), pp. 31–48. A slight exception is the absence of a preferential vote in the nationwide second ballot.

19. Young, *Politics in the Congo,* p. 271.

20. Kahin, "Indonesia," pp. 627–28.

nonelected predecessor. An even more significant result was that the four parties representing Indonesia's four main cultural segments or alirans—the Masjumi and Nahdatul Ulama parties of, respectively, the reformist and orthodox santris (devout Moslems), and the Nationalist and Communist parties representing, respectively, the traditionalist and modernist non-santri and secular segments—together won more than three-fourths of the votes and of the parliamentary seats.[21]

Unfortunately, several of the plural societies under consideration here—Rwanda, Burundi, the Netherlands Antilles, and, in one important respect, Indonesia also—are afflicted by an imbalance of power between their segments. Proportionality may not be a sufficient response in such situations, and the protection of minority interests may require the deliberate overrepresentation of the minority or parity of representation. The huge Hutu-Tutsi disequilibrium in Rwanda and Burundi made a solution along these lines very difficult and none was attempted. In Indonesia, the inequality between densely populated Java with about two-thirds of the country's population and the Outer Islands was not dampened by the proportional election method in 1955: Java received about two-thirds of the parliamentary seats. Dissatisfaction with this outcome in the Outer Islands was strengthened by the fact that three of the four large political parties were mainly Javanese parties and that only the Masjumi had polled well outside of Java, and by the contrast with the 1950–55 nonelected parliament in which the Outer Islands had been overrepresented.

Only in the Netherlands Antilles was this problem faced squarely. The population disparity among these islands was similar to that of Indonesia, albeit on a much smaller scale. In the years after the Second World War, close to two-thirds of the Antillian population lived on Curaçao. The Aruban population was only about half of Curaçao's, and the number of eligible voters on Aruba was an even smaller proportion. The remaining

21. For a systematic brief description of the *alirans*, see Donald Hindley, "Dilemmas of Consensus and Division: Indonesia's Search for a Political Format," *Government and Opposition* 4, no. 1 (winter 1969): 70–73.

small minority was divided between Bonaire and the three Windward Islands. The antagonism between the two principal islands of Curaçao and Aruba stems partly from divergent traditions and historical events—during the colonial period, the Arubans often resented the overbearing administration of their island from Curaçao more than Dutch colonialism itself—but also from the fact that, although the populations of both islands are racially mixed, there are clear differences in physical appearance between them: the average Curaçaoan has a considerably darker skin than the average Aruban.

When plans were made for the first elections by universal suffrage in the Antilles, the apportionment of seats to the different islands became a contentious issue. In order to check the growing separatist tendencies of Aruba and to maintain Antillian unity, the Curaçaoans consented not only to parity of representation with Aruba but also to the overrepresentation of the small islands. The Dutch government reluctantly agreed and allotted 8 seats each to Curaçao and Aruba, 2 to Bonaire, and 1 each to the Windward Islands in the 21-member legislature to be elected in 1949. The electoral method was not at issue: each island was a constituency, and in the multimember constituencies the Dutch list system of proportional representation was used.

The Curaçaoans soon began to regret their generosity, and the Dutch government also decided that the 1949 apportionment of legislative seats entailed too great a deviation from proportionality. Instead they proposed a drastic decentralization of the Antillian government—thereby going a long way toward acceding to Aruba's demand for independence from Curaçao—combined with a reapportionment of parliamentary seats that would still involve an overrepresentation of the other islands but not one as far-reaching as parity between Curaçao and Aruba or even between Curaçao and the other islands combined: 12 seats for Curaçao, 8 for Aruba, 1 for Bonaire, and 1 for the three Windward Islands in the new 22-member legislature. However, the non-Curaçaoan majority in the Antillian parliament elected in 1949 refused to consider any change in the apportionment of the seats. Their objections were finally overruled by the Dutch government which described its own proposal as the only acceptable "middle course between pure proportionality and parity," and which questioned the democratic legitimacy of the Antillian parliament in its 1949 composition "in which representatives of 30 percent of the eligible voters can impose their will on the others."[22] The 1950 elections were held under this new arrangement. It was obviously not one copied by the ex-colony from the metropolitan example but rather the application of a general consociational norm, adapted to the requirements of the territory being decolonized, and *imposed* on it by the mother-country. It turned out to be a workable compromise and was inserted without change in the 1955 constitution of the self-governing Netherlands Antilles.

ADAPTATION OF THE AUTONOMY PRINCIPLE

The principle of segmental autonomy in Belgian and Dutch consociational democracy has mainly taken the concrete form of a nonterritorial "federalism," and only since 1970 has Belgium adopted a clearly territorial kind of semifederalism. Especially in view of the long time it took the Belgians to follow the example of their own well-established practice of subcultural autonomy and to apply it in its territorial adaptation to the Flemish-Walloon linguistic problem, it is remarkable that the Belgian and Dutch governments did not resist—and even encouraged—federal or semifederal constitutions for those of their colonies that were plural societies with geographically concentrated segments: Indonesia, the Congo, and the Netherlands Antilles. However, these federal and semifederal solutions had no more than a mixed record of success.

The new state of Indonesia which the Dutch officially recognized as an independent country in 1949 was the formally federal Republic of the United States of Indonesia, but this federation lasted less than a year and was replaced by the unitary

22. W. H. van Helsdingen, *De Staatsregeling van de Nederlandse Antillen van 1955: Historische toelichting en praktijk* (The Hague: Staatsdrukkerij- en Uitgeverijbedrijf, 1956), pp. 156, 173.

Republic of Indonesia in 1950. The Congolese constitution of 1960 was formally unitary but decentralized to such an extent that Young describes its philosophy as "implicit federalism" and the state it created as a "federal system" because of the "recasting of the province from an administrative into a political structure"; it has also been characterized as a "federal constitution that dares not tell its name."[23] The democratic experiment in the Congo did not last long enough to give its at least partly federal structure a fair test. Only the highly decentralized system of the Netherlands Antilles, also verging on federalism, has worked satisfactorily since its introduction in 1951.

There were two serious flaws in Indonesia's federalism which doomed it from the beginning. The same weaknesses were also present in the implicit federalism of the Congo but have not afflicted the Antilles. The first and major flaw was the haphazard delimitation of the component states and provinces. Their boundaries did not correspond to segmental boundaries, thus defeating the rationale for federalism in plural societies. Most of the states of federal Indonesia were entities created by the Dutch in the areas they controlled during the Indonesian struggle for independence as a counterweight to the nationalist-controlled Republic. Especially in Java, as Herbert Feith states, "the Dutch-built states had virtually no social reality. Their boundaries corresponded to no ethnic entities, but simply to the limits to which the Dutch had been able to extend their military occupation." The revolutionary Republic became a single state consisting of noncontiguous areas in Java and Sumatra. The new provincial boundaries in unitary Indonesia did not coincide with the earlier state boundaries, but they, too, "paid little heed to regional or ethnic group feeling."[24]

The six provinces that the Congo consisted of when it became independent were the same as the old administrative provinces of Belgian colonial rule, and all of them were ethnically heterogeneous. In 1962, the six provinces were subdivided into

23. Young, *Politics in the Congo*, pp. 512, 515; Geerts, *Binza 10*, p. 282.

24. Herbert Feith, *The Decline of Constitutional Democracy in Indonesia* (Ithaca: Cornell University Press, 1962), pp. 72, 99. See also A. Arthur Schiller, *The Formation of Federal Indonesia: 1945–1949* (The Hague: Van Hoeve, 1955).

twenty-one smaller and more homogeneous units: the majority of the new provinces were either "clearly homogeneous" or "partially so," and this factor strengthened them a great deal, according to Young.[25] The Mobutu regime returned to the colonial pattern of unitary and centralized administration and a smaller number of provinces virtually coinciding with the old colonial provinces. Only in the Netherlands Antilles did the division into geographic components not present a problem, but here the right solution was so obvious that it could hardly be missed: the islands constitute the segments of the Antillian plural society and they are also the natural geographic units for a federal or semifederal organization. Accordingly, the 1951 basic law set up four *eilandgebieden* (island territories). The three Windward Islands were combined into one eilandgebied because of their very small populations, but the more important islands, especially Curaçao and Aruba, became separate autonomous units in the semifederal structure.

The second difficulty in adapting the autonomy principle to the federal needs of Indonesia and the Congo was the suspicion that the metropolitan powers advocated a federal or semifederal structure because they wanted to keep their ex-colonies weak and divided and hence subject to continuing, though indirect, colonial control. A major ground for this skepticism was that Belgium and the Netherlands themselves were not federal states. In the Indonesian case, the suspicion of Dutch motives was largely well-founded. Kahin aptly describes the short-lived Indonesian federation as "a weirdly unbalanced and distorted organism" and claims that in sponsoring it the Dutch government was "more concerned with promoting a strategy of divide and rule, calculated to eventuate in a political order which they could indirectly control, than in establishing a federal system honestly dedicated to Indonesia's very real need for a political decentralization consistent with basic geographic, economic, and cultural factors."[26] That Indonesia required some form of federalism is also argued by F. G. Carnell: "In view of this

25. Young, *Politics in the Congo,* pp. 529, 551–53.
26. Kahin, "Indonesia," p. 591.

country's enormous area and extreme regional diversities, this form of government would seem to be especially appropriate."[27] In particular, federalism could and should have given the Outer Islands autonomy from and countervailing power against Javanese predominance. Mohammad Hatta, the major spokesman for non-Javanese interests in independent Indonesia, was strongly in favor of federalism: "A federal system is, in fact, suitable for such a far-flung archipelago as Indonesia, and might be expected to strengthen the feeling of unity." But, he continued, "the manner and timing of the move [to federalism] by the Netherlands Indies Government had aroused such antipathy towards ideas of federation" that the federal system had to be abolished.[28] And it was a cabinet under Hatta as prime minister that effected the transition to a unitary state in 1950.

There were similar suspicions about Belgian motives in the Congo. For instance, Thomas Kanza, who was a minister in the first Congolese cabinet headed by Patrice Lumumba, writes that the Belgian government persuaded the Congolese leaders to accept "formulae whereby their democracy would be totally patterned on the Belgian model," and then claims, rather inconsistently, that this borrowing entailed severe restrictions on central government powers, which enabled the provinces "to make decisions against the national interest, but to the advantage of foreign big business."[29] Similarly, a resolution passed at a 1960 conference of Lumumba's party charged that federalism was a device for the installation of "neo-colonialism, the brother of the reactionary form which has just been buried."[30] Such suspicions were much less justified than in the Dutch-Indonesian case. The Belgian government originally even favored a unitary Congo, and it slowly moved to a semifederal approach as a middle ground between the contending Congolese groups. Joseph

27. F. G. Carnell, "Political Implications of Federalism in New States," in Ursula K. Hicks et al., *Federalism and Economic Growth in Underdeveloped Countries* (London: Allen and Unwin, 1961), p. 27.

28. Mohammad Hatta, "Indonesia's Foreign Policy," *Foreign Affairs* 31, no. 3 (April 1953): 449.

29. Thomas Kanza, *Conflict in the Congo: The Rise and Fall of Lumumba* (Harmondsworth: Penguin Books, 1972), p. 89.

30. Quoted in Gérard-Libois and Verhaegen, *Congo 1960*, 1: 176.

Kasavubu, the country's first president, strongly favored a federal Congo which, he argued, required a deliberate deviation from the Belgian constitutional blueprint: the Belgian example "tends to give to the Congolese a Belgian independence and not an African independence. . . . We need . . . a federal government on the Swiss model." It is interesting to note that Belgium even served as a negative example in this respect. A statement by Kasavubu's ethnically based party offers the following shrewd analysis:

> It suffices to observe the perpetual mistrust and misunderstandings between Flemings and Walloons to convince oneself of the danger there is to unite men of different origins. We do not want to meddle in the internal affairs of our Belgian friends, but we cannot help saying that if the union between Flemings and Walloons were conceived on a federal basis, the almost interminable quarrels which have often broken forth between these two tribes would have been avoided. Belgium herself offers us proof of the danger there is in uniting men of different origin.[31]

Suspicions concerning the federalizing motives of the Dutch were avoided in the Netherlands Antilles partly because the demand for some form of island autonomy originated with the Antillians and had no strong opponents in the Antilles, but also because the system that was adopted was squarely based on a Dutch model: the Dutch law on the governance of the municipalities. As a result, the 1951 basic law on the eilandgebieden institutes island executives and island legislatures that are a virtual carbon copy of the Dutch pattern of burgomasters, aldermen, and municipal councils. The application of the Dutch local government model also means that the Antilles lack some of the important features usually associated with federalism, such as separate island constitutions.[32] On the

31. Quoted in Young, *Politics in the Congo,* pp. 165–66, 267–68.

32. See J. W. Ellis, M. P. Gorsira, and F. C. J. Nuyten, *De zelfstandigheid der eilandgebieden: Een bijdrage tot herziening van de Eilandenregeling Nederlandse Antillen* (Willemstad: Eilandgebied Curaçao, 1954), pp. 13–14; and W. C. J. van Leeuwen, *Verslag aan de Parlementaire Statuutcommissie uit de Staten van de Neder-*

other hand, a few federal devices were grafted onto the Dutch model: a carefully defined division of powers guaranteeing a high degree of decentralization, and a provision that the basic law can be amended only by a two-thirds majority of all members of the Antillian parliament, which gives the eight members from Aruba an absolute veto; it should be noted that the Antillian constitution itself can be amended more easily, namely, by a two-thirds majority of the members present and voting.

In one other important respect, a thoroughly federal model would have served the Dutch ex-colonies better than the adapted Dutch example: the typical federal idea of a bicameral legislature, with one chamber either representing the component states on an equal basis or overrepresenting the smaller states, contains an attractive solution to the competing claims of proportionality and parity in plural societies with a numerically dominant segment. In Indonesia, a second chamber with an overrepresentation of the Outer Islands alongside the proportionally constituted chamber might have contributed to an easing of the regional tensions. There was originally a senate in federal Indonesia with two senators from each of the sixteen states—which means that the Republic with its near-majority of the total population was extremely underrepresented—but it was abolished in 1950. A federal-style bicameral legislature would also have been a logical compromise in the Antillian dilemma posed by Curaçao's popular majority and Aruba's claim to equal status. At one point during the negotiations on the apportionment of seats in the Antillian parliament, the Dutch government proposed a bicameral legislature with one purely proportional chamber and one federal council based on parity between Curaçao and Aruba and overrepresentation of the other islands.[33] This proposal was made with obvious reluctance, and, when it received no more than an indifferent response in the Antilles, it was quickly dropped.

landse Antillen met betrekking tot onze toekomstige staatkundige structuur (Willemstad: Staten van de Nederlandse Antillen, 1970), pp. 68–73.

33. M. P. Gorsira, *De staatkundige emancipatie van de Nederlandse Antillen* (The Hague: Staatsdrukkerij- en Uitgeverijbedrijf, 1950), pp. 27–34.

INFORMAL CONSOCIATIONAL PRACTICES: INDONESIA

The most important consociational principle—government by grand coalition and, as its close corollary, the minority veto—was also the most difficult to transplant from Belgium and Holland to their former colonies in the Third World, because the Belgian and Dutch examples of government by grand coalition represented informal extraconstitutional and largely extracabinet applications of the principle: grand coalition was not prescribed by any constitutional or legal rule and was never fully practiced at the cabinet level in Holland and only infrequently in Belgium. The degree of difficulty in perceiving the example of grand coalition is demonstrated by the fact that there is strong evidence of its deliberate imitation in only one of our six cases: Indonesia.

According to Ruth T. McVey, the Dutch example significantly affected the thinking of Soekarno and other Indonesian leaders: "Since the Netherlands was the Western democratic model presented to Indonesians in the colonial period, much of the Dutch approach to politics was absorbed by the Indonesian nationalists even as they reacted against colonial rule and European ways."[34] The Dutch style of consociational decision-making in a religiously and ideologically plural society seemed to fit the Indonesian conditions very well. The principal cleavages in the preindependence period were those between the alirans—religious and ideological segments very similar in nature to the Dutch *zuilen.* After independence, these alirans greatly increased their organizational scope and effectiveness under the guidance of the four large aliran-based political parties. Geertz describes the situation in the following words: "As well as its political organization proper, each party has connected with it, formally or informally, women's clubs, youth and student groups, labor unions, peasant organizations, charitable associations, private schools, religious or philosophical societies, veterans' organizations, savings clubs, and so forth." The complex of each party with its

34. Ruth T. McVey, "Nationalism, Islam and Marxism: The Management of Ideological Conflict in Indonesia," introduction to Soekarno, *Nationalism, Islam and Marxism,* trans. Karel H. Warouw and Peter D. Weldon (Ithaca: Modern Indonesia Project, Cornell University, 1969), p. 19.

ancillary associations provides "a general framework within which a wide range of social activities can be organized, as well as an over-all ideological rationale to give those activities point and direction."[35]

Soekarno's political tract *Nationalism, Islam and Marxism,* published in 1926, was an appeal to the leaders of the alirans to transcend their differences and work together for the common goal of Indonesian independence. In later years, McVey claims, Soekarno continued to think in terms of "the idea of permanent vertical cleavages in the society, capable of arbitration at the top," and he saw the political elite as "the representative and pacifying agent of the vertical cleavages in the society"—completely in line with the grand coalition principle. In the years of constitutional democratic or near-democratic government between 1950 and 1957, political cooperation at the elite level took two forms. The first was the dual leadership of Soekarno, a Javanese and a non-santri, as president, and Hatta, a Sumatran santri, as vice-president. As Geertz writes, these two leaders "supplemented one another not only politically but primordially," and Hatta's resignation in late 1956 "withdrew the stamp of legitimacy from the central government so far as many of the leading military, financial, political, and religious groups in the Outer Islands were concerned."[36] The second site for elite collaboration was the usually quite broadly based cabinet. The Masjumi participated in all but one and the Nationalists in all but two of the six cabinets in the 1950–57 period; the Nahdatul Ulama was represented in all cabinets formed after its disaffiliation from the Masjumi in 1952. Of the four large parties, only the Communists were consistently kept out of the cabinet.

35. Clifford Geertz, *Peddlers and Princes: Social Change and Economic Modernization in Two Indonesian Towns* (Chicago: University of Chicago Press, 1963), p. 14. See also Basuki Gunawan and O. D. van den Muijzenberg, "Verzuilingstendenties en sociale stratificatie in Indonesië," *Sociologische Gids* 14, no. 3 (May-June 1967): 146–58; and B. Gunawan, "Aliran en sociale structuur," in C. Baks et al., *Buiten de grenzen: Sociologische opstellen* (Meppel: Boom, 1971), pp. 69–85.

36. Clifford Geertz, "The Integrative Revolution: Primordial Sentiments and Civil Politics in the New States," in *Old Societies and New States: The Quest for Modernity in Asia and Africa,* ed. Clifford Geertz (New York: Free Press, 1963), p. 132.

Disagreement about the role of the Communists in Indonesian politics placed a great strain on the Soekarno-Hatta duumvirate. Especially after the 1955 elections, Soekarno repeatedly urged their inclusion in the government. At the opening of the newly elected parliament, he told its members to work on the basis of "real Indonesian democracy" and not on the majoritarian basis of "50 per cent plus one are always right."[37] About a year later, he proposed the formation of a grand coalition cabinet for which he used the Indonesian term *gotong rojong,* or "mutual assistance": "I expressly use the term *gotong rojong* because this is an authentic Indonesian term which provides us with the purest likeness of the Indonesian spirit. . . . At present we have a cabinet which includes a part of the political parties and groups. Let us now try to form one which comprises all political parties and groups." He also supported this idea by quoting, in Dutch, a Dutch saying to the effect that "all members of the family [should be] at the eating table and at the working table."[38]

Hatta's reaction was uncompromisingly negative, although, it should be noted, he was not opposed to the grand coalition idea itself: "When we come to examine Bung Karno's conception of a *Gotong Rojong* Cabinet, we are faced with an idea which is intrinsically good and idealistic but in practice cannot be put into effect. . . . Especially as between the [Communists] on the one hand and the religious parties and some nationalist groups on the other, there is a difference of ideology and goals which is very fundamental, so that it is difficult to bring these two together in a *Gotong Rojong* Cabinet." The Communists, he said, were committed to nondemocratic ideals and to a slavishly pro-Soviet foreign policy. Hence a grand coalition had to fail: "It is like trying to mix oil and water."[39] In the ideologically charged atmosphere of the 1950s, both in Indonesia and elsewhere, it

37. Quoted in Feith, *Decline of Constitutional Democracy,* p. 515.

38. Soekarno, "Saving the Republic of the Proclamation," in *Indonesian Political Thinking: 1945–1965,* ed. Herbert Feith and Lance Castles (Ithaca: Cornell University Press, 1970), pp. 85–86.

39. Mohammad Hatta, "Oil and Water Do Not Mix," in *Indonesian Political Thinking,* pp. 365–67.

was indeed difficult if not impossible to bridge the fundamental incompatibility between communists and noncommunists noted by Hatta. In the end, Soekarno's views prevailed, and he clung to the idea of cooperation among nationalist, religious, and communist aliran leaders even while he turned against the multiparty system and parliamentary democracy.

INTERSEGMENTAL COALITIONS IN SURINAM AND THE NETHERLANDS ANTILLES

The Dutch example of elite cooperation did not exert as much direct influence on the thinking of the leaders of the other two former Dutch colonies. Nevertheless, both countries benefited from the formation of intersegmental coalitions that, though not truly grand coalitions, approximated this consociational principle very closely. In Surinam, after an initial period of Creole predominance, a pattern of shifting coalitions developed that gave all significant ethnic parties a chance to participate in the cabinet. After the first parliamentary elections in 1949, the Dutch governor of Surinam unsuccessfully urged the formation of a cabinet resting "on as broad a base as possible," but six years later an interethnic cabinet was formed with representatives of both Creole and Javanese parties. The cabinets in the long period from 1958 to 1973 were even more significant instances of interethnic cooperation because they were coalitions of Creole and East Indian parties representing the country's two largest ethnic segments. Creole–East Indian cooperation was especially close and fruitful from 1958 to 1967, when the two main Creole parties and the large East Indian party were united in the cabinet coalition. Edward Dew calls the latter period one in which "Surinam enjoyed its most balanced and progressive period of development."[40]

The Dutch example does not seem to have been a factor in the

40. Edward Dew, "Surinam: The Struggle for Ethnic Balance and Identity," *Plural Societies* 5, no. 3 (autumn 1974): 7. See also R. A. J. van Lier, *Frontier Society: A Social Analysis of the History of Surinam* (The Hague: Nijhoff, 1971), p. 391.

formation of these coalitions except in an indirect way: there was no criticism, which might have been inspired by the British normative model, of the almost grand nature of the cabinet coalitions and of the weak opposition they faced in the legislature. A foreign model that did influence the Surinam elites was the negative example of ethnic strife between Creoles and East Indians in neighboring Guyana in the early 1960s.[41] It is interesting to note that Creole leader J. A. Pengel, who became prime minister in 1963, did not acknowledge any foreign examples as inspirations for his nearly grand coalition cabinet in his first official statement to parliament. Instead he held up interethnic cooperation in Surinam as a shining example for *other* countries: "A monument has been erected here which is an example for the entire world."[42]

The Antillian cabinet coalitions have been less broadly based but more consistently intersegmental than the ones in Surinam. From 1950 on, all cabinets have been interisland coalitions. As table 11 shows, there have always been both Curaçaoan and Aruban parties in the Antillian cabinets; in addition, they have consistently included representatives of Bonaire and the Windward Islands. The table also shows, however, that these interisland coalitions have usually had a narrow base. Until 1966, the major government parties never held more than half of the twenty seats allotted to Curaçao and Aruba in the Antillian parliament. For their majorities, the cabinets were therefore dependent on the two legislators from the other islands and sometimes on minor parties. For the unity of the Antilles, the participation of both Curaçaoan and Aruban leaders in all cabinets has been of immeasurable importance.

The emergence of this pattern of interisland coalitions was an intentional by-product of the legislative reapportionment that the Dutch government decided on for the Antilles in 1950 after the Antillians were unable to reach a compromise among them-

41. Edward Dew, "De beheersing van raciale en culturele polarisatie in een onafhankelijk Suriname," *Beleid en Maatschappij* 2, no. 9 (September 1975): 227.

42. J. A. Pengel, *Regeringsverklaring op 7 juni 1963 in de Staten van Suriname uitgesproken door J. A. Pengel, Minister-President van Suriname* (Paramaribo, 1963), p. 6.

TABLE 11. Major Parties in the Netherlands Antilles Government and in the Curaçao and Aruba Island Governments, 1950–1977[1]

Period	Netherlands Antilles Government			Curaçao Govt.	Aruba Govt.
	Curaçaoan Parties	Aruban Parties	Share of Seats[2]		
1950–54[3]	NVP	AVP	45%	NVP, DP	AVP
1954–55	DP	PPA	50	NVP, DP	AVP
1955–59	DP	PPA	50	NVP, DP	PPA
1959–61	DP	PPA	50	NVP[4]	PPA
1961–63	DP	PPA	50	DP	PPA
1963–67	DP	PPA	50[5]	NVP	PPA
1967–69	DP	PPA	55	DP	AVP
1969–71	DP, NVP, FO	PPA	80	DP	PPA, AVP
1971–73	DP, NVP	PPA, AVP	85	DP, NVP	PPA, AVP
1973–75	NVP, PSD	MEP	65	NVP, PSD	PPA, AVP
1975–76	NVP, FO	MEP	65	FO, PSD	MEP
1976–77	NVP, FO	PPA	55	FO, PSD	MEP

1. The major Curaçaoan parties are the NVP (National People's party), DP (Democratic party), and, more recently, the FO (Workers' Front) and PSD (Social Democratic party). The major Aruban parties are the AVP (Aruban People's party), PPA (Aruban Patriotic party), and the new MEP (People's Electoral Movement).

2. The percentage of the 20 seats allotted to Curaçao and Aruba that were won by the major government parties in the national legislative elections. The actual parliamentary strength of the government has usually been somewhat broader as a result of Bonaire, Windward Islands, and minor party support.

3. The first island elections took place and the first island governments were formed in 1951.

4. Party government in Curaçao was temporarily suspended in 1960–61.

5. The DP-PPA share of seats rose to 55 percent in the 1966 election.

SOURCE: Based on data supplied by A. J. Booi, B. Fijnje, and E. Monte, whose assistance is gratefully acknowledged.

selves. Because Curaçao had a clear majority of the Antillian population, the Dutch government felt that it was imperative to give the island more than half of the parliamentary seats, but they described this majority position as one "tempered to the utmost." Of course, the twelve seats held by Curaçao made it theoretically possible for Curaçao to exclude Aruba with its eight seats and the other islands with their two seats from the government, but the Dutch government pointed out that Curaçao and Aruba had several parties and that it was therefore most unlikely that "all of the Curaçaoan members of parliament would be united against all Aruban members." And they considered their proposal to be not only "the most equitable solution," but also "a solution that offers the best guarantee that the different islands will continue to cooperate well and successfully in the common interest and in the interest of each of the islands."[43] This "guarantee" proved to be a strong one, and Peter Verton, surveying the developments since 1950, argues that interisland cooperation was in fact "dictated" by the apportionment of seats in the legislature.[44] As pointed out earlier, this beneficial arrangement was not freely borrowed by the Antillians from the Dutch example but was a Dutch solution imposed by Dutch fiat. In the years that followed, however, the pattern of interisland coalitions that was set in motion by Dutch design was strengthened by the increasing Antillian recognition of its value and by its gradual growth into a legitimate tradition.

Politics in Curaçao was dominated until the early 1970s by the Democratic party and the National People's party, which were fiercely competitive although there were no outstanding programmatic differences between them. The National People's party tended to appeal to the rural voters and native Curaçaoans and the Democrats to the urban electorate and to immigrants from the other islands and Surinam attracted by the oil industry, but there was no sharp division between the respective party

43. Van Helsdingen, *De Staatsregeling van de Nederlandse Antillen,* pp. 174, 176, 184.

44. Peter Verton, *Kiezers en politieke partijen in de Nederlandse Antillen* (Aruba: De Wit, 1973), p. 15.

clienteles.[45] Aruba had a similar pragmatic two-party system: the Aruban People's party, mainly supported by autochthonous Arubans, faced the immigrant-supported Aruban Patriotic party. Their main policy difference was the somewhat more moderate stand of the Patriotic party on the issue of island independence. At the national level the four parties confronted each other in stable interisland alliances: the Democrats and the Aruban Patriotic party versus the National and Aruban People's parties, a pattern reminiscent of the stable coalitions between Conservatives and Bleus and between Reformers and Rouges in the United Province of Canada.

The interisland character of the Antillian government coalitions served the purpose, identical to that of a grand coalition, of including representatives of all segments in the decision-making process. But the narrowness of the cabinet coalitions, in terms of the parties rather than of the segments included in them, had one significant disadvantage: the fact that the parties in the Antilles cabinet were not always government parties in the islands could cause grave strains between the two levels of government. As table 11 shows, there was a long period of such inconsonance in the 1960s: from 1963 to 1967 the Curaçaoan government party was not in the Antilles cabinet and from 1967 to 1969 the Aruban government party was in the same position. The report of the official commission of investigation into the serious riots and violence that shook Curaçao in 1969 attributed most of the blame to internal Curaçaoan factors but also mentioned the discordant relationship between the national and island governments in the 1963–67 period.[46] From 1969 on,

45. Colonial Curaçao was a plural society consisting of small Dutch Protestant and Sephardic Jewish segments and a large Negro segment, but these cleavages have become diffuse and increasingly irrelevant to party politics in democratic Curaçao. See H. Hoetink, *De gespleten samenleving in het Caribisch gebied: Bijdrage tot de sociologie der rasrelaties in gesegmenteerde maatschappijen* (Assen: Van Gorcum, 1962), pp. 191–97; and R. A. Römer, *Naar de voltooiing van de emancipatie: Beschouwingen naar aanleiding van het verschijnsel 30 mei* (Willemstad: Hogeschool van de Nederlandse Antillen, 1974, pp. 10–11.

46. R. A. Römer et al., *De Meidagen van Curaçao* (Curaçao: Ruku, 1970), pp. 84–85, 105–06, 164.

government coalitions became more broadly based and in 1971–73 there were grand coalitions including all four of the formerly competing parties at both the national and island levels. This cooperation, however, caused a split in the Aruban People's party and the establishment of the more intensely separatist People's Electoral Movement. This new party won a majority of the Aruban seats in the national elections in 1973 and also gained an overwhelming victory in the 1975 Aruban island election, giving it a strong political position to press for greater decentralization and federalism or to prepare for Aruba's secession from the Antilles. The likelihood of the latter course of action was increased by the Antilles cabinet crisis of late 1975 and the expulsion of the People's Electoral Movement from the cabinet in early 1976.

COALITIONS IN THE FORMER BELGIAN TERRITORIES

In the Belgian ex-dependencies, the metropolitan example of inter-subcultural grand coalitions did not have any significant influence. Neither by a process of free borrowing nor by direct Belgian pressure does this example appear to have been transmitted. As far as the Congo is concerned, two slight exceptions must be noted. One is the provision in the 1960 Congolese constitution that the cabinet had to "include at least one member from each province"—similar to an unwritten Belgian political rule.[47] In spite of the multiethnic composition of all six provinces, this constitutional prescription had the indirect effect of encouraging a broad ethnic base for Congolese cabinets. The second exception was the insistence by the Belgian resident minister in the Congo that "the only acceptable formula" for the first Congolese cabinet to be formed after the 1960 elections "was one of a broad coalition in which as many tendencies as possible were to be represented." Both Lumumba and Kasavubu, who were in turn given the responsibility of forming

47. Gérard-Libois and Verhaegen, *Congo 1960*, 1: 111; André Mast, *Les pays du Benelux* (Paris: Librairie Générale de Droit et de Jurisprudence, 1960), pp. 94–95.

a government, favored narrow coalitions, and it was at least partly due to Belgian pressure that the Lumumba cabinet that finally emerged was a grand coalition: it was based on parties holding 88 percent of the seats in the lower house of the legislature. But it was not proportionally constituted–Kasavubu's party in particular was underrepresented—and it obtained only a weak 54 percent vote of confidence when it presented itself to the chamber.[48] It lasted but a few months, and Congolese democracy did not survive much longer.

In Rwanda, there was a short period of coalition government in which both Hutus and Tutsis participated, but it came into existence after urgent entreaties by the United Nations rather than under Belgian pressure. Particularly in Rwanda, the Belgian government was caught uncomfortably between the demands of Tutsis and Hutus. The Belgians had administered their trust territory through the elite of the Tutsi minority, and in the late 1950s the call for Rwandese independence came from the Tutsi leaders. However, the Hutu majority feared a perpetuation of the Tutsis' dominant status in independent Rwanda and therefore favored continued Belgian trusteeship until their own position could be improved. The 1960 U. N. Visiting Mission was greeted by the contradictory slogans: "Immediate independence—Get rid of the Belgians for us" (the Tutsi demand), and "Down with Tutsi feudalism—Long live Belgian trusteeship" (the Hutu view).[49]

The Belgians finally chose the side of the Hutu majority. Lemarchand characterizes this policy as "blatant favouritism" which unleashed a trend towards Hutu "racial supremacy." He charges that it was the Belgian administration which helped the Hutus to "rid themselves of Tutsi chiefs and subchiefs; which ceaselessly denounced the sins of feudalism while deliberately ignoring the murders, thefts and provocations of its protégés; and which, in the end, joined hands with the [Hutu] republicans to bring the downfall of the [Tutsi] monarchy."[50] The United

48. Lemarchand, *Political Awakening,* pp. 229–31; Gérard-Libois and Verhaegen, *Congo 1960,* 1: 299.

49. Richard F. Nyrop et al., *Area Handbook for Rwanda* (Washington: U. S. Government Printing Office, 1969), p. 18.

50. Lemarchand, *Rwanda and Burundi,* p. 197.

Nations, on the other hand, valiantly strove to encourage Hutu-Tutsi cooperation. In early 1961, the General Assembly called for the establishment of a broadly based caretaker government until national elections could be held, and a year later, in February 1962, the United Nations was instrumental in securing two ministerial posts for Tutsis in the postelection Rwandese government. This grand coalition lasted only one year: the two Tutsi ministers were dismissed from the cabinet in February 1963 as the first step toward the complete elimination of the Tutsis from Rwandese politics.[51]

In Burundi prior to independence, ethnic cleavages had much less political salience than in Rwanda, and the first national elections in 1961 were won overwhelmingly by a nonethnic party that was led by Prince Louis Rwagasore and included both Tutsis and Hutus among its other leaders and its followers. Rwagasore's personal characteristics made him an ideal leader of this nonethnic political party: he was a son of the Tutsi king, though not the heir to the throne, and he was married to a Hutu. After his electoral victory, he formed an ethnically balanced cabinet, but he was assassinated a few weeks later and his party split into ethnic factions. During the years that followed, the increasingly powerful Tutsi king continued to include both Hutus and Tutsis in the government: "Instead of taking sides . . . the crown engaged in a complicated 'ethnic arithmetic' designed to give each faction an equal share of whatever power was left to the government." Especially between 1963 and 1965, when the cabinets had become primarily responsible to the king instead of to parliament, Lemarchand points out, "the court went to great lengths to insure a parity of representation in government." Moreover, the prime-ministership alternated between the two ethnic segments: "Every government headed by a Tutsi was automatically followed by a Hutu-led cabinet once the former had lost the confidence of the court."[52] This policy was motivated by rational calculations designed to preserve and enhance the monarchy, and neither Belgian pressure nor the force of the

51. Vanderlinden, *La République Rwandaise,* pp. 25–26.
52. Lemarchand, *Rwanda and Burundi,* pp. 296, 368.

Belgian example played a role. The ethnic equilibrium was upset by the translation of the numerical strength of the Hutu majority into a clear Hutu victory in the 1965 elections. Their electoral gains were nullified first by the king's countermeasures and then, after an abortive Hutu coup, by brutal repression: almost all Hutu political leaders were apprehended and many of them were executed, including, according to the observer sent by the International Commission of Jurists, all of the officers of the two houses of parliament.[53]

COUNTERCONSOCIATIONAL ELEMENTS IN THE BELGIAN AND DUTCH EXAMPLES

The foregoing review of the development of grand coalition or more narrowly based governments in countries that might have benefited from the Belgian and Dutch grand coalition examples shows that these examples had only a very limited effect. The main reason, already suggested earlier, was the extraconstitutional and mainly extracabinet character of the Belgian and Dutch grand coalitions, which prevented the examples from being clear, straightforward, and easy to imitate. In the one case of the Netherlands Antilles, direct Dutch pressure substantially strengthened the influence of the metropolitan example, but this was an exception. In Belgium and the Netherlands, there was generally no clear recognition of the special relevance of their own political systems for the dependencies under their responsibility.

A revealing statement in this respect is the following one, made shortly before the Congo's independence by Raymond Scheyven, who, as Belgium's minister of Congo economic affairs, participated in the negotiations with the Congolese leaders:

> I do not think that underdeveloped countries are ready for democratic formulas exactly the same as we know them. . . . We have presented to the Congo a political system like our own. . . . There are communes,

53. Ibid., p. 419.

> provincial assemblies, a bicameral system, a political system where the Chief of State is not responsible before Parliament, whereas most young countries need a single executive. We have set up a government which can be reversed in the course of the legislature, whereas the continuity of executive action is essential in a country in construction. We have installed an electoral system which fragmented representation.[54]

There are four striking features in Scheyven's comments. First, he emphasizes the differences between developed Belgium and the underdeveloped Congo and fails to note their similarities as plural societies. Second, among the typical elements of the Belgian model that he lists, the consociational elements of grand coalition and segmental autonomy are conspicuously absent. Third, he deprecates the proportional method of election, the only consociational practice that he does mention. Fourth, he recommends a single executive—which is an obstacle to consociational democracy in plural societies.

In fact, there were two concrete aspects of the metropolitan examples which demonstrably *hindered* the successful transplantation of the grand coalition principle. One was the monarchical form of the Belgian and Dutch governmental systems and the ambiguous provisions regarding the monarchy in their constitutions. When transferred to the constitutions of, in particular, the Congo and Indonesia, these constitutional rules gave powers to the presidents that interfered with parliamentary and cabinet government. The Congolese constitution contained an article stating: "The head of state appoints and dismisses the prime minister and the ministers"—copied almost literally from an article in the 1831 Belgian constitution and unchanged since then, but obviously no longer giving the Belgian king any real political power.[55] The constitutional crisis over President Kasavubu's use of this article to dismiss Prime Minister Lumumba, although Lumumba still had the legislature's confidence, was the ostensible reason for Mobutu's first military

54. Quoted in Young, *Politics in the Congo,* pp. 176–77.

55. Gérard-Libois and Verhaegen, *Congo 1960*, 1: 110; Godelieve Craenen, Wilfried Dewachter, and Edith Lismont, *De Belgische Grondwet van* 1831 *tot heden: Nederlandse en Franse teksten* (Louvain: Acco, 1971), pp. 74–75.

coup. A more appropriate imitation of the same article of the Belgian constitution was its literal transfer to the 1962 constitution of the Kingdom of Burundi. Here its effect was not so much anticonsociational, since the king at first acted in an ethnically impartial manner, as antidemocratic. In the absence of the unwritten constitutional tradition that in Belgium strictly limits the monarch's power, this article was used to defend the growing power of the Burundi king at the expense of the system of parliamentary government.[56]

An instance of literal constitutional imitation that was less immediately fatal but also disruptive was the article in the 1950 Indonesian constitution stating: "The President and the Vice-President are inviolable." This phrase was copied from a Dutch constitutional provision relating to the political accountability of the cabinet and implying a very limited role for the king. But President Soekarno took advantage of it to increase his own power at the expense of the coalition cabinets and eventually to terminate parliamentary democracy: "Sitting in his constitutionally unassailable position and responsible constitutionally to no one, Soekarno was free to interpret a number of ambiguous provisions in the constitution in ways which allowed him to play a role far in excess of what was usually regarded as its spirit and intent."[57]

The second case of directly negative influence exerted by the metropolitan example was the effect of the Dutch anticonsociational reaction beginning in the late 1960s on Surinam politics. The pattern of close cooperation between Creole and East Indian parties broke down in 1973, and the election campaign that followed it became a virtually straight confrontation between a Creole bloc of parties and the large East Indian party, although both groups were also allied to Javanese junior partners. During the campaign, Dew writes, "one felt as if a Northern Ireland was in the making." One of the "ominous signs" that struck him was the symbolic use of colors by the two major antagonists: orange,

56. "Constitution définitive du Royaume du Burundi, en date du 16 octobre 1962," *Chronique de politique étrangère* 16, no. 4–6 (July–November 1963): 638; Lemarchand, *Rwanda and Burundi,* p. 364n.

57. Kahin, "Indonesia," p. 602.

the color of the Dutch House of Orange under which the East Indians wanted to remain united in the Netherlands Kingdom, and green, the color of the main Creole party.[58] The Creoles won the election and formed a narrowly based cabinet: for the first time in many years, there were no East Indians in the government and among the government parties and no Creoles in the opposition.

The new cabinet resolutely pressed for a quick rupture of the ties with the Netherlands and the Antilles against clearly expressed East Indian preferences. A particularly sensitive issue was the adoption of a new constitution by the two-thirds majority required by the existing constitution. The Creole-dominated government, which had only a narrow parliamentary majority far short of a two-thirds margin, declared that a regular majority would suffice; this was not only a constitutionally questionable policy but also a highly perilous course of action since a fundamental question was at stake in a plural society. Significantly, the majoritarian-minded Dutch government failed to voice any public disapproval. However, the final text of the new constitution—which, according to a Dutch expert on public law, is "in many respects a better constitution" than the Dutch one because it is deeply influenced by officially proposed revisions not yet incorporated in the Dutch constitution[59]—was passed by unanimous vote in Surinam's parliament after a miraculous reconciliation in the last days before independence in late 1975, auguring well for a resumption of Creole–East Indian coalition governments.

THE SWISS MODEL IN URUGUAY

In view of the many difficulties of transplanting the grand coalition model, it may be instructive to take a brief look at Uruguay's experiments with a Swiss-style plural executive in which grand

58. Dew, "Surinam: The Struggle for Ethnic Balance and Identity," p. 5.

59. D. Roemers, "Ontwerp Surinaamse grondwet dichtbij ontwerp Cals-Donner," *NRC-Handelsblad,* October 13, 1975. See also H. T. J. F. van Maarseveen, "De Grondwet van Suriname," *Nederlands Juristenblad* 50, no. 43 (December 13, 1975): 1381–90.

coalitions of the two dominant parties were constitutionally prescribed. It should be stated at the outset, however, that the case of Uruguay does not provide additional evidence to test Lewis's hypothesis, depicted in figure 4 above, because of the absence of a colonial relationship between Switzerland and Uruguay and because Uruguay is not a plural but a quite homogeneous society. Its significance for our analysis is therefore limited to three aspects: first, it is an intriguing instance of grand coalition government that was not just an informal practice but a formal constitutional requirement; second, it demonstrates the possibility of a deliberate deviation from established political traditions; and third, it may throw some light on the viability of a system of government that is transplanted to a very different social and cultural environment.

From 1919 to 1933 and again from 1952 to 1967, Uruguay was governed by a collegial executive composed of nine representatives of the two major parties—the *colegiado*—patterned after the seven-member Federal Council of Switzerland. The leading advocate of replacing presidential government by a Swiss-style executive body was José Batlle y Ordóñez, who was twice elected president in the early twentieth century and who, between his two terms in office, traveled widely in Europe and became an admirer of the Swiss system of government. As a result of his enthusiastic and persistent efforts, the colegiado was embodied in the 1917 constitution. Batlle's victory was not complete, however, because the collegial council had to share power with a popularly elected president who appointed and supervised the ministers in charge of the "political" departments of the interior, foreign relations, and war, leaving the other more administrative departments to the councillors. A presidential coup d'état in 1933 abolished both the council and the legislature and terminated the first period of what was only a limited and halfhearted experiment with a Swiss-style council.[60]

The restoration of the colegiado in the early 1950s on the

60. Göran G. Lindahl, *Uruguay's New Path: A Study in Politics during the First Colegiado, 1919–33* (Stockholm: Library and Institute of Ibero-American Studies, 1962).

initiative of President Andrés Martínez Trueba, who was a faithful *batllista* (Batlle himself had died in 1929), provided a better test because it now reappeared in undiluted form. Like the earlier council, it consisted of six representatives of the majority and three of the minority party, but it did not have to exercise executive authority jointly with an independently elected president. Nevertheless, it still differed from its Swiss counterpart in a number of important respects. First, the Uruguayan council with its nine members was slightly larger than the Swiss council, but it was restricted to representatives of the two major parties, unlike the multiparty Swiss council. Second, Uruguay's council was elected by popular vote instead of by parliament. Third, the councillors were ineligible for immediate reelection after their four-year terms in contrast to the strong Swiss tradition of reelecting incumbent councillors. Fourth, the presidency of the council rotated annually among the six majority party members instead of among all of the councillors as in Switzerland. Fifth, the nine councillors were not in charge of the executive departments but appointed, by majority vote, ministers for this purpose; such a separate cabinet operating under the supervision of the council does not exist in Switzerland. Finally, the Uruguayan council operated within a unitary system in contrast with the Swiss federal structure.[61]

Most of these deviations from the Swiss model did not affect the consociational aspects of the model to a significant extent. Because Uruguay had a two-party system in spite of its long devotion to the proportional representation method of election, the council composed exclusively of members of the Colorado and Blanco parties can undoubtedly be regarded as a grand coalition. Only the fact that the presidency of the council was restricted to members of the majority party violated the grand coalition principle. Proportional representation for legislative elections predated the establishment of the council. On the council itself, the six-to-three ratio was not strictly proportional since the two parties were usually closely matched in voter sup-

61. See Russell H. Fitzgibbon, "Adoption of a Collegiate Executive in Uruguay," *Journal of Politics* 14, no. 4 (November 1952): 620–22, 633–38.

port. A somewhat more serious infringement of the proportionality principle was that its application was not extended to the appointment of cabinet ministers by the council. On all other matters, too, the council decided by majority vote and without minority veto.

However, the fact of Uruguay's unitary form of government again calls attention to the fact that, although especially in the nineteenth century the country was frequently torn by civil strife, Uruguayan society cannot really be considered plural. Because consociational democracy is defined as a particular type of democratic regime in a plural society, the Swiss-style governmental system in Uruguay from 1952 to 1967 cannot be labeled consociational. It should also be pointed out that the regime's coalescent characteristics were a coincidence rather than its major purpose. Batlle's interest was in diffusing executive power among a number of persons in order to prevent what he believed to be an inherent tendency of presidents to become dominant and dictatorial. A letter that he wrote from Switzerland to a friend in Montevideo shows which aspect of Swiss government he was most impressed with: Can you "believe that the people do not know who is president?" And he reported that when he had taken a taxi in Berne and had asked the chauffeur to take him to the "government house"—a term with only one meaning to a Latin American—he was driven first to the town hall and then to the parliament building.[62] The Federal Council that Batlle observed during his visit in Switzerland was dominated by the majority party by a six-to-one ratio; it did not become a grand coalition of the four major parties until 1943. His own preference was for a colegiado composed of members of the majority party only, and the idea of *coparticipación* was added as a tactical concession to the minority in order to get his proposal adopted.

It is difficult to judge the success of Uruguay's application of the Swiss model. The major complaint about its performance concerns its indecisiveness and inefficiency. Of course, as Philip B. Taylor points out, this was partly deliberate: "Batlle's plan for

62. Quoted ibid., p. 617.

an Executive Council was designed deliberately to curtail its efficiency."[63] Actually, it functioned quite well during its early years. Alexander T. Edelmann comments that it "got off to a good start, effectively coping with its first domestic and international problems," but that from about 1956 on its performance declined, justifying the conclusion that in its last decade it was "on many counts a failure as an effective, viable executive body."[64] Much of the blame for this failure attaches to the Blancos, who grudgingly accepted the colegiado when they were in the minority, but who began to sabotage it as soon as they became the majority party in the 1958 election—a tendency that may be compared with the opposition to power-sharing by the Protestant majority in Northern Ireland, the Greek majority in Cyprus, and the Hutu majority in Rwanda. It is a moot question whether a presidential regime would have served Uruguay better in the late 1950s and early 1960s. The Uruguayan political leaders and voters became convinced of this, however, and a referendum in 1966 abolished the colegiado and restored the presidency. Presidential government soon proved to have the weakness diagnosed and feared by Batlle: it turned into dictatorial rule in 1973.

THE VALUE OF THE CONSOCIATIONAL HERITAGE

On the basis of the evidence presented in this chapter, we should now be able to complete figure 4, which was left only partly completed at the beginning of the chapter. How should the six cases examined above—the seventh case, that of nonplural Uruguay, falls outside the scheme—be classified in figure 4: do they fit relationship I, in accordance with Lewis's implicit hypothesis, or relationship II? Figure 5 schematically portrays

63. Philip B. Taylor, Jr., "Interests and Institutional Dysfunction in Uruguay," *American Political Science Review* 57, no. 1 (March 1963): 72.

64. Alexander T. Edelmann, "The Rise and Demise of Uruguay's Second Plural Executive," *Journal of Politics* 31, no. 1 (February 1969): 126, 128. See also Martin Weinstein, *Uruguay: The Politics of Failure* (Westport, Conn.: Greenwood Press, 1975), pp. 113–39.

FIG. 5. Type of Democracy and Democratic Performance in the Former Belgian and Dutch Dependencies

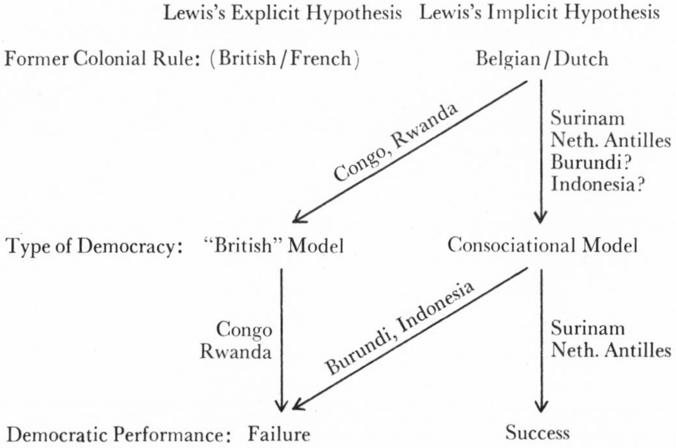

our overall conclusions. The dichotomous classification entails an oversimplification which must be qualified with regard to a few of the cases. All six contain at least some elements of consociationalism, and it is not always easy to decide whether or not these elements add up to a sufficient degree of it to permit their classification as consociational democracies.

Two cases can be assigned without difficulty to the category of former dependencies of consociational democracies that have adopted the consociational model: Surinam (at least until 1973) and the Netherlands Antilles. Dew concludes that the year 1955, shortly after Surinam attained full internal self-government, "marks the emergence of full-fledged consociational democracy in the true sense that Lijphart defines the term."[65] If we accept the Antillian interisland coalitions as the functional equivalent of grand coalitions, the Antilles can be placed in the same category.

65. Edward Dew, "Surinam: The Test of Consociationalism," *Plural Societies* 3, no. 3 (autumn 1972): 45. Similar conclusions are stated by R. Hoppe, "Het politiek systeem van Suriname: Elite-kartel demokratie," *Acta Politica* 11, no. 2 (April 1976): 163; and by Christopher Bagley, *The Dutch Plural Society: A Comparative Study in Race Relations* (London: Oxford University Press, 1973), pp. 233–34.

On the other hand, Rwanda unquestionably fits the other category; the brief and grudging inclusion of Tutsi in the cabinet cannot mask the basically majoritarian and adversarial character of the model of government that was adopted. The Congo should probably be included in the same category although the extremely short duration of its democratic regime hardly permits a confident judgment. The Lumumba cabinet was at least superficially a grand coalition, and the ethnically balanced distribution of the two highest offices might have fashioned a Lumumba-Kasavubu duumvirate similar to the dual Soekarno-Hatta leadership in Indonesia. However, these potentially consociational characteristics were nullified by the cabinet's weak parliamentary support and the adversarial and constitutionally muddled relations between the two top leaders, as well as by the limited and inappropriate application of the federal principle. Indonesia and Burundi are included in the first category—but with a question mark to indicate that it might have been more desirable to create an intermediate category for them. Although Indonesian democracy from 1950 to 1957 contained several strong consociational features, there were two serious deficiencies: the absence of an appropriate federal system and the systematic exclusion of the Communist party, representing one of the four large segments, from the government coalitions. Burundi's series of grand coalition cabinets from 1961 to 1965 might permit its classification as a consociational democracy if it were not for the nondemocratic nature of the political actor primarily responsible for these coalitions: the monarch as a potent but benevolently impartial arbiter.

The evidence summarized in figure 5 lends only weak and ambivalent support to the first part of Lewis's hypothesis: two cases are in accord with it, two only partially so, and two contradict it. But it is strengthened considerably when the *degree* of influence exerted by the metropolitan power is taken into consideration. It is significant that the two unambiguous cases of consociational democracy are also the only two countries where the transition from colonial status to self-government and (in the Surinam case) sovereign independence was a gradual process, and where this process of decolonization was effected in a spirit of harmony and goodwill with the mother-country. In order to end their dependent status, neither Surinam nor the Antilles had to resort to forcible methods which easily entail not only the rejection of the political authority of the colonial power but also its intellectual and moral authority. The other extreme is the Congo. The Belgian administration did next to nothing to prepare the Congolese for independence and, as Young remarks, kept them in "almost total isolation" from the rest of the world: until 1958 "literally only a handful of educated Congolese had been abroad."[66] Total independence was then granted very soon after the first revolutionary incidents, and only two weeks after independence the new Congolese government broke off its diplomatic relations with Belgium.

The second step of the hypothesis sketched in figure 5 is largely confirmed by the six cases under consideration. Only the two clearly consociational democracies can boast satisfactory democratic performances. When the entire three-variable relationship is examined in both figure 4 and figure 5, it is clear that a Belgian or Dutch colonial heritage was neither a necessary condition for successful consociational democracy—as demonstrated by Lebanon and Malaysia—nor a sufficient condition for it—as shown by four of the six cases examined in this chapter. The only firm conclusion that can be drawn is that such a heritage is a helpful factor, and hence similar in its effect to the other conditions favorable for consociational democracy treated in chapter 3.

It is worth emphasizing, however, that Indonesia and Burundi—the two cases of democracy or near-democracy characterized by a Belgian-Dutch heritage, the adoption of a partly consociational regime, and eventual democratic failure—were in fact strengthened considerably albeit not sufficiently by these consociational elements. For instance, Geertz argues that regional tensions in Indonesia were contained until 1957 not only by the solidarity created in the struggle for independence but also by the "broadly representative multiparty system"—including, it should be added, a broad pattern of participation in the cabinet—and the

66. Young, *Politics in the Congo,* p. 279.

dual leadership of Soekarno and Hatta.[67] And Lemarchand notes that, in spite of Burundi's severe ethnic tensions between 1962 and 1965, its political climate was "surprisingly tolerant and refreshingly free of the 'mobilisation' features that one might have encountered during these years in other African states," and he credits this happy state of affairs to the practice of grand coalition government: "The diffusion of authority among the representatives of each group meant that neither side felt directly threatened by the system."[68]

One final question remains to be answered: can the helpful effect attributed to a favorable colonial heritage be ascribed instead to the other favorable conditions? Because so many variables have to be considered, it is not possible to establish strict scientific controls, but our tentative conclusion would obviously be weakened or even disconfirmed if the success of consociational democracy in Surinam and the Netherlands Antilles were also found to be favored overwhelmingly by all or most of the other helpful factors. However, a comparison of these two countries with the other four that were less successful in their attempts at democracy, shows that the former have not enjoyed disproportionate advantages.

The only strongly favorable condition in Surinam, other than its colonial heritage, is the moderately multiple balance of power among its ethnic segments. It is considerably better off in this respect than the Netherlands Antilles which is afflicted with a distribution of power closely approximating the most unfavorable pattern of dual imbalance. A similar dual imbalance also characterizes Indonesia in terms of the Java–Outer Islands relationship, but not in terms of its alirans, and in extreme degree both Rwanda and Burundi. The principal favorable factor for the Netherlands Antilles is its almost perfect segmental isolation since its segments are island populations. A trait that Surinam and the Antilles have in common is their very small populations of well under half a million people. However, according to our earlier analysis, such small populations—even smaller than those

67. Geertz, "Integrative Revolution," p. 130.
68. Lemarchand, *Rwanda and Burundi,* p. 296.

of Lebanon, Cyprus, and Northern Ireland—do not offer optimal conditions for consociational democracy. Rwanda and Burundi with about three million people each and the Congo with a population of some fifteen million at the time of independence were closer to the optimal point, but Indonesia as the world's sixth most populous country in the 1950s—its population was then already approaching the 100 million mark—was in the most unfavorable situation. One factor usually associated with small size is a relatively light foreign policy load. This advantage has also accrued to Surinam and the Antilles as a result of their membership in the Kingdom of the Netherlands, in which they have been overshadowed by the more populous and wealthier European Netherlands and, consequently, almost totally relieved of the responsibilities of making foreign policy.[69]

It should also be pointed out that both Surinam and the Antilles are clearly plural societies and that their plural character is not offset by overarching loyalties. Surinam's segments are separated from each other by mutually reinforcing cultural, religious, linguistic, and racial cleavages, and there is hardly any overarching nationalism. Social scientists who have done research on Surinam society and politics are virtually unanimous in their judgment that Surinam is "probably one of the finest examples of a plural society," that it is "without any doubt . . . one of the most segmented societies in the Caribbean area," and that it "possibly illustrates the greatest incidence of cultural pluralism" in the Western hemisphere.[70] The Antilles are divided both by geographic differences and differences in skin color, but the two main islands and Bonaire are united by the Roman Catholic religion and by the Papiamento language that is exclusively spoken in these islands—although, significantly, Curaçao and Aruba are at odds about the proper spelling of this

69. Membership in the kingdom also entailed the presence of small and mainly symbolic Dutch military contingents which are sometimes credited with having had a pacifying influence.

70. Van Lier, *Frontier Society,* p. 11; J. D. Speckmann, "De plurale Surinaamse samenleving," in A. N. J. den Hollander et al., *De plurale samenleving: Begrip zonder toekomst?* (Meppel: Egel Reeks, 1966), p. 52; and Dew, "Surinam: The Test of Consociationalism," p. 36.

language. On the whole, their differences far outweigh their common bonds and, as Albert L. Gastmann states, these differences have "stifled any sense of loyalty to the Netherlands Antilles as a whole."[71]

Moreover, economic inequalities reinforce the segmental cleavages in both countries. There is a substantial ethnic division of labor in Surinam as well as ethnic differences in economic development; the most advantaged Creole segment has only recently been challenged by the East Indians. In the Antilles, the smaller islands are economically dependent on the larger ones, but the most important divisive factor is that Aruba is considerably more prosperous than Curaçao. Nor is Antillian unity strengthened by a foreign threat. All Antillians are vividly aware of the potential challenge posed by the proximity of Venezuela—Curaçao, Aruba, and Bonaire are situated on the continental shelf close to the Venezuelan coast—but it does not forge a common Antillian bond since the Arubans contemplate the possibility of closer ties with the light-skinned Venezuelans with much greater equanimity than the Curaçaoans. Surinam's only contentious foreign policy problem is a border dispute with Guyana, but this does not qualify as a serious threat.

The conclusions of this chapter do not unequivocally strengthen the case for consociational democracy as a normative model for plural societies in the Third World. One positive result is the discovery of two additional empirical examples that demonstrate the feasibility of consociationalism in Third World conditions. But our findings also include an additional factor—a favorable colonial heritage—that has been present very rarely and the influence of which is receding into the past. Hence it is especially important that the consociational model be disseminated by other means such as by the forceful arguments presented by Lewis—and possibly also by the comparative explorations of this book.

71. Gastmann, *Politics of Surinam and the Netherlands Antilles*, p. 3.

7 Consociational Engineering

This book's message to the political leaders of plural societies is to encourage them to engage in a form of political engineering: if they wish to establish or strengthen democratic institutions in their countries, they must become consociational engineers. Political scientists have generally been far too reluctant to make macro-level policy recommendations. Particularly as far as issues of development are concerned, the contrast with their colleagues in economics is a stark one. As Giovanni Sartori puts it, "with reference to economic development the economist is a planner; with reference to political development the political scientist is a spectator. The economist intervenes: His knowledge is applied knowledge. The political scientist awaits: He explains what happens, but does not make it happen."[1] Yet we find ourselves in a genuine dilemma. On the one hand, if we conceive of political development not as any change but as induced change toward an intended goal—such as stable democracy—the need to specify the means whereby this end can be reached is self-evident. On the other hand, are we justified in engaging in political engineering or in advising political engineers when our knowledge is imperfect? Specifically, is our knowledge sufficient to justify the recommendation of the means of consociational democracy for the objective of an effective and durable democratic regime in a plural society?

The ideal circumstances for giving such advice with complete confidence are the following: (1) The political engineer must accept democracy as a basic goal. (2) The consociational structures and procedures to be instituted must be clearly described. (3) The application of the consociational model must be a necessary means for the attainment of stable democracy (or, if there

1. Giovanni Sartori, "Political Development and Political Engineering," in *Public Policy*, vol. 17, ed. John D. Montgomery and Albert O. Hirschman (Cambridge, Mass.: Harvard University Press, 1968), p. 261.

are other means to the same end, the consociational method must be preferable in some other respect). (4) The consociational method must be a sufficient means to the end of stable democracy. (5) The other consequences of consociational democracy must be known, and the balance of the advantages and disadvantages of these by-products must be acceptable according to the political engineer's norms.[2] The first two criteria are primarily concerned with the relevance of the advice for policy-making; the fourth guarantees that the advice is failsafe; and the third and fifth guarantee that, on balance, it yields the intended result at the smallest cost.

These requirements cannot be fully met, and it is therefore not possible to recommend consociational engineering with unqualified confidence. Two of the criteria pose relatively few problems. The disadvantages that can be the by-products of consociational democracy have already been discussed in chapter 2 and were found to be relatively mild. Specific and detailed advice on consociational institutions and procedures can be given only for a specific plural society and depend on the individual characteristics of that society, especially on the balance of power among its segments and the extent of their territorial concentration. The various concrete examples examined in this book illustrate the ways in which the basic principles of grand coalition, mutual veto, proportionality, and autonomy can be implemented. One general recommendation that can be made concerns the traditional categories of constitutional engineering. While consociational democracy is not incompatible with presidentialism, majority or plurality electoral systems, and unitary forms of government, a better institutional framework is offered by their opposites: parliamentary systems (or semiparliamentary systems with a plural executive such as in Switzerland), list systems of proportional representation, and, in the case of societies with geographically concentrated segments, federal systems.

The weakest links in the chain of arguments on which the recommendation of consociational engineering is based are that

2. This list of criteria was inspired by A. Hoogerwerf, "Rationalisering en democratisering van beleid," *Bestuurswetenschappen* 27, no. 5 (September 1973): 306–07.

it cannot claim to be either a necessary or a sufficient method for achieving stable democracy. The relative success of nonconsociational India and the failure of consociational Cyprus point up these weaknesses. Moreover, skeptics are likely to argue that, of the four cases of reasonably successful consociational democracy in the Third World, two survived for many years but were not ultimately successful (Lebanon and Malaysia), and the other two have not yet proved their stability under conditions of complete independence (Surinam and the Netherlands Antilles). Another criticism that such skeptics could bring forward is that the factors found to be favorable to consociational democracy were first derived from the empirical analysis of the European cases and subsequently applied and tested in several non-European cases, but that this analytical procedure masks a few important differences between the two sets of cases which, when uncovered, severely damage the feasibility of consociational engineering in the Third World. Two differences stand out: the disparities in levels of economic development and in the degrees of depth and intensity of segmental cleavages. Do these disparities cause irreparable damage to consociational democracy as a normative model for Third World countries?

ALTERNATIVE OR PRIOR GOALS

Before examining—and trying to allay—these final doubts about the feasibility of consociational democracy outside the Western world, it is necessary to take a brief look at the first of the criteria listed above: the conviction that democracy is a goal worth striving for.[3] One can be a convinced democrat and yet tend to agree with Rupert Emerson that the single-party system or another nondemocratic regime has "evident virtues" in a plural and

3. This is not the appropriate place to argue the general question of the merits of democracy. Robert A. Dahl does this very effectively by giving a series of affirmative and very persuasive answers to the question: does democracy matter? For instance, compared with nondemocratic regimes, democratic regimes provide a larger measure of the classic liberal freedoms, a more representative political leadership, and a higher probability that a wide variety of interests are served by public policies; see Robert A. Dahl, *Polyarchy: Participation and Opposition* (New Haven: Yale University Press, 1971), pp. 17–32.

underdeveloped society where "unity is the first requisite, where a new . . . society must be brought into being, and where the hardships and disciplines of development must take priority over private preferences."[4] This is partly a question of values: should economic development and nation-building be rated more highly on our scale of values than democracy? But it is also an empirical question: can a nondemocratic regime achieve these objectives with greater speed and effectiveness than a democratic one?

It is highly doubtful that the latter question can be answered affirmatively: the performance of nondemocratic regimes in plural societies has been far from outstanding. Most observers who have reviewed the record of such regimes arrive at decidedly unfavorable conclusions. Aristide R. Zolberg argues that the African leaders have been misled by "the view that authoritarian measures are necessary to maintain order and to bring about modernization in the political, the economic, and other spheres." In Africa, such "imitative authoritarianism" is "doomed to failure."[5] Arthur Lewis, who is a renowned expert on the conditions of economic growth, states that the single-party system's claim to be able to accelerate economic development is "bogus," and that this type of regime is "largely irrelevant" to the economic problems of West Africa.[6] A democratic government may be unable to foster rapid economic development because popular demands may force the diversion of resources into private consumption and welfare services, but nondemocratic regimes may waste a nation's resources in other ways: "At times, a dictatorship can stimulate the rate of production; at times, it can decisively retard it."[7]

4. Rupert Emerson, *Political Modernization: The Single-Party System,* Monograph Series in World Affairs, no. 1 (Denver: University of Denver, 1963–64), p. 30.

5. Aristide R. Zolberg, *Creating Political Order: The Party-States of West Africa* (Chicago: Rand McNally, 1966), p. 158.

6. W. Arthur Lewis, *Politics in West Africa* (London: Allen and Unwin, 1965), p. 44.

7. William McCord, *The Springtime of Freedom: Evolution of Developing Societies* (New York: Oxford University Press, 1965), p. 285.

The claim that nondemocratic governments are required to build integrated nations in plural societies is of equally doubtful validity. As Arnold Rivkin states, they have not yet proved effective in welding together diverse populations because the possibility of *imposing* unity is very limited.[8] The basic problem is that primordial loyalties have extremely deep and strong roots, and that single leaders or oligarchies almost inevitably are exponents of particular segments and hence unacceptable to other segments. A good example is the case of Soekarno, who was often regarded by foreign observers—and by himself—as a truly national, charismatic leader. Actually, he was only a Javanese and a representative of one of Indonesia's subcultures. As a result, R. William Liddle states in his case study of ethnicity and national integration, Soekarno's "charisma and his ideology had profound meaning for only a segment of the Indonesian population (and were explicitly rejected by many others)." Liddle concludes that, at least in Indonesia, authoritarianism and centralization were not effective at all as nation-building devices.[9] The only nondemocratic regime that can avoid this problem is what may be termed a "consociational *oligarchy*," such as a single-party system that is truly a grand coalition of all significant segments.

Not only have nondemocratic regimes failed to be good nation-builders; they have not even established good records of maintaining intersegmental order and peace in plural societies. It is significant that the worst recent outbreaks of intersegmental violence in plural societies took place in Indonesia and Burundi many years *after* the termination of democratic rule in these countries. In 1965 and 1966, at least half a million people were killed in the aftermath of the military coup that drove Soekarno from power. The nearly one hundred thousand people, mainly Hutus, who were massacred in Burundi in 1972 represent an even more terrifying "selective genocide," because it was deliberately aimed at the educated and semieducated strata of the

8. Arnold Rivkin, *Nation-Building in Africa: Problems and Prospects* (New Brunswick: Rutgers University Press, 1969), p. 56.

9. R. William Liddle, *Ethnicity, Party, and National Integration: An Indonesian Case Study* (New Haven: Yale University Press, 1970), pp. 220, 229.

Hutu segment and because of the much smaller size of this country's population: approximately 3.5 percent of the total population was killed in a few weeks.[10]

In fact, it can be more plausibly argued that democracy, especially in its consociational form, is a better nation-builder than nondemocratic regimes. Although, in the short run, consociational democracy tends to strengthen the plural character of a plural society, an extended period of successful consociational government may be able to resolve some of the major disagreements among the segments and thus to depoliticize segmental divergences, and it may also create sufficient mutual trust at both elite and mass levels to render itself superfluous. This growth of consensus resulting from the cumulative experience of the successful settlement of conflicts is very similar to the process according to which Ali A. Mazrui argues that national integration should take place in African countries: "The resolution of conflict is an essential mechanism of integration. The whole experience of jointly looking for a way out of a crisis, of seeing your own mutual hostility subside to a level of mutual tolerance, of being intensely conscious of each other's positions and yet sensing the need to bridge the gulf—these are experiences which, over a period of time, should help two groups of people move forward into a relationship of deeper integration."[11] The Austrian grand coalition, which was designed to prevent the breakdown of democracy after the Second World War, paved the way for the resumption of a government-versus-opposition pattern of politics in 1966 without any danger to democratic stability. By that time, enough of a consensual nation had been built by the indirect method of

10. René Lemarchand and David Martin, *Selective Genocide in Burundi,* report no. 20 (London: Minority Rights Group, n.d.); Bernard Aupens, "L'engrenage de la violence au Burundi," *Revue française d'études politiques africaines* 8, no. 91 (July 1973): 48–69; Thomas Patrick Melady, *Burundi: The Tragic Years* (Maryknoll, N. Y.: Orbis Books, 1974).

11. Ali A. Mazrui, "Pluralism and National Integration," in *Pluralism in Africa,* ed. Leo Kuper and M. G. Smith (Berkeley: University of California Press, 1969), p. 335 (italics omitted).

consociational democracy to render further use of consociationalism superfluous. In contrast, as William T. Bluhm points out, the attempt at direct nation-building by the "Fatherland Front" and a one-party dictatorship in the 1930s failed miserably.[12]

A somewhat different argument is that economic development and national integration should take precedence over democratization, not because they are intrinsically more important than democracy, but because they form the prerequisite substructure for democracy. This is encouraged both by political development theories and by much of Western democratic theory (of the nonconsociational variety) which relies heavily on the empirical correlation between the presence of democracy and various social and economic characteristics of Western countries. This correlation does not carry the policy implication, however, that favorable conditions for democracy should be created by nondemocratic methods. Furthermore, nondemocratic regimes have a poor record of paving the way for democracy. Although they often justify their rule in terms of democratic objectives, they are more likely to be be more concerned with the maintenance of their nondemocratic power: "From having been a means, the political monoply becomes a self-justifying goal."[13] Rivkin notes that there is not one example of a single-party regime in Africa which "has not used its monopoly of public power to crush actual or potential opposition in the name of unity, which has become synonymous for this purpose with whatever the will or leadership of the controlling party dictates."[14]

12. William T. Bluhm, *Building an Austrian Nation: The Political Integration of a Western State* (New Haven: Yale University Press, 1973), pp. 38–40. The following comment by Stein Rokkan on the consociational method of proportional representation as an (indirect) nation-building device in the European plural societies should also be noted: "The introduction of PR was essentially part of a strategy of national integration—an alternative to monopolization of influence or civil war." Stein Rokkan, *Citizens, Elections, Parties: Approaches to the Comparative Study of the Processes of Development* (Oslo: Universitetsforlaget, 1970), p. 168.

13. Zolberg, *Creating Political Order,* p. 62. He also calls attention to the danger of an "inflationary spiral of coercion and violence" (p. 87).

14. Rivkin, *Nation-Building in Africa,* p. 50.

ECONOMIC UNDERDEVELOPMENT AND CONSOCIATIONAL ENGINEERING

The argument cited in the previous paragraph is based on the assumption that economic development and nation-building are prerequisites for democracy and hence also presumes that consociational engineering in the economically underdeveloped plural societies of the Third World is doomed to failure. As far as the factor of economic development is concerned, this pessimistic view is supported by one of the best-known empirical relationships in comparative politics: that between level of economic development and democracy.[15] In addition, since consociational democracy entails a system of proportional allocation of resources, it requires the creation of new resources in order to minimize zero-sum redistributions even more than other types of democracy do. Finally, to add even more weight to this argument, it must be pointed out that Lebanon and Malaysia belong to the most developed category among Asian and African countries, and that Surinam and the Netherlands Antilles are quite prosperous by South American standards.

Nevertheless, these facts do not change the nature of the correlation, which is merely statistical, is far from perfect, and has many notable exceptions. To the extent that it indicates a causal relationship, it may well be that democracy rather than economic development is the cause. It is interesting to read Michael C. Hudson's appraisal of the role of these variables in Lebanese politics; his testimony is of special interest, because Hudson has made significant contributions to macro-quantitative statistical analyses in comparative politics. He raises the question of "whether or not it is Lebanon's high living standard that supports its democracy. There is little doubt that there is a rough association between wealth and stable democracy in the world." But although this correlation clearly holds for Lebanon, he argues that it is not a causal relationship: "If there is a causal relation in Lebanon it would . . . seem to be the other way

15. For a critical review of this literature, see John D. May, *Of the Conditions and Measures of Democracy* (Morristown, N. J.: General Learning Press, 1973).

around." Furthermore, the country would not become "much more or much less democratic than it now is if the per capita income were either half or twice its present level."[16]

At most, economic underdevelopment can be considered an unfavorable factor for consociational engineering; it does not render it impossible. Instead of writing off consociational engineering in economically underdeveloped countries altogether, it is more constructive to take the requirements of economic modernization into account when a consociational democracy is engineered in an underdeveloped country. One interesting suggestion of this kind has been made by David E. Apter and Martin R. Doornbos: they propose the establishment of a "development upper house" staffed by professionals and responsible for long-term economic planning as part of a democratic "development constitution" specifically designed for the developing countries.[17]

INTENSE CLEAVAGES AND CONSOCIATIONAL ENGINEERING

The potentially most damaging challenge to the idea of consociational engineering is that the lessons drawn from Western consociational experiences are not applicable to non-Western plural societies because there is literally a world of difference between the plural societies in the First and Third Worlds.[18] According to this objection, the differences between the segments of non-Western plural societies are generally so much greater than those in the Western plural societies that the chances of bridging them by consociational methods are nil or infinitesimally small. One obvious answer is to point to the

16. Michael C. Hudson, "Democracy and Social Mobilization in Lebanese Politics," *Comparative Politics* 1, no. 2 (January 1969): 246n.

17. David E. Apter and Martin R. Doornbos, "Development and the Political Process: A Plan for a Constitution," in David E. Apter, *Political Change: Collected Essays* (London: Frank Cass, 1973), pp. 118–46; and David E. Apter, *Choice and the Politics of Allocation* (New Haven: Yale University Press, 1971), pp. 167–75.

18. David Nicholls, *Three Varieties of Pluralism* (London: Macmillan, 1974), p. 58.

example of consociationalism in Malaysia with its extremely deep racial, cultural, and economic cleavages among the population segments. But it will also be instructive to examine in some detail the arguments presented by the principal critics.

The most extreme view is that of Alvin Rabushka and Kenneth A. Shepsle. They maintain that stable democracy in plural societies is inherently impossible and claim that scholars who think otherwise are led astray by their democratic commitments: "Many scholars display a bias for democratic political arrangements [which] has led, we think, to some wishful and as yet unsuccessful attempts to demonstrate that stable democracy can be maintained in the face of cultural diversity." The flaw in their own—largely deductive—argument that democracy is impossible is that they view politics in plural societies in terms of a zero-sum game: "The world of ethnic communities is Hobbesian and often implies 'a war of all against all.' " In particular, they argue that a grand coalition is unworkable because it is "inherently oversized" according to the criterion of Riker's size principle, which states that under zero-sum conditions a coalition with a bare majority will be formed. The zero-sum assumption is not realistic, however, except in the most extreme case of a plural society. If there is at least either some common loyalty or a rational perception that politics is not one "game" but a continuing series of games so that part of the payoff is the advantage of peaceful relationships in the long run, the zero-sum assumption becomes invalid—and so does the hypothesis that grand coalitions cannot operate successfully.[19]

The authors also cite a great deal of empirical evidence concerning the failure of democracy in plural societies. Much of this evidence does not concern *consociational* democracies, however, and some of it should not be considered proof of failure from the point of view of the consociational model. For instance, the *apanjaht* ("vote for your own kind") politics of Guyana is not at all incompatible with consociational democracy, in which the pres-

19. Alvin Rabushka and Kenneth A. Shepsle, "Political Entrepreneurship and Patterns of Democratic Instability in Plural Societies," *Race* 12, no. 4 (April 1971): 462, 467, 470.

ence of parties that clearly represent particular ethnic groups is an advantage. Similarly, Flemish-Walloon federalism should be considered a step toward the solution of linguistic conflict in Belgium rather than evidence of democratic failure.[20] The zero-sum bias is just as unrealistic as prodemocratic wishful thinking, but it is more debilitating because it precludes creative attempts at making democracy work in spite of unfavorable conditions.

Rabushka and Shepsle's blanket condemnation of democratic engineering in plural societies covers both the First and Third Worlds, but by implication it has special relevance for the Third World because of the greater incidence of plural societies there and their more strongly plural character. In particular, the plural societies of the Third World may be argued to be more plural than those of the First in two respects: cultural differences tend to be greater and they also tend to be reinforced by highly visible and often ineradicable differences in physical appearance.

The second dimension is emphasized by Brian Barry when he counsels caution in extending to ethnically divided societies the consociational formula that has been successful in the resolution of religious and ideological conflicts among political subcultures in Europe. He argues that "religious and class conflict is a conflict of organizations. Ethnic conflict is a conflict of solidary groups [which] do not need organization to work up a riot or a pogrom so long as they have some way of recognizing who belongs to which group." But highly visible differences, whether of a physical or cultural nature, may also serve the positive function of clearly demarcating segmental boundaries—thus limiting intersegmental contacts and minimizing opportunities for intersegmental conflict. Barry also argues that, unlike ethnic segments, religious and ideological segments are defined in terms of organizations and by the fact that they follow certain leaders; as a result, the leaders can count on the loyal support of their followers for agreements that they make with the leaders of

20. Alvin Rabushka and Kenneth A. Shepsle, *Politics in Plural Societies: A Theory of Democratic Instability* (Columbus, Ohio: Merrill, 1972), esp. pp. 62–92.

rival segments. This argument overlooks the tendency of plural societies of all kinds to become organized along segmental lines and the tendency of intrasegmental loyalties to increase as intersegmental differences increase. Finally, he claims that religious and ideological issues are comparatively more susceptible to consociational solutions because the question is "how the country is to be run" rather than "whether it should be a country at all."[21] However, this is not merely a matter of different kinds and intensities of cleavages but also of the presence or absence of overarching loyalties.

All of Barry's arguments concentrate too much on the problem of elite control of the segments and too little on the problem of arriving at intersegmental elite agreements. Religious and ideological differences present special obstacles in the latter respect: they may lead to tensions as a result of attempts at religious and ideological conversion, and they may be *logically* and not just emotionally incompatible. The fierce resistance to the inclusion of communists in grand coalition cabinets in Italy and Indonesia abundantly shows the intensity that ideological cleavages can have. This is not to deny that racial and ethnic cleavages strengthen the plural character of plural societies and weaken the possibilities of consociational democracy; the conclusion is merely that different *kinds* of segmental cleavages produce different *degrees* of intensity and that these differences in degree should not be exaggerated.

Cultural differences are stressed by Pierre van den Berghe, who, like Rabushka and Shepsle, tends to view plural societies as inherently conflictual but also concedes that under certain conditions a few moderately plural societies have been fairly democratic. The examples of plural but democratic systems that he mentions are Switzerland, Belgium, Canada, India, and Israel. From an inspection of these five cases he derives a set of five "limiting conditions," which are worthy of examination because of the light they can throw on the overall prospects of democracy in plural societies. Two of Van den Berghe's conditions are

21. Brian Barry, "Political Accommodation and Consociational Democracy," *British Journal of Political Science* 5, no. 4 (October 1975): 502–03.

characteristics of consociational democracy. He emphasizes the importance of agreement on certain procedural norms such as "a precise *modus vivendi* and *modus operandi* ensuring that the distribution of power in the society is roughly proportional to the size of the groups." Democracy also depends on agreement as to how segmental cleavages are to be treated, including "general norms accepting the legitimacy of pluralism and more specific counteracculturative norms ensuring the continued integrity of the groups. The most important issues here are those of cultural and regional autonomy." These conditions are "limiting" mainly in the sense that they limit the forms of democracy that are viable in a plural society to those of the consociational type—a view that is in accord with the thesis of this book.

The other three conditions involve societal characteristiscs. One of these is the degree to which different cleavages cut across or reinforce each other, a matter discussed in chapter 3. The crucial condition, which Van den Berghe lists first, is that the prospects for democracy in plural societies are "directly proportional to the degree of consensus about basic values and, hence, inversely proportional to the degree of cultural pluralism." The view that there are different degrees of pluralism and that the probability of stable democracy is inversely related to the degree of pluralism is indeed highly plausible. The more important question is at what point democracy becomes impossible or highly improbable. Van den Berghe argues that Belgian and Swiss democracy is compatible with the pluralism of these countries because theirs is only an "intermediate cultural pluralism." Other examples of intermediate pluralism include Yugoslavia and, within South Africa, the relations between Afrikaners and English-speaking whites. A minimal degree of pluralism, also within South Africa, exists between Afrikaners and Afrikaans-speaking Coloreds, and a maximal one between Afrikaners and Zulus. In the case of maximal cultural pluralism, Van de Berghe says, the chances of democracy are severely reduced. According to these rough criteria, most of the plural societies of Asia and Africa belong to the intermediate category. The extreme degree of pluralism, as in Afrikaner-Zulu relations, occurs very rarely. Hence this "limiting condition" does not entail a restrictive and pessimistic view either. His final condition is that democracy depends on the technological and scientific levels of the different segments: democracy is unlikely in a situation "where one group by virtue of its superior technology can easily achieve a monopoly over the means of violence." Except in the white-settler societies of South Africa and Rhodesia, such an extreme discrepancy in levels of development is also quite rare.[22]

Although the prospects for consociational democracy become less and less favorable as the degree of pluralism increases, as the numerical balance among the segments becomes more uneven or severely fragmented, and so forth, they remain more favorable than the prospects for stable British-style democracy. In the extreme cases of plural societies, such as South Africa, the outlook for democracy of any kind is poor, but if there is to be democracy at all it will almost certainly have to be of the consociational type. It is worth noting that strong foes of *apartheid* policies like Alan Paton are increasingly thinking of possible solutions of the South African dilemma that resemble the consociational model. Paton reaffirms his passionate belief in "the common society, in one country South Africa, belonging to all, in whose government all persons participate," but he argues that "the goal of the common society must now be striven for in the framework of separate development. . . . These territorial creations [the African 'homelands'], for all their poverty, have a potential dynamism," which may well "hasten the inevitable progress towards a common society." One way in which this may occur would be the abandonment of *total* separation into sovereign homelands and the creation of "some kind of federal society, with a federal parliament in which all states or provinces are represented [and] a large measure of state or provincial autonomy." He also emphasizes that evolution in this direction should be accompanied by progress toward political and economic equality.[23] Paton's solution is basically a consociational

22. Pierre L. van den Berghe, "Pluralism and the Polity: A Theoretical Exploration," in Kuper and Smith, *Pluralism in Africa,* pp. 70, 74–77.

23. Alan Paton, "Some Thoughts on the Common Society," in *Directions of Change in South African Politics,* ed. Peter Randall (Johannesburg: Study Project on Christianity in Apartheid Society, 1971), pp. 46, 49–50.

one, although he overlooks the possibility of nonterritorial or only partly territorial segmental autonomy combined with segmental political representation, which may be a more attractive implementation of consociational principles, both morally and practically, since it does not entail a large-scale resettlement policy. Consociational solutions of this kind offer the best—that is, the least unfavorable—prospects for peaceful democratic change.

In the final analysis, it remains true that the proposal of consociational engineering fails the two requirements, stated at the beginning of the chapter, that consociationalism be both a necessary and a sufficient means for the attainment of stable democracy. But the claim made by this book is more modest though still of crucial practical importance for plural societies. It is summarized in figure 6, which uses a very rough and nonoperationalized index to express the degree to which a soci-

FIG. 6. Probabilities of Success of Two Normative Democratic Models

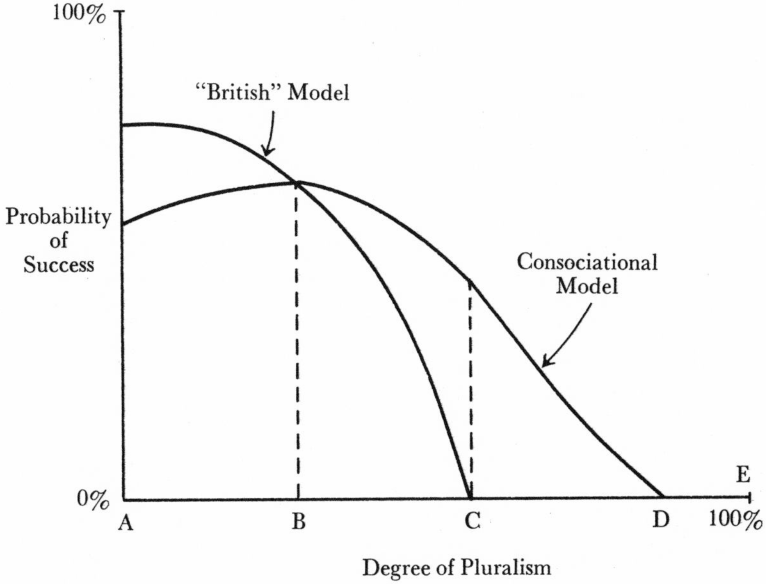

ety is plural (assuming all other factors to be equal) and an equally rough measurement of the probability of success of the two types of democratic engineering.[24] In homogeneous societies (the area between points A and B in figure 6), the application of the British model must be recommended because of the relative weakness of "depoliticized" democracy.[25] For the most extreme plural societies (D–E) neither model offers any hope. As the degree of pluralism increases from B to D, the chances of success of *both* models decrease, but those of the British model decrease at a much more rapid rate than those of the consociational model. In other words, the consociational model's *relative* prospects even *improve* in this area compared to the prospects of the British model. Between B and C, the consociational model offers better chances than the British one, but neither model is either a sufficient or a necessary method. Between C and D, however, the consociational method does become a necessary method although its chances of success continue to decrease. For many of the plural societies of the non-Western world, therefore, the realistic choice is not between the British normative model of democracy and the consociational model, but between consociational democracy and no democracy at all.

24. It is also assumed that the consociational and British models are the ideal-type alternatives and that there is no as yet undiscovered third alternative model.

25. See above, pp. 106–08.

Index